Azure Data Factory Cookbook

Build and manage ETL and ELT pipelines with
Microsoft Azure's serverless data integration service

Dmitry Anoshin

Dmitry Foshin

Roman Storchak

Xenia Ireton

BIRMINGHAM—MUMBAI

Azure Data Factory Cookbook

Group Product Manager: Kunal Parikh

Publishing Product Manager: Devika Battike

Commissioning Editor: Sunith Shetty

Acquisition Editor: Devika Battike

Senior Editor: Mohammed Yusuf Imaratwale

Content Development Editor: Sean Lobo

Technical Editor: Manikandan Kurup

Copy Editor: Safis Editing

Project Coordinator: Aishwarya Mohan

Proofreader: Safis Editing

Indexer: Pratik Shirodkar

Production Designer: Vijay Kamble

First published: December 2020

Production reference: 1231220

Published by Packt Publishing Ltd.
Livery Place
35 Livery Street
Birmingham
B3 2PB, UK.

ISBN 978-1-80056-529-6

`www.packt.com`

`Packt.com`

Subscribe to our online digital library for full access to over 7,000 books and videos, as well as industry leading tools to help you plan your personal development and advance your career. For more information, please visit our website.

Why subscribe?

- Spend less time learning and more time coding with practical eBooks and Videos from over 4,000 industry professionals

- Improve your learning with Skill Plans built especially for you

- Get a free eBook or video every month

- Fully searchable for easy access to vital information

- Copy and paste, print, and bookmark content

Did you know that Packt offers eBook versions of every book published, with PDF and ePub files available? You can upgrade to the eBook version at `packt.com` and as a print book customer, you are entitled to a discount on the eBook copy. Get in touch with us at `customercare@packtpub.com` for more details.

At `www.packt.com`, you can also read a collection of free technical articles, sign up for a range of free newsletters, and receive exclusive discounts and offers on Packt books and eBooks.

Contributors

About the authors

Dmitry Anoshin is an Analytics and Data Engineer Leader with over 10 years of experience working in Business Intelligence, Data Warehouse and Data Integration, BigData, Cloud, and ML space across North America and Europe. He has worked on leading Data Engineering initiatives while working on a petabyte size data platform built using Cloud and BigData technologies for supporting machine learning experiments, data science models, business intelligence reporting, and data exchange with internal and external partners. With expertise in data modeling, Dmitry also has a background in handling privacy compliance and security-critical datasets. He is also an active speaker at data conferences and helps people to adopt cloud analytics.

Dmitry Foshin is a business intelligence team leader, whose main goals are delivering business insights to the management team through data engineering, analytics, and visualization. He has led and executed complex full-stack BI solutions (from ETL processes to building DWH and reporting) using Azure technologies, Data Lake, Data Factory, Data Bricks, MS Office 365, Power BI, and Tableau. He has also successfully launched numerous data analytics projects – both on-premises and cloud – that help achieve corporate goals in international FMCG companies, banking, and manufacturing industries.

Roman Storchak has a PhD, and is a chief data officer whose main interest lies in building data-driven cultures through making analytics easy. He has led teams that have built ETL-heavy products in AdTech and retail and often uses Azure Stack, Power BI, and Data Factory.

Xenia Ireton is a software engineer at Microsoft and has extensive knowledge in the field of data engineering, big data pipelines, data warehousing, and systems architecture.

About the reviewers

Steph Martin is a senior customer engineer in the FastTrack for Azure team at Microsoft. She has a background in SQL Server database design and development and extensive knowledge of SSIS and ETL patterns and practices. Steph helps customers to achieve success with their projects, providing architecture design reviews, best practice guidance, and in-depth knowledge-sharing across the platform, covering migration to Azure as well as cloud-first deployments. She has wide experience in Azure data services, specializing in Azure SQL Database and Managed Instance, and Azure Data Factory. Steph is an active member of the data platform community, running a PASS affiliated Meetup in the UK and helping to co-ordinate the volunteer team at SQLBits.

Sawyer Nyquist is a consultant based in Grand Rapids, Michigan, USA. His work focuses on business intelligence, data analytics engineering, and data platform architecture. He holds the following certifications from Microsoft: MCSA BI Reporting, Data Analyst Associate, and Azure Data Engineer Associate. Over his career, he has worked with dozens of companies to strategize and implement data, analytics, and technology to drive growth. He is passionate about delivering enterprise data analytics solutions by building ETL pipelines, designing SQL data warehouses, and deploying modern cloud technologies for custom dashboards and reporting. Sawyer currently works as a data analytics engineer for Skyline Technologies.

Pavel Novichkov graduated from the University as a software engineer. Now it is a branch of the Bauman Moscow State Technical University, one of the most famous technical universities in Russia. For the last 8 years, he has been working in the field of web technologies, focusing on performance and data-driven marketing. During this time, he has worked in top Russian advertising agencies and as an independent contractor. He is one of those "crazy" people who love their job and are in constant search of new knowledge. Recently, he has been actively interested in cloud technologies and plans to promote them in Russia.

Packt is searching for authors like you

If you're interested in becoming an author for Packt, please visit `authors.packtpub.com` and apply today. We have worked with thousands of developers and tech professionals, just like you, to help them share their insight with the global tech community. You can make a general application, apply for a specific hot topic that we are recruiting an author for, or submit your own idea.

Table of Contents

2
Orchestration and Control Flow

3
Setting Up a Cloud Data Warehouse

4

Working with Azure Data Lake

5

Working with Big Data – HDInsight and Databricks

8
Working with Azure Services Integration

9
Managing Deployment Processes with Azure DevOps

10
Monitoring and Troubleshooting Data Pipelines

Other Books You May Enjoy

Index

Preface

Azure Data Factory (**ADF**) is a modern data integration tool available on Microsoft Azure. This ADF cookbook helps you get up and running by showing you how to create and execute your first job in ADF. You'll learn how to branch and chain activities, create custom activities, and schedule pipelines. This book will help you to discover the benefits of cloud data warehousing, specifically Azure Synapse Analytics and Azure Data Lake Storage Gen2, which are frequently used for big data analytics. With practical recipes, you'll learn how to actively engage with analytical tools from Azure data services and leverage your on-premises infrastructure with cloud-native tools to get relevant business insights.

As you advance, you'll be able to integrate the most commonly used Azure services into ADF and understand how Azure services can be useful in designing ETL pipelines. The book will take you through common errors that you may encounter while working with ADF and guide you in using the Azure portal to monitor pipelines. You'll also understand error messages and resolve problems in connectors and data flows with the debugging capabilities of ADF.

By the end of this book, you'll be able to use ADF as the main ETL and orchestration tool for your data warehouse or data platform projects.

Who this book is for

This book is for ETL developers, data warehouse and ETL architects, software professionals, and anyone who wants to learn about the common and not-so-common challenges faced while developing traditional and hybrid ETL solutions using Microsoft's ADF. You'll also find this book useful if you are looking for recipes to improve or enhance your existing ETL pipelines. Basic knowledge of data warehousing is expected.

What this book covers

Chapter 1, Getting Started with ADF, will briefly show you the Azure data platform. In this chapter, you will learn about the ADF interface and options as well as common use cases. You will perform hands-on exercises in order to find ADF in the Azure portal and create your first job.

Chapter 2, Orchestration and Control Flow, will introduce you to the building blocks of the data processing in Azure Data Factory. The chapter contains hands-on exercises which show you how to set up linked services and datasets for your data sources, use various types of activities, design data-processing workflows, and create triggers for the data transfers.

Chapter 3, Setting up a Cloud Data Warehouse, covers key features and benefits of cloud data warehousing and Azure Synapse Analytics. You will learn how to connect and configure Azure Synapse Analytics, load data, build transformation processes, and operate data flows.

Chapter 4, Working with Azure Data Lake, will go through the features of Azure Data Lake Storage Gen2. This is multi-modal cloud storage that is frequently used for big data analytics. We will load and manage the datasets that we will use for analytics in the next chapter.

Chapter 5, Working with Big Data – HDInsight and Databricks, is where we will actively engage with analytical tools from the Azure data services. We will start with munging data with Azure Databricks, then train some models on big data, and analyze them to draw business insights. Also, we will go through Stream Analytics.

Chapter 6, Integration with MS SSIS, covers using the Azure data platform and ADF on-premises. This chapter will help you leverage your on-premises infrastructure together with cloud-native tools to get relevant business insights.

Chapter 7, Data Migration – Azure Data Factory and Other Cloud Services, explains how to use Azure Data factory to transfer data between Azure and other cloud providers, such as AWS or Google Cloud, using ADF built-in connectors. We also show how to integrate a provider not currently supported by a built-in ADF connector, using Dropbox as an example.

Chapter 8, Working with Azure Services Integration, will cover how to do integrations of the most commonly used Azure services into ADF. You will also learn how Azure services can be useful in designing ETL pipelines.

Chapter 9, Managing Deployment Processes with Azure DevOps, will cover the key features of Azure DevOps. You will learn how to build CI/CD processes and continuous monitoring with Microsoft Azure. You will create a platform for application deployment and integrate it with ADF.

Chapter 10, Monitoring and Troubleshooting Data Pipelines, will teach readers how to use the Azure Data Factory Monitor interface to evaluate the progress of your data transfers, how to understand error messages and set up alerts for the pipelines. This chapter contains hands-on recipes highlighting the debugging capabilities of ADF.

To get the most out of this book

Basic knowledge of data warehousing is expected. You'll need an Azure subscription to follow all the recipes mentioned in the book. If you're using a paid subscription, make sure to pause or delete the services after using them to avoid high usage costs.

Software/hardware covered in the book	OS requirements
An Azure subscription	Windows, Mac OS X, and Linux (any)
SQL Server Management Studio (SSMS)	
AWS S3 and Google Cloud Storage (for *Chapter 7, Data Migration – Azure Data Factory and Other Cloud Services*)	

If you are using the digital version of this book, we advise you to type the code yourself or access the code via the GitHub repository (link available in the next section). Doing so will help you avoid any potential errors related to the copying and pasting of code.

Download the example code files

You can download the example code files for this book from GitHub at `https://github.com/PacktPublishing/Azure-Data-Factory-Cookbook`. In case there's an update to the code, it will be updated on the existing GitHub repository.

We also have other code bundles from our rich catalog of books and videos available at `https://github.com/PacktPublishing/`. Check them out!

Download the color images

We also provide a PDF file that has color images of the screenshots/diagrams used in this book. You can download it here: `https://static.packt-cdn.com/downloads/9781800565296_ColorImages.pdf`.

Conventions used

There are a number of text conventions used throughout this book.

`Code in text`: Indicates code words in text, database table names, folder names, filenames, file extensions, pathnames, dummy URLs, user input, and Twitter handles. Here is an example: "Execute `databricks configure --token` in the Azure CLI."

A block of code is set as follows:

```
from pyspark.ml.evaluation import RegressionEvaluator
regEval = RegressionEvaluator(
                    predictionCol="predictions", \
                         labelCol="rating", \
                         metricName="mse")
predictedTestDF = alsModel.transform(testDF)
testMse = regEval.evaluate(predictedTestDF)

print('MSE on the test set is {0}'.format(testMse))
```

When we wish to draw your attention to a particular part of a code block, the relevant lines or items are set in bold:

```
CREATE TABLE [dbo].[CommonCrawlPartitions](
    [YearAndMonth] [varchar](255) NULL,
    [Path] [varchar](255) NULL,
    [UpdatedAt] [Datetime]
)
```

Bold: Indicates a new term, an important word, or words that you see onscreen. For example, words in menus or dialog boxes appear in the text like this: Go to the Azure portal and find **Azure Active Directory**.

> **Tips or important notes**
> Appear like this.

Sections

In this book, you will find several headings that appear frequently (*Getting ready*, *How to do it...*, *How it works...*, *There's more...*, and *See also*).

To give clear instructions on how to complete a recipe, use these sections as follows:

Getting ready

This section tells you what to expect in the recipe and describes how to set up any software or any preliminary settings required for the recipe.

How to do it...

This section contains the steps required to follow the recipe.

How it works...

This section usually consists of a detailed explanation of what happened in the previous section.

There's more...

This section consists of additional information about the recipe in order to make you more knowledgeable about the recipe.

See also

This section provides helpful links to other useful information for the recipe.

Get in touch

Feedback from our readers is always welcome.

General feedback: If you have questions about any aspect of this book, mention the book title in the subject of your message and email us at customercare@packtpub.com.

Errata: Although we have taken every care to ensure the accuracy of our content, mistakes do happen. If you have found a mistake in this book, we would be grateful if you would report this to us. Please visit www.packtpub.com/support/errata, selecting your book, clicking on the Errata Submission Form link, and entering the details.

Piracy: If you come across any illegal copies of our works in any form on the Internet, we would be grateful if you would provide us with the location address or website name. Please contact us at copyright@packt.com with a link to the material.

If you are interested in becoming an author: If there is a topic that you have expertise in and you are interested in either writing or contributing to a book, please visit authors. packtpub.com.

Reviews

Please leave a review. Once you have read and used this book, why not leave a review on the site that you purchased it from? Potential readers can then see and use your unbiased opinion to make purchase decisions, we at Packt can understand what you think about our products, and our authors can see your feedback on their book. Thank you!

For more information about Packt, please visit packt.com.

1
Getting Started with ADF

Microsoft Azure is a public cloud vendor. It offers different services for modern organizations. The Azure cloud has several key components, such as compute, storage, databases, and networks. They serve as building blocks for any organization that wants to reap the benefits of cloud computing. There are many benefits to using the cloud, including utilities, metrics, elasticity, and security. Many organizations across the world already benefit from cloud deployment and have fully moved to the Azure cloud. They deploy business applications and run their business on the cloud. As a result, their data is stored in cloud storage and cloud applications.

Microsoft Azure offers a cloud analytics stack that helps us to build modern analytics solutions, extract data from on-premises and the cloud, and use data for decision-making progress, searching patterns in data, and deploying machine learning applications.

In this chapter we will meet Azure Data Platform services and meet main cloud data integration service - **Azure Data Factory** (**ADF**). We will login to the Azure and navigate to the Data Factories service in order to create the first data pipeline and run Copy activity. Then, we will do the same exercise but will use different methods of data factories management and control by using Python, PowerShell and Copy Data Tool.

If you don't have an Azure account, we will cover, how you can get a free Azure Account.

In this chapter, we will cover the following recipes:

- Introduction to the Azure data platform
- Creating and executing our first job in ADF
- Creating an ADF pipeline by using the Copy Data tool
- Create an ADF pipeline using Python
- Creating a data factory using PowerShell
- Using templates to create ADF pipelines

Introduction to the Azure data platform

The Azure data platform provides us with a number of data services for databases, data storage, and analytics. In *Table 1.1*, you can find a list of services and their purpose:

Service Name	Definition
Azure Synapse Analytics	A limitless analytics service with unmatched time to insight (formerly SQL Data Warehouse)
Power BI	A business intelligence solution for building reports and dashboards and data visualization
Azure Stream Analytics	Real-time analytics on fast-moving streams of data from applications and devices
ADF	Hybrid data integration at an enterprise scale made easy
Azure Databricks	Apache Spark-based analytics platform optimized for the Microsoft Azure cloud services platform
Azure Cognitive Services	Cloud-based services with REST **application programming interfaces** (**APIs**) and client library **Software Development Kits** (**SDKs**), available to help developers build cognitive intelligence into applications without having direct **artificial intelligence** (**AI**) or data science skills or knowledge
Azure Event Hubs	Big data streaming platform and event ingestion service
Azure Data Lake Storage	Set of capabilities dedicated to big data analytics, built on Azure Blob storage
Azure HDInsight	Provisions cloud Hadoop, Spark, R Server, HBase, and Storm clusters
Azure Cosmos DB	Fast NoSQL database with open APIs for any scale
Azure SQL Database	Managed, intelligent SQL in the cloud

Table 1.1 – Azure data platform services

Using the Azure data platform services can help you build a modern analytics solution that is secure and scalable. The following diagram shows an example of a typical modern cloud analytics architecture:

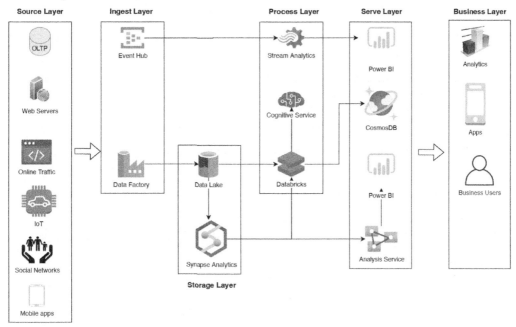

Figure 1.1 – Modern analytics solution architecture

You can find most of the Azure data platform services here. ADF is a core service for data movement and transformation.

Let's learn more about the reference architecture in *Figure 1.1*. It starts with source systems. We can collect data from files, databases, APIs, IoT, and so on. Then, we can use Event Hubs for streaming data and ADF for batch operations. ADF will push data into Azure Data Lake as a staging area, and then we can prepare data for analytics and reporting in Azure Synapse Analytics. Moreover, we can use Databricks for big data processing and machine learning models. Power BI is an ultimate data visualization service. Finally, we can push data into Azure Cosmos DB if we want to use data in business applications.

Getting ready

In this recipe, we will create a free Azure account, log in to the Azure portal, and locate ADF services. If you have an Azure account already, you can skip the creation of the account and log straight into the portal.

How to do it...

Open `https://azure.microsoft.com/free/`, then take the following steps:

1. Click **Start Free**.

2. You can sign in to your existing Microsoft account or create a new one. Let's create one as an example.

3. Enter an email address in the format `someone@example.com` and click **Next**.

4. Enter a password of your choice.

5. Verify your email by entering the code, and click **Next**.

6. Fill in the information for your profile (**Country, Name**, and so on). It will also require your credit card information.

7. After you have finished the account creation, it will bring you to the Microsoft Azure portal, as shown in the following screenshot:

Figure 1.2 – Azure portal

8. Now, we can explore the Azure portal and find Azure data services. Let's find Azure Synapse Analytics. In the search bar, enter `Azure Synapse Analytics` and choose **Azure Synapse Analytics (formerly SQL DW)**. It will open the Synapse control panel, as shown in the following screenshot:

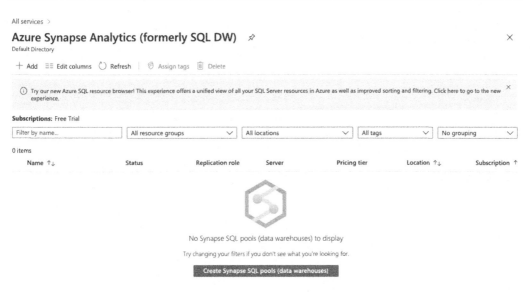

Figure 1.3 – Azure Synapse Analytics menu

Here, we can launch a new instance of a Synapse data warehouse.

Let's find and create some data factories. In the next recipe, we will create a new data factory.

Before doing anything with ADF, though, let's review what we have covered about an Azure account.

How it works...

Now that we have created a free Azure account, it gives us the following benefits:

- 12 months of free access to popular products
- $250 worth of credit
- 25+ always-free products

The Azure account we created is free and you won't be charged unless you choose to upgrade.

Moreover, we discovered the Azure data platform products, which we will use over the course of the book. The Azure portal has a friendly UI where we can easily locate, launch, pause, or terminate the service. Aside from the UI, Azure offers us other ways of communicating with Azure services, using the **command-line interface (CLI)**, APIs, SDKs, and so on.

Using the Microsoft Azure portal, you can choose the **Analytics** category and it will show you all the analytics services, as shown in the following screenshot:

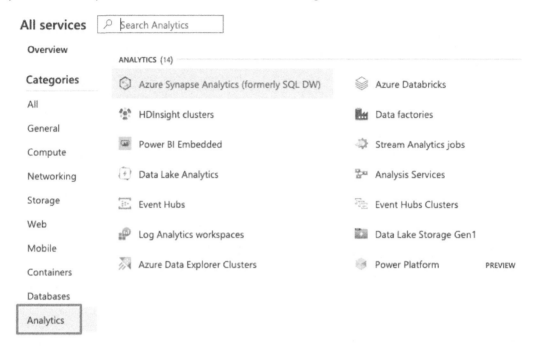

Figure 1.4 – Azure analytics services

We just located Azure Synapse Analytics in the Azure portal. Next, we should be able to create an ADF job.

Creating and executing our first job in ADF

ADF allows us to create workflows for transforming and orchestrating data movement. You may think of ADF as an **ETL** (short for **Extract, Transform, Load**) tool for the Azure cloud and the Azure data platform. ADF is **Software as a Service (SaaS)**. This means that we don't need to deploy any hardware or software. We pay for what we use. Often, ADF is referred to as a code-free ETL as a service. The key operations of ADF are listed here:

- **Ingest**: Allows us to collect data and load it into Azure data platform storage or any other target location. ADF has 90+ data connectors.
- **Control flow**: Allows us to design code-free extracting and loading.
- **Data flow**: Allows us to design code-free data transformations.

- **Schedule**: Allows us to schedule ETL jobs.
- **Monitor**: Allows us to monitor ETL jobs.

We have learned about the key operations in ADF. Next, we should try them.

Getting ready

In this recipe, we will continue on from the previous recipe, where we found Azure Synapse Analytics in the Azure console. We will create a data factory using a straightforward method – through the ADF UI via the Azure portal UI. It is important to have the correct permissions in order to create a new data factory. In our example, we are a super admin, and so we should be good to go.

During the exercise, we will create a new resource group. A resource group is a collection of resources that share the same life cycle, permissions, and policies.

How to do it...

Let's get back to our data factory:

1. If you have closed the **Data Factory** console, you should open it again. Search for `Data factories` and click **Enter**.

2. Click **Create data factory**, or **Add** if you are on the **Data factories** screen, and it will open the project details, where we will choose a subscription (in our case, **Free Trial**).

3. We haven't created a resource group yet. Click **Create new** and type the name `ADFCookbook`. Choose **East US** for **Region**, give the name as `ADFcookbookJob1-<YOUR NAME>` (in my case, `ADFcookbookJob1-Dmitry`), and leave the version as `V2`. Then, click **Next: Git Configuration**.

4. We can use GitHub or Azure DevOps. We won't configure anything yet and so we will select **Configure Git later**. Then, click **Next: Networking**.

5. We have an option to increase the security of our pipelines using **Managed Virtual Network** and **Private endpoint**. For this recipe, we will use the default settings. Click **Next**.

6. Optionally, you can specify tags. Then, click **Next: Review + Create**. ADF will validate your settings and will allow you to click **Create**.

7. Azure will deploy the data factory. We can choose our data factory and click **Author and Monitor**. This will open the ADF UI home page, where we can find lots of useful tutorials and webinars.

8. From the left panel, choose the blue pencil icon, as shown in the following screenshot, and it will open a window where we will start the creation of the pipeline. Choose **New pipeline** and it will open the **pipeline1** window, where we have to provide the following information: input, output, and compute. Add the name ADF-cookbook-pipeline1 and click **Validate All**:

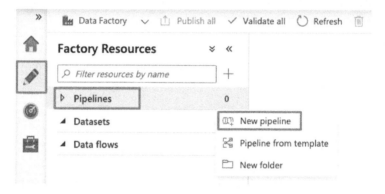

Figure 1.5 – ADF resources

9. When executing *Step 8*, you will find out that you can't save the pipeline without the activity. For our new data pipeline, we will do a simple *copy data* activity. We will copy the file from one blob folder to another. In this chapter, we won't spend time on spinning resources such as databases, Synapse, or Databricks. Later in this book, you will learn about using ADF with other data platform services. In order to copy data from Blob storage, we should create an Azure storage account and a blob container.

10. Let's create the Azure storage account. Go to **All Services | Storage | Storage Accounts**.

11. Click + **Add**.

12. Use our **Free Trial** subscription. For the resource group, we will use ADFCookbook. Give a name for the storage account, such as adfcookbookstorage, then click **Review and Create**. The name should be unique to you.

13. Click **Go to Resource** and select **Containers**:

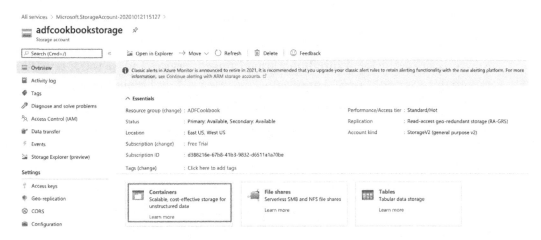

Figure 1.6 – Azure storage account UI

14. Click **+ Container** and enter the name `adfcookbook`.

15. Now, we want to upload a data file into the `SalesOrders.txt` file. You can get this file from the book's GitHub account. Go to the `adfcookbook` container and click **Upload**. We will specify the folder name as `input`. We just uploaded the file to the cloud! You can find it with the `/container/folder/file – adfcookbook/input/SalesOrders.txt` path.

16. Next, we can go back to ADF. In order to finish the pipeline, we should add an input dataset and create a new linked service.

17. In the ADF studio, click the **Managed** icon from the left sidebar. This will open the linked services. Click **+ New** and choose **Azure Blob Storage**, then click **Continue**.

18. We can optionally change the name or leave it as the default, but we have to specify the subscription and choose the storage account that we just created.

19. Click **Test Connection** and if all is good, click **Create**.

20. Next, we will add a dataset. Go to our pipeline and click **New dataset**, as shown in the following screenshot:

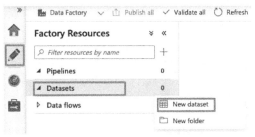

Figure 1.7 – ADF resources

21. Choose **Azure Blob Storage** and click **Continue**. Choose the **Binary** format type for our text file and click **Continue**.

22. Now, we can specify the **AzureBlobStorage1** linked services and we will specify the path to the `adfcookbook/input/SalesOrders.txt` file and click **Create**.

23. We can give the name of the dataset in **Properties**. Type in `SalesOrdersDataset` and click **Validate all**. We shouldn't encounter any issues with data.

24. We should add one more dataset as the output for our job. Let's create a new dataset with the name `SalesOrdersDatasetOutput`.

25. Now, we can go back to our data pipeline. We couldn't save it when we created it without a proper activity. Now, we have all that we need in order to finish the pipeline. Add the new pipeline and give it the name `ADF-cookbook-pipeline1`. Then, from the activity list, expand **Move & transform** and drag and drop the **Copy data** step to the canvas.

26. We have to specify the parameters of the step – the source and sink information. Click the **Source** tab and choose our dataset, **SalesOrdersDataset**.

27. Click the **Sink** tab and choose **SalesOrdersDatasetOutput**. This will be our output folder.

28. Now, we can publish two datasets and one pipeline.

29. Then, we can trigger our pipeline manually. Click **Add trigger**, as shown in the following screenshot:

Figure 1.8 – ADF canvas with the Copy data activity

30. Select **Trigger Now**. It will launch our job.

31. We can click on **Monitor** from the left sidebar and find the pipeline runs. In the case of failure, we can pick up the logs here and find the root cause. In our case, the `ADF-cookbook-pipeline1` pipeline succeeds. In order to see the outcome, we should go to **Azure Storage** and open our container. You can find the additional **Output** folder and a file named `SalesOrders.txt` there.

We just created our first job using the UI. Let's learn more about ADF.

How it works...

Using the ADF UI, we created a new pipeline – an ETL job. We specified input and output datasets and used Azure Blob storage as a linked service. The linked service itself is a kind of connection string. ADF is using the linked service in order to connect external resources. On the other hand, we have datasets. They represent the data structure for the data stores. We performed the simple activity of copying data from one folder to another. After the job ran, we reviewed the **Monitor** section with the job run logs.

There's more...

An ADF pipeline is a set of config JSON files. You can also view the JSON for each pipeline, dataset, and so on in the portal by clicking the three dots in the top-right corner. We are using the UI in order to create the configuration file and run the job. You can review the config JSON file by downloading a JSON file, as shown in the following figure:

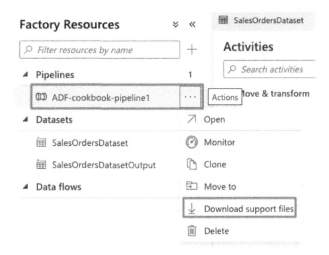

Figure 1.9 – Downloading the pipeline config files

This will save the archive file. Extract it and you will find a folder with the following subfolders:

- `Dataset`
- `LinkedService`
- `Pipeline`

Each folder has a corresponding JSON config file.

See also

You can find more information about ADF from this Microsoft video, *Introduction to Azure Data Factory*: `https://azure.microsoft.com/en-us/resources/videos/detailed-introduction-to-azure-data-factory/`.

Creating an ADF pipeline by using the Copy Data tool

We just reviewed how to create the ADF job using UI. However, we can also use the **Copy Data tool** (CDT). The CDT allows us to load data into Azure storage faster. We don't need to set up linked services, pipelines, and datasets as we did in the previous recipe. In other words, depending on your activity, you can use the ADF UI or the CDT. Usually, we will use the CDT for simple load operations, when we have lots of data files and we would like to ingest them into Data Lake as fast as possible.

Getting ready

In this recipe, we will use the CDT in order to do the same task of copying data from one folder to another.

How to do it...

We created the ADF job with the UI. Let's review the CDT:

1. In the previous recipe, we created the Azure Blob storage instance and container. We will use the same file and the same container. However, we have to delete the file from the output location.

2. Go to **Azure Storage Accounts**, choose **adfcookbookstorage**, and click **Containers**. Choose **adfcookbook**. Go to the **Output** folder and delete the `SalesOrders.txt` file.

3. Now, we can go back to the **Data Factories** portal. On the home page, we can see the icon for copy data. Click on it. It will open with the CPD wizard. Give it the name CDP-copy-job and choose **Run once now**. Click **Next**.

4. Click **Create a new connection**. Choose the free trial subscription and adfcookbookstorage as the account name. It will create the AzureBlobStorage2 connection. Click **Next**.

5. You can browse the blob storage and you will find the filename. The path should look like adfcookbook/input/SalesOrders.txt. Mark **Binary copy**. When we are choosing the binary option, the file will be treated as binaries and won't enforce the schema. This is a great option to just copy the file as is. Click **Next**.

6. Next, we will choose the destination. Choose **AzureBlobStorage2** and click **Next**. Enter the adfcookbook/output output path and click **Next** until you reach the end. As a result, you should get a similar output as I have, as you can see in the following screenshot:

Figure 1.10 – CDT UI

7. If we go to the storage account, we will find that CDT copied data into the **Output** folder.

We have created a copy job using CDT.

How it works...

CPD basically created the data pipeline for us. If you go to **ADF author**, you will find a new job and new datasets.

There's more...

You can learn more about the CDT at the Microsoft documentation page: `https://docs.microsoft.com/en-us/azure/data-factory/copy-data-tool`.

Creating an ADF pipeline using Python

We can use PowerShell, .NET, and Python for ADF deployment and data integration automation. Here is an extract from the Microsoft documentation:

> *Azure Automation delivers a cloud-based automation and configuration service that provides consistent management across your Azure and non-Azure environments. It consists of process automation, update management, and configuration features. Azure Automation provides complete control during deployment, operations, and decommissioning of workloads and resources.*

In this recipe, we want to cover the Python scenario because Python is one of the most popular languages for analytics and data engineering. We will use Jupyter Notebook with example code.

Getting ready

For this exercise, we will use Python in order to create a data pipeline and copy our file from one folder to another. We need to use the `azure-mgmt-datafactory` and `azure-mgmt-resource` Python packages as well as some others.

How to do it...

We will create data factory pipeline using Python. We will start from preparation steps.

1. We will start with the deletion of our file in the output directory. Go to **Azure Storage Accounts**, choose **adfcookbookstorage**, and click **Containers**. Choose **adfcookbook**. Go to the **Output** folder and delete the `SalesOrders.txt` file.

2. We will install the Azure management resources Python package by running this command from the CLI. In my example, I used Terminal on macOS:

    ```
    pip install azure-mgmt-resource
    ```

3. Next, we will install the ADF Python package by running this command from the CLI:

```
pip install azure-mgmt-datafactory
```

4. Also, I installed these packages in order to run code from Jupyter:

```
pip install msrestazure
pip install azure.mgmt.datafactory
pip install azure.identity
```

5. When we finish installing the Python packages, we should use these packages in order to create the data pipeline, datasets, and linked service, as well as to run the code. Python gives us flexibility and we could embed this into our analytics application or Spark/Databricks.

    The code itself is quite big and you can find the code in the attachment to this chapter, `ADF_Python_Run.ipynb`. This is the Jupyter notebook. It has 10 sections, and you can run them one by one and see the output.

6. In order to control Azure resources from the Python code, we have to register the app with Azure Active Directory and assign a contributor role to this app in **Identity and Access Management (IAM)** under our subscription. We have to get `tenant_id`, `client_id`, and `client_secret`.

7. Go to Azure Active Directory and click **App registrations**. Click **+ New registration**. Enter the name `ADFcookbookapp` and click **Register**. From the app properties, you have to copy `Application (client) ID` and `Directory (tenant) ID`.

8. Still in `ADFcookbookapp`, go to **Certificates & secrets** on the left sidebar. Click **+ New client secret** and add new client secret. Copy the value.

9. Next, we should give permissions to our app. Go to the subscriptions. Choose **Free Trial**. Click on **Access control (IAM)**. Click on **Add role assignments**. Select the **Contributor** role. Assign access to a user, group, or service principal. Finally, search for our app, `ADFcookbookapp`, and click **Save**. As a result, we just granted access to the app and we can use these credentials in our Python code.

10. Open `ADF_Python_Run.ipynb` and make sure that you have all the libraries in place by execute the first code block. You can open the file in Jupyter Notebook:

```
from azure.identity import ClientSecretCredential
from azure.mgmt.datafactory import
DataFactoryManagementClient
from azure.mgmt.datafactory.models import *
from msrest.authentication import
```

```
BasicTokenAuthentication
from azure.core.pipeline.policies import
BearerTokenCredentialPolicy
from azure.core.pipeline import PipelineRequest,
PipelineContext
from azure.core.pipeline.transport import HttpRequest
from azure.identity import DefaultAzureCredential
```

11. You should run this piece without any problems. If you encounter an issue, it means you are missing the Python package. Make sure that you have installed all of the packages. Run sections 2 and 3 in the notebook. You can find the notebook in the GitHub repository with the book files.

12. In section 4, *Authentificate Azure*, you have to enter the `tenant_id`, `client_id`, and `client_secret` values. The resource group and data factory name we can leave as is. Then, run sections 4 and 5.

13. The Python code will also interact with the Azure storage account and we should provide the storage account name and key. For this chapter, we are using the `adfcookbookstorage` storage account and you can find the key under the **Access keys** section of this storage account menu. Copy the key value and paste it into section 6, *Created a Linked Service*, and run it.

14. In sections 7 and 8, we are creating input and output datasets. You can run the code as is. In section 9, we will create the data pipeline and specify the `CopyActivity` activity.

15. Finally, we will run the pipeline at section 10, *Create a pipeline run*.

16. In section 17, *Monitor a pipeline run*, we will check the output of the run. We should get the following:

```
Pipeline run status: Succeeded
```

We just created an ADF job with Python. Let's add more details.

How it works...

We used Azure Python packages in order to control Azure resources. We registered an app in order to authenticate the Python code and granted contributor permissions. Using Jupyter Notebook, we ran the code step by step and created a data factory, as well as executed the `copy` command.

There's more...

We used notebooks in order to demonstrate the sequence of steps and its output. We can also create a Python file and run it.

See also

There are lots of useful resources available online about the use of Python for ADF. Here are a few of them:

- Serverless Python in ADF: `https://medium.com/asos-techblog/serverless-python-in-azure-data-factory-42f841e06dc3`

- ADF libraries for Python: `https://docs.microsoft.com/en-us/python/api/overview/azure/datafactory?view=azure-python`

- Tutorial: *Run Python scripts through ADF using Azure Batch*: `https://docs.microsoft.com/en-us/azure/batch/tutorial-run-python-batch-azure-data-factory`

Creating a data factory using PowerShell

Often, we don't have access to the UI and we want to create infrastructure as code. It is easily maintainable and deployable and allows us to track versions and have code commit and change requests. In this recipe, we will use PowerShell in order to create a data factory. If you have never used PowerShell before, you can find information about how to get PowerShell and install it onto your machine at the end of this recipe.

Getting ready

For this exercise, we will use PowerShell in order to create a data pipeline and copy our file from one folder to another.

How to do it...

Let's create an ADF job using PowerShell.

1. In the case of macOS, we can run the following command to install PowerShell:

   ```
   brew install powershell/tap/powershell
   ```

2. Check that it is working:

   ```
   pwsh
   ```

Optionally, we can download PowerShell for our OS from `https://github.com/PowerShell/PowerShell/releases/`.

3. Next, we have to install the Azure module. Run the following command:

```
Install-Module -Name Az -AllowClobber
```

4. Next, we should connect to the Azure account by running this command:

```
Connect-AzAccount
```

It will ask us to open the `https://microsoft.com/devicelogin` page and enter the code for authentication, and will tell us something like this:

```
Account                SubscriptionName
TenantId                         Environment
-------                ---------------- -----
---                              ----------
datalearn4all@gmail.com Free Trial      1c204124-0ceb-
41de-b366-1983c14c1628 AzureCloud
```

5. Run the command in order to check the Azure subscription:

```
Get-AzSubscription
```

6. Now, we can create a data factory. As usual, we should specify the resource group:

```
$resourceGroupName = "ADFCookbook"
```

Then, run the code that will create or update the existing resource group:

```
$ResGrp = New-AzResourceGroup $resourceGroupName
-location 'East US'
```

You can choose your region, then specify the ADF name:

```
$dataFactoryName = "ADFCookbook-PowerShell"
```

Now, we can run the command that will create a data factory under our resource group:

```
$DataFactory = Set-AzDataFactoryV2 -ResourceGroupName
$ResGrp.ResourceGroupName `
    -Location $ResGrp.Location -Name $dataFactoryName
```

As a result, PowerShell will create for us a new data factory.

7. The next steps would be the same as we did in Python – creating a linked service, datasets, and pipeline. In the case of PowerShell, we should use JSON config files where we would specify the parameters.

We used PowerShell in order to create an ADF job. Let's add more details.

How it works...

We used PowerShell in order to connect to Azure and control Azure resources. We created a new data factory using the PowerShell command. In the same way, we can create datasets, data flows, linked services, and pipelines using JSON files for configuration, and then execute the command with PowerShell. For example, we can define a JSON file for the input dataset using the following code block:

```
{
    "name": "InputDataset",
    "properties": {
        "linkedServiceName": {
            "referenceName": "AzureStorageLinkedService",
            "type": "LinkedServiceReference"
        },
        "annotations": [],
        "type": "Binary",
        "typeProperties": {
            "location": {
                "type": "AzureBlobStorageLocation",
                "fileName": "emp.txt",
                "folderPath": "input",
                "container": "adftutorial"
            }
        }
    }
}
```

Save it as `input.json` and then execute the following PowerShell command:

```
Set-AzDataFactoryV2Dataset -DataFactoryName $DataFactory.
DataFactoryName `
    -ResourceGroupName $ResGrp.ResourceGroupName -Name
"InputDataset" `
    -DefinitionFile ".\Input.json"
```

This command will create a dataset for our data factory.

There's more...

You can learn about the use of PowerShell with ADF by reviewing the available samples from Microsoft at `https://docs.microsoft.com/en-us/azure/data-factory/samples-powershell`.

See also

You can refer to the following links to get more information about the use of PowerShell:

- You can find information about installing Azure PowerShell on Windows here: `https://docs.microsoft.com/en-us/powershell/azure/get-started-azureps`

- If you have macOS, you can use this doc: `https://docs.microsoft.com/en-us/powershell/scripting/install/installing-powershell-core-on-macos?view=powershell-7`

Using templates to create ADF pipelines

Modern organizations are operating in a fast-pace environment. It is important to deliver insights faster and have shorter analytics iterations. Moreover, Azure found that many organizations have similar use cases for their modern cloud analytics deployments. As a result, Azure built a number of predefined templates. For example, if you have data in Amazon S3 and you want to copy it into Azure Data Lake, you can find a specific template for this operation; or say you want to move an on-premises Oracle data warehouse to the Azure Synapse Analytics data warehouse – you are covered with ADF templates.

Getting ready

ADF provides us with templates in order to accelerate data engineering development. In this recipe, we will review the common templates and see how to use them.

How to do it...

We will find and review an existing template using Data Factories.

1. In the Azure portal, choose **Data Factories**.

2. Open our existing data factory, `ADFcokbookJob1-Dmitry`.

3. Click **Author and Monitor** and it will open the ADF portal.

4. From the home page, click on **Create pipeline from template**. It will open the page to the list of templates.

5. Let's open **Slow Changing Dimension Type 2**. This is one of the most popular techniques for building a data warehouse and dimensional modeling. From the description page, we can review the documentation, examples, and user input. For this particular example, we have **Delimited Text** as input and the **Azure SQL** database as output. If you would like to proceed and use this template, you have to fill in the user input and click **Use this template**. It will import this template into ADF and you can review the steps in detail as well as modify them.

   Let's review one more template.

6. Let's choose the **Distinct Rows** template. For the user input, let's choose the existing **AzureBlobStorage1** and click **Use this template**.

7. It will import the pipeline, datasets, and data flows, as shown in the following screenshot:

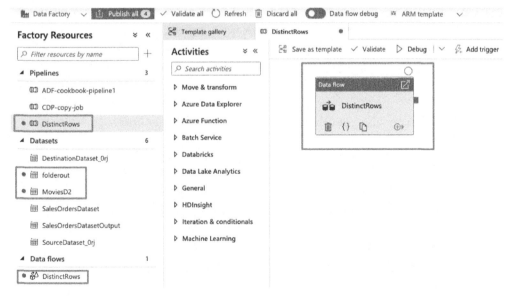

Figure 1.11 – ADF data flow activity

8. We should review the datasets and update the information about the file path for the input dataset and output location. We won't run this job.

9. You can also review the data flow's **DistinctRows** feature, where you can see all the logic, as shown in the following screenshot:

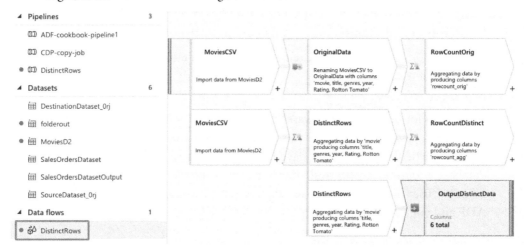

Figure 1.12 – ADF data flow

You can review other templates and see many examples of ADF design.

How it works...

We learned that ADF is a set of JSON files with configuration. As a result, it is relatively easy to create new components and share them as a template. We can deploy each template right to ADF or we can download the template bundle and modify the JSON file. These templates help us learn best practices or avoid reinventing the wheel.

See also

There are useful materials about the use of templates available online:

*   You can learn more about ADF templates using the Microsoft blog: `https://azure.microsoft.com/en-us/blog/get-started-quickly-using-templates-in-azure-data-factory/`

*   You can learn more about SCD 2 templates at this blog post: `https://mssqldude.wordpress.com/2019/04/15/adf-slowly-changing-dimension-type-2-with-mapping-data-flows-complete/`

*   You can learn more about the Distinct Rows data flow at this blog post: `https://mssqldude.wordpress.com/2019/09/18/adf-data-flows-distinct-rows/`

2
Orchestration and Control Flow

Azure Data Factory is an excellent tool for designing and orchestrating your **Extract, Transform, Load** (ETL) processes. In this chapter, we introduce several fundamental data factory concepts and guide you through the creation and scheduling of increasingly complex data-driven workflows. All the work in this chapter is done using the Microsoft data factory online portal. You'll learn how to create and configure **Linked Services** and datasets, take advantage of built-in expressions and functions, and, most importantly, learn how and when to use the most popular **Data Factory** activities.

This chapter covers the following topics:

- Using parameters and built-in functions
- Using the Metadata and Stored Procedure activities
- Using the ForEach and Filter activities
- Chaining and branching activities within a pipeline
- Using the Lookup, Web, and Execute Pipeline activities
- Creating event-based pipeline triggers

Technical requirements

> **Note**
>
> To fully understand the recipes, we make naming suggestions for the accounts, pipelines, and so on throughout the chapter. Many services, such as Azure Storage and SQL Server, require that the names you assign are unique. Follow your own preferred naming conventions, making appropriate substitutions as you follow the recipes. For the Azure resource naming rules, refer to the documentation at `https://docs.microsoft.com/azure/azure-resource-manager/management/resource-name-rules`.

In addition to Azure Data Factory, we shall be using three other Azure Services: **Logic Apps**, **Blob Storage**, and **Azure SQL Database**. You will need to have Azure Blob Storage and Azure SQL Database accounts set up to follow the recipes. The following steps describe the necessary preparation:

- Create an Azure Blob Storage account and name it `adforchestrationstorage`. When creating the storage account, select the same region (that is, East US) as you selected when you created the Data Factory instance. This will save us costs when moving data.

- Create a container named `data` within this storage account, and upload two CSV files to the folder: `airlines.csv` and `countries.csv` (the files can be found on GitHub: `https://github.com/PacktPublishing/Azure-Data-Factory-Cookbook/tree/master/data`).

- Create an Azure SQL Database instance and name it `AzureSQLDatabase`. When you create the Azure SQL Database instance, you will have the option of creating a server on which the SQL database will be hosted. Create that server, and take note of the credentials you entered. You will need these credentials later when you log in to your database.

  Choose the basic configuration for your SQL server to save on costs. Once your instance is up and running, configure the firewall and network settings for the SQL server: make sure that you set the **Allow Azure services and resources to access this database** option to **Yes**. You may also need to create a rule to allow your IP to access the database:

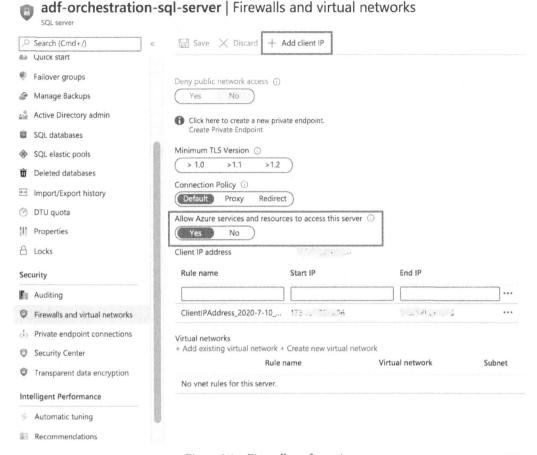

Figure 2.1 – Firewall configuration

Download the SQL scripts from GitHub at `https://github.com/PacktPublishing/Azure-Data-Factory-Cookbook/tree/master/Chapter02/sql-scripts`:

- `CreateAirlineTable.sql` and `CreateCountryTable.sql`: These scripts will add two tables, `Country` and `Airline`, which are used in several recipes, including the first one.

- `CreateMetadataTable.sql`: This will create the `FileMetadata` table and a stored procedure to insert data into that table. This table is necessary for the *Using Metadata and Stored Procedure activities* and *Filtering your data and looping through your files* recipes.

- `CreateActivityLogsTable.sql`: This will create the `PipelineLog` table and a stored procedure to insert data into that table. This table is necessary for the *Chaining and branching activities within your pipeline* recipe.

- `CreateEmailRecipients.sql`: This script will create the `EmailRecipients` table and populate it with a record. This table is used in the *Using the Lookup, Web, and Execute Pipeline activities* recipe. You will need to edit it to enter email recipient information.

Using parameters and built-in functions

In this recipe, we shall demonstrate the power and versatility of ADF by performing a common task: importing data from several files (blobs) from a storage container into tables in Azure SQL Database. We shall create a pipeline, define datasets, and use a `Copy` activity to tie all the pieces together and transfer the data. We shall also see how easy it is to back up data with a quick modification to the pipeline.

Getting ready

In this recipe, we shall be using most of the services that were mentioned in the *Technical requirements* section of this chapter. Make sure that you have access to Azure SQL Database (with the `AzureSQLDatabase` instance we created) and the Azure storage account with the necessary `.csv` files already uploaded.

How to do it...

First, open your Azure Data Factory instance in the Azure portal and go to the **Author and Monitor** interface. Here, we shall define the datasets for input files and database tables, and the linked services (for Azure Blob Storage and Azure SQL Database):

1. Start by creating linked services for the Azure storage account and `AzureSQLDatabase`.

2. Create the linked service for the `adforchestrationstorage` storage account:

    (a) In the **Manage** tab, select **Linked Services** and click on the **New** button. On the **New linked service** blade, select **Azure Blob Storage**:

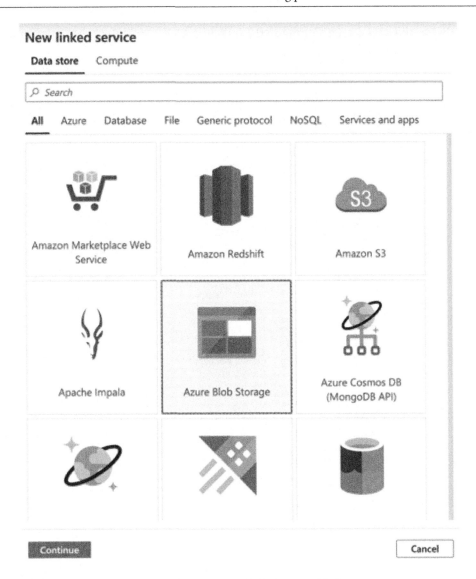

Figure 2.2 – The New linked service blade

(b) On the next screen, configure the linked service connection properties as shown in the following screenshot:

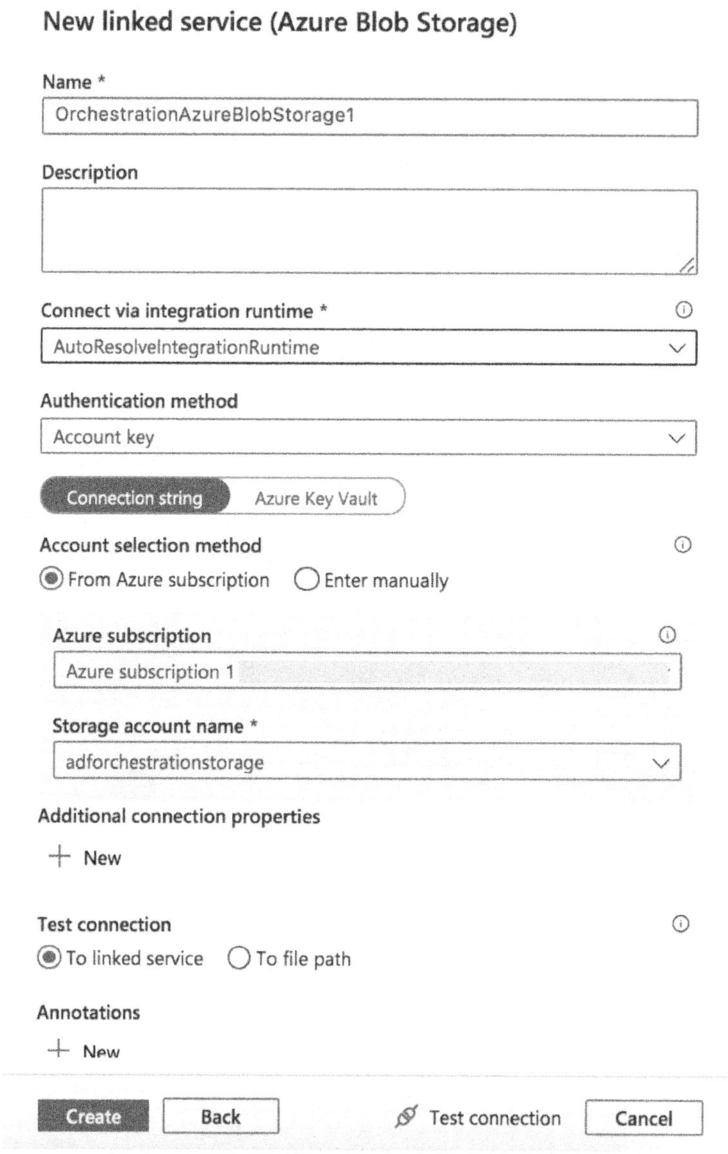

New linked service (Azure Blob Storage)

Name *

OrchestrationAzureBlobStorage1

Description

Connect via integration runtime *   ⓘ

AutoResolveIntegrationRuntime   ⌄

Authentication method

Account key   ⌄

[**Connection string**] (Azure Key Vault)

Account selection method   ⓘ

◉ From Azure subscription   ◯ Enter manually

Azure subscription   ⓘ

Azure subscription 1

Storage account name *

adforchestrationstorage   ⌄

Additional connection properties

+ New

Test connection   ⓘ

◉ To linked service   ◯ To file path

Annotations

+ New

[Create] [Back]   🖉 Test connection [Cancel]

Figure 2.3 – Connection configurations for Azure Blob Storage

Name your linked service according to your naming convention (in our example, we named it `OrchestrationAzureBlobStorage1`).

Select the appropriate subscription and enter the name of your storage account (where you store the `.csv` files).

For **Integration Runtime**, select **AutoResolveIntegrationRuntime**.

For **Authentication method**, select **Account Key**.

Note:

In this recipe, we are using **Account Key** authentication to access our storage account. However, in your work environment, it is recommended to authenticate using Managed Identity, taking advantage of the Azure Active Directory service. This is more secure and allows you to avoid using credentials in your code. Find the references for more information about using Managed Identity with Azure Data Factory in the *See also* section of this recipe.

(c) Click the **Test Connection** button at the bottom and verify that you can connect to the storage account.

(d) Finally, click on the **Create** button and wait for the linked service to be created.

3.   Create the second linked service for `AzureSQLDatabase`:

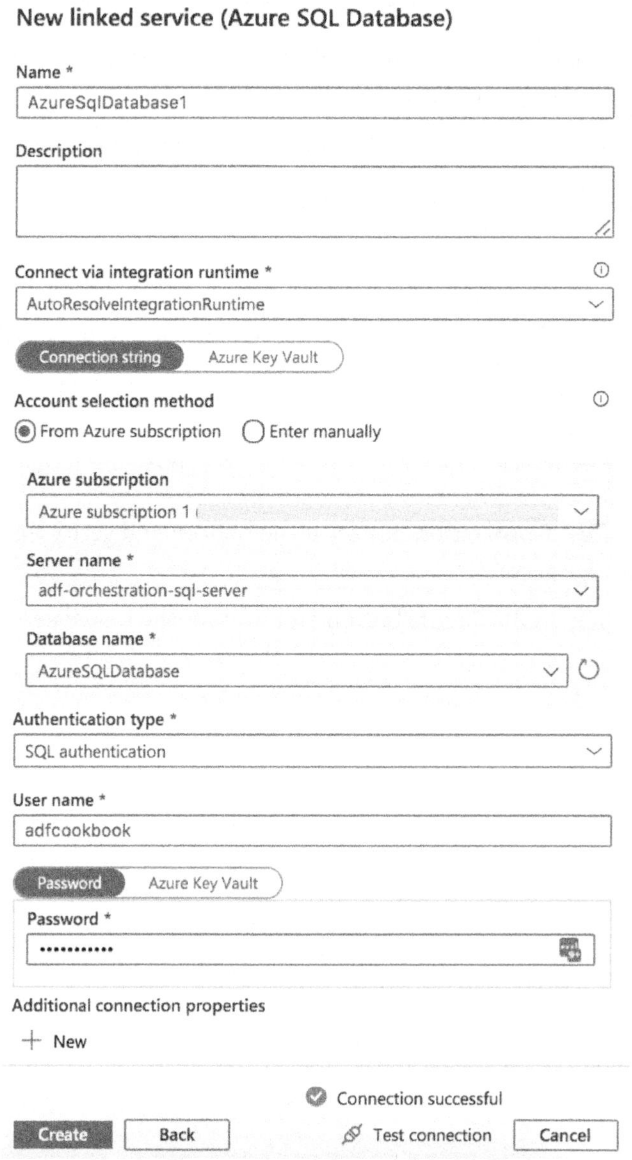

New linked service (Azure SQL Database)

Name *

AzureSqlDatabase1

Description

Connect via integration runtime *

AutoResolveIntegrationRuntime

Connection string   Azure Key Vault

Account selection method

● From Azure subscription   ○ Enter manually

Azure subscription

Azure subscription 1

Server name *

adf-orchestration-sql-server

Database name *

AzureSQLDatabase

Authentication type *

SQL authentication

User name *

adfcookbook

Password   Azure Key Vault

Password *

••••••••••

Additional connection properties

+ New

✓ Connection successful

Create   Back   Test connection   Cancel

Figure 2.4 – Connection properties for Azure SQL Database

(a) In the **Manage** tab, create a new linked service, but this time select **Azure SQL** from choices in the **New linked service** blade. You can enter `Azure SQL` into the search field to find it easily.

(b) Select the subscription information and the SQL server name (the dropdown will present you with choices). Once you have selected the SQL server name, you can select your database (`AzureSQLDatabase`) from the dropdown in the **Database Name** section.

(c) Select **SQL Authentication** for **Authentication Type**. Enter the username and password for your database.

(d) Make sure to test the connection. If the connection fails, ensure that you configured access correctly in **Firewall and Network Settings**. Once you have successfully tested the connection, click on **Create** to save your linked service.

Now, we shall create two datasets, one for each linked service.

4. In the **Author** tab, define the dataset for Azure Storage as shown in the following screenshot:

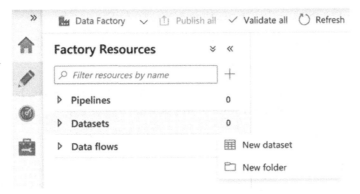

Figure 2.5 – Create a new dataset

(a) Go to **Datasets** and click on **New dataset**. Select **Azure Blob Storage** from the choices and click **Continue**.

(b) In the **Select Format** blade, select **Delimited Text** and hit **Continue**.

(c) Call your new dataset `CsvData` and select **OrchestrationAzureBlobStorage** in the **Linked Service** dropdown.

(d) With the help of the **folder** button, navigate to your Azure folder and select any file from there to specify the file path:

Figure 2.6 – Dataset properties

(e) Check the **First Row as Header** checkbox and click on **Create**.

5.   In the same **Author** tab, create a dataset for the Azure SQL table:

(a) Go to **Datasets** and click on **New dataset**.

(b) Select **Azure SQL** from the choices in the **New Dataset** blade.

(c) Name your dataset AzureSQLTables.

(d) In the **Linked Service** dropdown, select **AzureSQLDatabase**. For the table name, select **Country** from the dropdown.

(e) Click on **Create**.

6.   Parameterize the `AzureSQLTables` dataset:

(a) In the **Parameters** tab, enter the name of your new parameter, `tableName`:

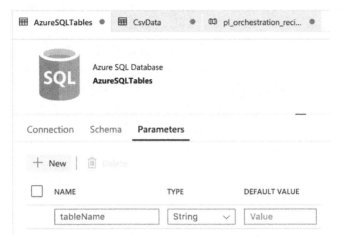

Figure 2.7 – Parameterizing the dataset

(b) Next, in the **Connection** tab, click on the **Edit** checkbox and enter `dbo` as schema and `@dataset().tableName` in the table text field, as shown in the following screenshot:

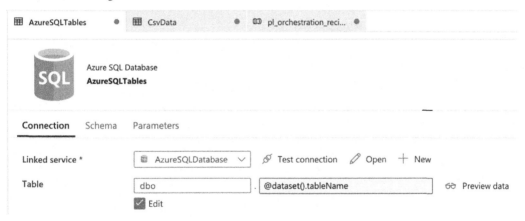

Figure 2.8 – Specifying a value for the dataset parameter

7. In the same way, parameterize and add dynamic content in the **Connection** tab for the `CsvData` dataset:

(a) Select your dataset, open the **Parameters** tab, and create a parameter named `filename`.

(b) In the **Connections** tab, in the **File Path** section, click inside the **File** text box, then click on the **Add Dynamic Content** link. This will bring up the **Dynamic Content** interface. In that interface, find the **Parameters** section and click on `filename`. This will generate the correct code to refer to the dataset's `filename` parameter in the dynamic content text box:

Figure 2.9 – Dynamic content interface

Click on the **Finish** button to finalize your choice.

Verify that you can see both datasets under the **Datasets** tab:

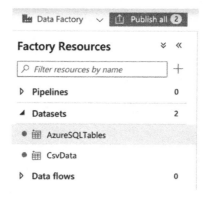

Figure 2.10 – Datasets in the Author tab

8. We are now ready to design the pipeline.

    In the **Author** tab, create a new pipeline. Change its name to `pl_
    orchestration_recipe_1`.

9. From the **Move and Transform** menu in the **Activities** pane (on the left), drag
    a **Copy** activity onto the canvas:

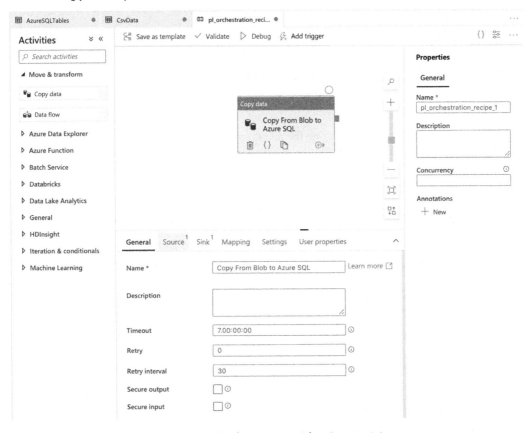

Figure 2.11 – Pipeline canvas with a Copy activity

On the bottom of the canvas, you will see some tabs: **General**, **Source**, **Sink**, and so on. Configure your **Copy** activity.

In the **General** tab, you can configure the name for your activity. Call it `Copy From Blob to Azure SQL`.

In the **Source** tab, select the `CsvData` dataset and specify `countries.csv` in the **filename** textbox.

In the **Sink** tab, select the `AzureSQLTables` dataset and specify `Country` in the **tableName** text field.

10. We are ready to run the pipeline in **Debug** mode:

> **Note**
>
> You will learn more about using the debug capabilities of Azure Data Factory in *Chapter 10, Monitoring and Troubleshooting Data Pipelines*. In this recipe, we introduce you to the **Output** pane, which will help you understand the design and function of this pipeline.

(a) Click the **Debug** button in the top panel. This will run your pipeline.

(b) Put your cursor anywhere on the pipeline canvas. You will see the report with the status of the activities in the bottom panel in the **Output** tab:

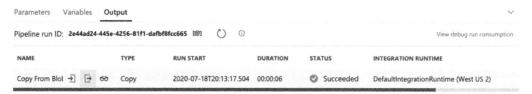

Figure 2.12 – Debug output

Hover your cursor over the row representing the activity to see the **inputs** and **outputs** buttons. We shall make use of these in later chapters.

After your pipeline has run, you should see that the dbo.Country table in your Azure SQL database has been populated with the countries data:

Query 1 ✕

▷ Run ☐ Cancel query ↓ Save query ↓ Export data as ⌄ ▦ Show only Editor

```
1   select * from [dbo].[Country]
```

Results   Messages

🔍 Search to filter items...

Name	Code
Aruba	AW
Antigua and Barbuda	AG
United Arab Emirates	AE
Afghanistan	AF
Algeria	DZ
Azerbaijan	AZ
Albania	AL
Armenia	AM
Angola	AO
American Samoa	AS
Argentina	AR

Figure 2.13 – Contents of the Country table in Azure SQL Database

We have copied the contents of the Countries.csv file into the database. In the next steps, we shall demonstrate how parameterizing the datasets gives us the flexibility to define which file we want to copy and which SQL table we want as the destination without redesigning the pipeline.

11. Edit the pipeline: click on the **Copy from Blob To Azure SQL** activity to select it, and specify airlines.csv for the filename in the **Source** tab and Airline for the table name in the **Sink** tab. Run your pipeline again (in **Debug** mode), and you should see that the second table is populated with the data – using the same pipeline!

12. Now, let's say we want to back up the contents of the tables in an Azure SQL database before overwriting them with data from .csv files. We can easily enhance the existing pipeline to accomplish this.

13. Drag another instance of the **Copy** activity from the **Activities** pane, name it `Backup Copy Activity`, and configure it in the following way:

    (a) For the source, select **AzureSQLDatabase** for the linked service, and add `Airline` in the text box for the table name.

    (b) In **Sink**, specify `CsvData` as the linked service, and enter the following formula into the **filename** textbox: `@concat('Airlines-', utcnow(), '.backup' )`.

    (c) Connect **Backup Copy Activity** to the **Copy from Blob to AzureSQL** copy activity:

Figure 2.14 – Adding backup functionality to the pipeline

14. Run the pipeline in debug mode. After the run is complete, you should see the backup file in your storage account.

15. We have created two linked services and two datasets, and we have a functioning pipeline. Click on the **Publish All** button at the top to save your work.

Let's look at how this works!

How it works...

In this recipe, we became familiar with all the major components of an Azure Data Factory pipeline: linked services, datasets, and activities:

- Linked services represent configured connections between your Data Factory instance and the service that you want to use.

- Datasets are more granular: they represent the specific view of the data that your activities will use as input and output.

- Activities represent the actions that are performed on the data. Many activities require you to specify where the data is extracted from and where it is loaded to. The ADF terms for these entities are source and sink.

Every pipeline that you design will have those components.

In *step 1* and *step 2*, we created the linked services to connect to Azure Blob Storage and Azure SQL Database. Then, in *step 3* and *step 4*, we created datasets that connected to those linked services and referred to specific files or tables. We created parameters that represented the data we referred to in *step 5* and *step 6*, and this allowed us to change which files we wanted to load into tables without creating additional pipelines. In the remaining steps, we worked with instances of the Copy activity, specifying the inputs and outputs (sources and sinks) for the data.

There's more...

We used a built-in function for generating UTC timestamps in *step 12*. Data Factory provides many convenient built-in functions and expressions, as well as system variables, for your use. To see them, click on **Backup SQL Data activity** in your pipeline and go to the **Source** tab below it. Put your cursor inside the **tableName** text field. You will see an **Add dynamic content** link appear underneath. Click on it, and you will see the **Add dynamic content** blade:

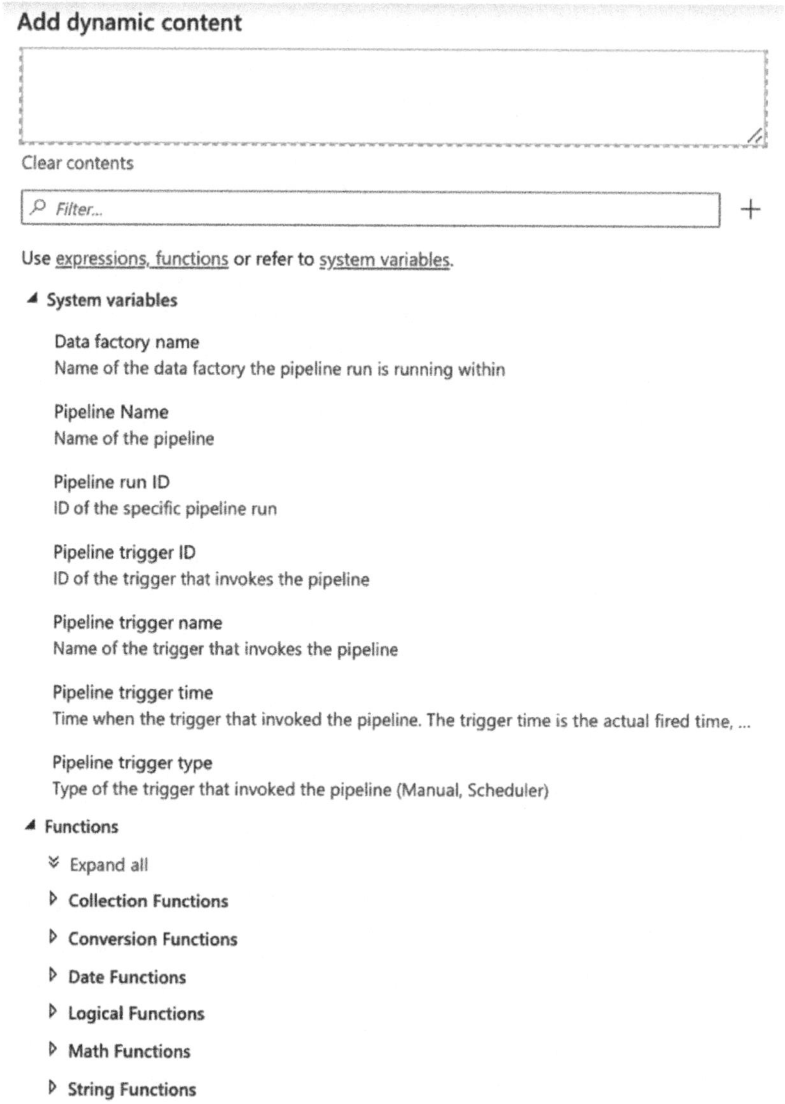

Add dynamic content

Clear contents

🔍 *Filter...*   +

Use expressions, functions or refer to system variables.

▲ **System variables**

    Data factory name
    Name of the data factory the pipeline run is running within

    Pipeline Name
    Name of the pipeline

    Pipeline run ID
    ID of the specific pipeline run

    Pipeline trigger ID
    ID of the trigger that invokes the pipeline

    Pipeline trigger name
    Name of the trigger that invokes the pipeline

    Pipeline trigger time
    Time when the trigger that invoked the pipeline. The trigger time is the actual fired time, ...

    Pipeline trigger type
    Type of the trigger that invoked the pipeline (Manual, Scheduler)

▲ **Functions**

    ≫ Expand all

    ▷ **Collection Functions**

    ▷ **Conversion Functions**

    ▷ **Date Functions**

    ▷ **Logical Functions**

    ▷ **Math Functions**

    ▷ **String Functions**

Figure 2.15 – Data Factory functions and system variables

This blade lists many useful functions and system variables to explore. We will use some of them in later recipes.

See also

Microsoft keeps extensive documentation on Data Factory. For a more detailed explanation of the concepts used in this recipe, refer to the following pages:

- Linked services in Azure Data Factory:

  `https://docs.microsoft.com/azure/data-factory/concepts-linked-services`

- Pipelines and activities in Azure Data Factory:

  `https://docs.microsoft.com/azure/data-factory/concepts-pipelines-activities`

- Setting up and using Managed Identity with Azure Data Factory:

  `https://docs.microsoft.com/azure/data-factory/data-factory-service-identity`

Using Metadata and Stored Procedure activities

In this recipe, we shall create a pipeline that fetches some metadata from an Azure storage container and stores it in an Azure SQL database table. You will work with two frequently used activities, the **Metadata** activity and the **Stored Procedure** activity.

Getting ready

- In the first recipe, we created two datasets and two linked services. We shall be using the `AzureSqlDatabase` and `OrchestrationAzureBlobStorage` linked services in this recipe as well, so if you did not create them before, please go through the necessary steps in the previous recipe.

- We shall be using `AzureSQLDatabase`. If you haven't done so already, create the `FileMetadata` table and the stored procedure to insert the data as described in the *Technical requirements* section of this chapter.

How to do it...

1. Create a new pipeline in the **Author** tab, and call it `pl_orchestration_ recipe_2`.

2. Create a new dataset named `CsvDataFolder`, pointing to the Azure Storage container (`adforchestrationstorage`) we specified in the *Technical requirements* section. Use the delimited text file format. This time, do not specify the filename; leave it pointing to the data container itself. Use the same linked service for Azure Blob Storage as we used in the previous recipe.

3. From the **Activities** pane on the left, find the **Get Metadata** activity (under the **General** Tab) and drag it onto the pipeline canvas. Using the configuration tabs at the bottom, configure it in the following way:

    (a) In the **General** tab, rename this **Metadata** activity `CsvDataFolder Metadata`.

    (b) In the **Source** tab, pick the `CsvDataFolder` dataset. In the same tab, under **Field list**, use the **New** button to add two fields, and select **Item Name** and **Last Modified** as the values for those fields:

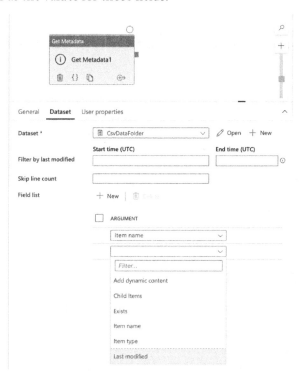

Figure 2.16 – Get Metadata activity configuration

4. In the **Activities** pane, find the **Stored Procedure** activity (under the **General** tab), and drag it onto the canvas. In the pipeline canvas, connect the **CsvDataFolder** Metadata activity to the **Stored Procedure** activity.

5. Configure the **Stored Procedure** activity in the following way:

   (a) In the **General** tab, change the activity name to Insert Metadata.

   (b) In the **Settings** tab, specify the linked service (AzureSqlDatabase) and the name of the stored procedure: [dbo].[InsertFileMetadata].

   (c) In the same **Settings** tab, click on **Import Parameters** to display the text fields to specify the parameters for the Stored Procedure activity. Use the following values:

   FileName: @activity('CsvDataFolder Metadata').output.itemName

   ModifiedAt: @convertFromUtc(activity('CsvDataFolder Metadata').output.lastModified, 'Pacific Standard Time')

   UpdatedAt: @convertFromUtc(utcnow(), Pacific Standard Time'):

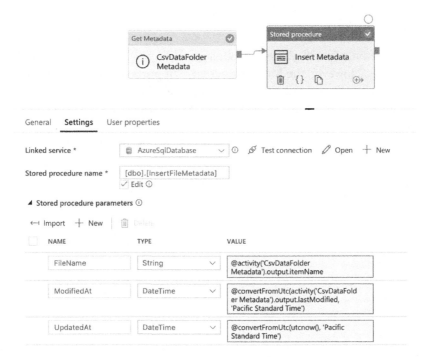

Figure 2.17 – Stored Procedure activity configuration

6. Run your pipeline in **Debug** mode. After the run is done, go to **AzureSqlDatabase** and verify that the **FileMetadata** table is populated with one record: the last modified date of the folder where we keep the `.csv` files.

7. Do not forget to publish your pipeline in order to save your changes.

How it works...

In this simple recipe, we introduced two new activities. In *step 2*, we have used the Metadata activity, with the dataset representing a folder in our container. In this step, we were only interested in the item name and the last modified date of the folder. In *step 3*, we added a Stored Procedure activity, which allows us to directly invoke a stored procedure in the remote database. In order to configure the Stored Procedure activity, we needed to obtain the parameters (`itemName`, `lastModified`, and `UpdatedAt`). The formulas used in *step 5* (such as `@activity('CsvDataFolder Metadata').output.itemName`) define which activity the value is coming from (the `CsvDataFolder` Metadata activity) and which parts of the output are required (`output.itemName`). We have used the built-in conversion function `convertFromUtc` in order to present the time in a specific time zone (Pacific Standard Time, in our case).

There's more...

In this recipe, we only specified the `itemName` and `lastModified` fields as the metadata outputs. However, the Metadata activity supports many more options. Here is the list of currently supported options from the Data Factory documentation at `https://docs.microsoft.com/azure/data-factory/control-flow-get-metadata-activity#capabilities`:

Metadata options

You can specify the following metadata types in the Get Metadata activity field list to retrieve the corresponding information:

Metadata type	Description
itemName	Name of the file or folder.
itemType	Type of the file or folder. Returned value is `File` or `Folder`.
size	Size of the file, in bytes. Applicable only to files.
created	Created datetime of the file or folder.
lastModified	Last modified datetime of the file or folder.
childItems	List of subfolders and files in the given folder. Applicable only to folders. Returned value is a list of the name and type of each child item.
contentMD5	MD5 of the file. Applicable only to files.
structure	Data structure of the file or relational database table. Returned value is a list of column names and column types.
columnCount	Number of columns in the file or relational table.
exists	Whether a file, folder, or table exists. Note that if `exists` is specified in the Get Metadata field list, the activity won't fail even if the file, folder, or table doesn't exist. Instead, `exists: false` is returned in the output.

Figure 2.18 – Metadata activity options

The Metadata type options that are available to you will depend on the dataset: for example, the `contentMD5` option is only available for files, while `childItems` is only available for folders.

Using the ForEach and Filter activities

In this recipe, we introduce you to the **Filter** and **ForEach** activities. We shall enhance the pipeline from the previous recipe to not just examine the data in the Azure Storage container, but filter it based on the file type and then record the last modified date for every `.csv` file in the folder.

Getting ready

The preparation steps are the same as for the previous recipe. We shall be reusing the pipeline from the *Using Metadata and Stored Procedure activities* recipe, so if you did not go through the steps then, do so now.

How to do it...

1. Clone the pipeline from the previous recipe and rename it `pl_orchestration_recipe_3`.

2. Delete the **Stored Procedure** activity.

3. Select the Metadata activity and configure it in the following way:

    (a) In the **Dataset** tab, verify that `CsvDataFolder` is selected as the dataset.

    (b) Verify that the **Item Name** and **Last Modified** fields are added as arguments. Add one more field, **Child Items**.

4. Now, select a Filter activity from the **Activities** pane on the left (find it in the **Iteration and Conditionals** section) and drop it in the pipeline canvas to the right of the Metadata activity.

5. Connect the Metadata activity to the Filter activity.

6. Configure the Filter Activity in the following way:

    (a) In the **General** tab, change the name to `FilterOnCsv`.

    (b) In the **Settings** tab, fill in the values as follows:

    Items: `@activity('CsvDataFolder Metadata').output.childItems`

    Condition: `@endswith(item().name, '.csv'):`

Figure 2.19 – Filter activity settings

7. Run this pipeline in **Debug** mode:

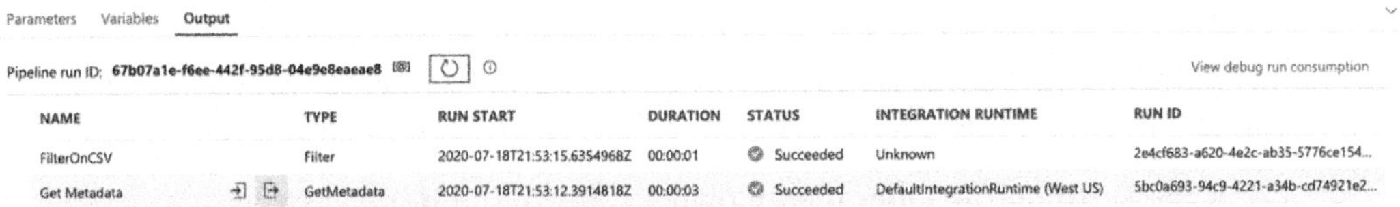

NAME	TYPE	RUN START	DURATION	STATUS	INTEGRATION RUNTIME	RUN ID
FilterOnCSV	Filter	2020-07-18T21:53:15.6354968Z	00:00:01	✓ Succeeded	Unknown	2e4cf683-a620-4e2c-ab35-5776ce154...
Get Metadata	GetMetadata	2020-07-18T21:53:12.3914818Z	00:00:03	✓ Succeeded	DefaultIntegrationRuntime (West US)	5bc0a693-94c9-4221-a34b-cd74921e2...

Parameters   Variables   **Output**

Pipeline run ID: 67b07a1e-f6ee-442f-95d8-04e9e8eaeae8   View debug run consumption

Figure 2.20 – Pipeline status overview in Debug mode

After the pipeline is finished running, hover over the row representing the **Get Metadata** activity run in the **Output** pane and examine the activity's output. You should see that the **Get Metadata** activity fetched the metadata for all the files in the folder, as follows:

Output

```
{
    "itemName": "data",
    "lastModified": "2020-07-11T02:36:47Z",
    "childItems": [
        {
            "name": "Airlines-2020-07-18T20:30:47.2924367Z.backup",
            "type": "File"
        },
        {
            "name": "Country-2020-07-18T21:51:23.0941216Z.backup",
            "type": "File"
        },
        {
            "name": "airlines.csv",
            "type": "File"
        },
        {
            "name": "countries.csv",
            "type": "File"
        }
    ],
    "effectiveIntegrationRuntime": "DefaultIntegrationRuntime (West US)",
    "executionDuration": 0,
    "durationInQueue": {
        "integrationRuntimeQueue": 0
    },
    "billingReference": {
        "activityType": "PipelineActivity",
        "billableDuration": [
            {
                "meterType": "AzureIR",
                "duration": 0.016666666666666666,
                "unit": "Hours"
            }
        ]
    }
}
```

Figure 2.21 – Get Metadata activity output

Do the same for the **FilterOnCSV** activity and verify that the outputs were filtered to only the `csv` files.

8. From the **Activities** pane, add an instance of the **ForEach** activity on the canvas, connect it to the **FilterOnCsv** activity, and configure it in the following way:

   (a) In the **Settings** tab, enter the following value in the **Items** textbox: @ `activity('FilterOnCSV').output.Value`.

   (b) Within the **ForEach** activity square, click on the pencil image. This will open another canvas. We shall configure the actions for the **ForEach** activity within this canvas.

9. Add an instance of **Get Metadata Activity** onto the **ForEach Activity** canvas, and configure it in the following way:

   (a) In the **General** tab, change the name to `ForEach Metadata`.

   (b) In the **Dataset** tab, specify `CsvData` (the parameterized dataset we created in the *Using parameters and built-in functions* recipe) as the dataset for this activity. If you do not have this dataset, please refer to the *Using parameters and built-in functions* recipe to see how to create a parameterized dataset.

   (c) For the **filename** parameter, enter `@item().name`.

   (d) In the same **Dataset** tab, in the **Field List** section, add two arguments: **Item Name** and **Last Modified Date**, as shown in the following screenshot:

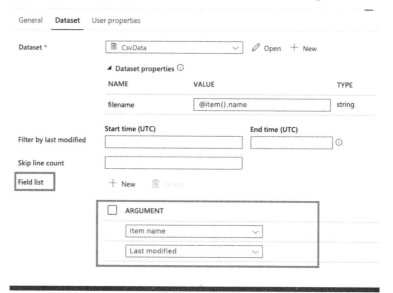

Figure 2.22 – Adding arguments in the Field List section

10. Add an instance of **Stored Procedure Activity** onto the **ForEach Activity** canvas. Connect **ForEach Metadata** to **Stored Procedure Activity** and configure **Stored Procedure Activity**:

(a) In the **Settings** tab at the bottom, select **AzureSQLDatabase** as the linked service and **[dbo][InsertFileMetadata]** as the stored procedure name.

(b) Click on **Import** under **Stored Procedure Parameters** and enter the following values:

FileName: `@{item().name}`

ModifiedAt: `@convertFromUtc(activity('ForEach Metadata').output.lastModified,'Pacific Standard Time')`

UpdatedAt: `@convertFromUtc(utcnow(), 'Pacific Standard Time')` (you can use your own time zone here, as well):

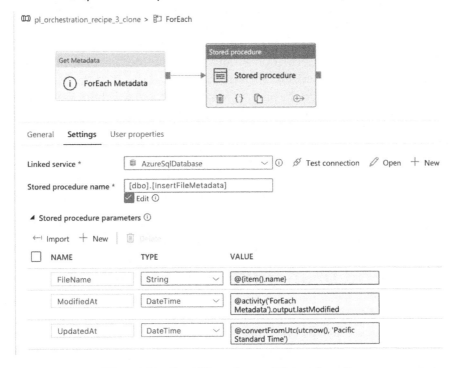

Figure 2.23 – Stored Procedure activity configuration

Run your whole pipeline in **Debug** mode. When it is finished, you should see the two additional rows in your **FileMetadata** table (in Azure SQL Database) for the last modified date for `airlines.csv` and `countries.csv`.

11. Publish your pipeline to save the changes.

How it works...

In this recipe, we used the Metadata activity again and took advantage of the **childItems** option to retrieve information about the folder. After this, we filtered the output to restrict processing to CSV files only with the help of the Filter activity.

Next, we needed to select only the CSV files from the folder for further processing. For this, we added a Filter activity. Using @activity('Get Metadata').output. childItems, we specified that the Filter activity's input is the metadata of all the files inside the folder. We configured the Filter activity's condition to only keep files whose name ends with csv (the built-in endswith function gave us a convenient way to do this).

Finally, in order to process each file separately, we used the ForEach activity, which we used in *step 6*. ForEach is what is called a *compound* activity, because it contains a group of activities that are performed on each of the items in a loop. We configured the Filter activity to take as input the filtered file list (the output of the Filter activity), and in *steps 7 and 8*, we designed the sequence of actions that we want to have performed on each of the files. We used a second instance of the Metadata activity for this sub-pipeline and configured it to retrieve information about a particular file. To accomplish this, we configured it with the parameterized CsvData dataset and specified the filename. In order to refer to the file, we used the built-in formula @item (which provides a reference to the current file in the ForEach loop) and indicated that we need the *name* property of that object.

The configuration of the Stored Procedure activity is similar to the previous step. In order to provide the filename for the Stored Procedure parameters, we again referred to the provided *current object* reference, @item. We could have also used @ activity('ForEach Metadata').output.itemName, as we did in the previous recipe.

Chaining and branching activities within a pipeline

In this recipe, we shall build a pipeline that will extract the data from the CSV files in Azure Blob Storage, load this data into the Azure SQL table, and record a log message with the status of this job. The status message will depend on whether the extract and load succeeded or failed.

Getting ready

We shall be using all the Azure services that are mentioned in the *Technical requirements* section at the beginning of the chapter. We shall be using the `PipelineLog` table and the `InsertLogRecord` stored procedure. If you have not created the table and the stored procedure in your Azure SQL database yet, please do so.

How to do it...

1. In this recipe, we shall reuse portions of the pipeline from the *Using parameters and built-in functions* recipe. If you completed that recipe, just create a clone of it and save it as `pl_orchestration_recipe_4`. If you did not, go through *steps 1-10* and create a parameterized pipeline.

2. Observe that each activity by default has a little green square on the right. This denotes a successful outcome of the activity. However, sometimes activities fail. We want to add an action on the failure of the **Copy from Blob to Azure SQL** activity. To denote failure, click on the **Add output** button inside the activity and select **Failure**:

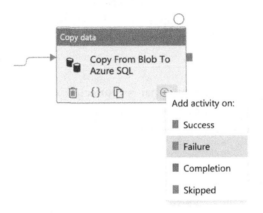

Figure 2.24 – Possible activity outcomes

3. From the **Activities** pane on the left, drag two Stored Procedure activities onto the canvas. Connect one of them to the green square of the **Copy From Blob to Azure SQL** activity and another one to the red square.

4. First, configure the **Stored Procedure** activity that is connected to the green square in the following way:

    (a) In the **General** tab, rename it On Success.

    (b) In the **Settings** tab, specify **AzureSQLTables** as the linked service and **[dbo]. [InsertPipelineLog]** as the Stored Procedure name. Click on **Test Connection** to verify that you can connect to the Azure SQL database.

    (c) Click on the **Import Parameters** button and fill in the values in the following way:

    PipelineID: @pipeline().Pipeline

    RunID: @pipeline().RunId

    Status: Success

    UpdatedAt: @utcnow()

    > **Note**
    > You can also use the **Add dynamic content** functionality to fill in the values. For each field, put your cursor into the field and then click on the little blue **Add dynamic content** link that appears underneath the field. You will see a blade that gives you a selection of system variables, functions, and activity outputs to choose from.

5. Now, select the stored procedure that is connected to the red square in the **Copy Data** activity. Configure it in a similar way to the previous step, but give it the name On Failure, and for the **Status** parameter, enter Failure:

Figure 2.25 – A full pipeline with On Success and On Failure branches

6. It is time to test the pipeline. Run it in Debug mode and verify that, when your pipeline succeeds, you have a corresponding entry in the **PipelineLog** table.

7. Now, in order to see the branching in action, let's imitate the failure of our pipeline. Edit your **Copy From Blob To Azure SQL** activity: in the **Sink** tab below the canvas, put any string into the **tableName** textbox.

8. Run your pipeline in debug mode. You will see that now the **Copy From Blob To Azure SQL** activity failed, and the **On Failure** stored procedure was invoked. Verify that the **PipelineLog** table in the Azure SQL database has a new record:

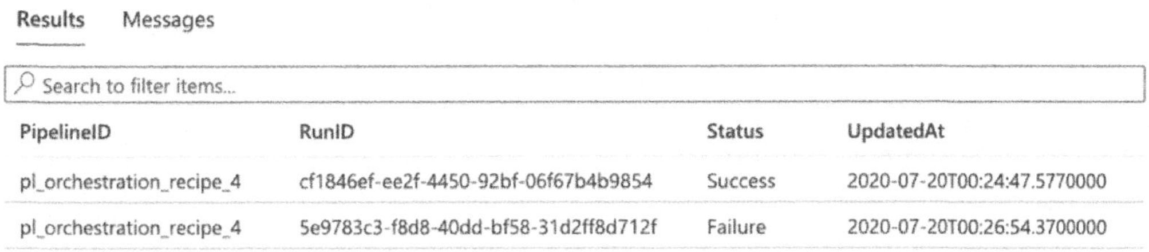

Results   Messages

🔎 Search to filter items...

PipelineID	RunID	Status	UpdatedAt
pl_orchestration_recipe_4	cf1846ef-ee2f-4450-92bf-06f67b4b9854	Success	2020-07-20T00:24:47.5770000
pl_orchestration_recipe_4	5e9783c3-f8d8-40dd-bf58-31d2ff8d712f	Failure	2020-07-20T00:26:54.3700000

Figure 2.26 – Entries in PipelineLog after successful and failed pipeline runs

9. Publish your changes to save them.

There's more...

ADF offers another option for branching out on a condition during pipeline execution: the If Condition activity. This activity is another example of a compound activity (like the ForEach activity in the previous recipe): it contains two activity subgroups and a condition. Only one of the activity subgroups is executed, based on whether the condition is true or false.

The use case for the `If Condition` activity is different than the approach we illustrated in this recipe. While the recipe branches out on the outcome (success or failure) of the previous activity, you design the condition in the `If Condition` activity to branch out on the inputs from the previous activity. For example, let's suppose that we want to retrieve metadata about a file, and perform one stored procedure if the file is a CSV and another stored procedure if the file is of a different type. Here is how we would configure an `If Condition` activity to accomplish this:

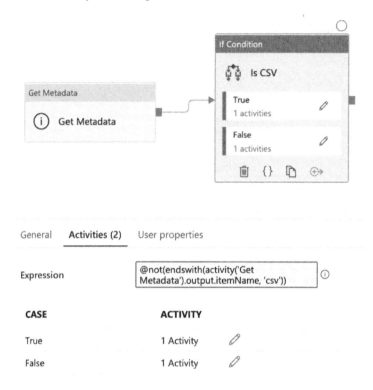

Figure 2.27 – Configuring the If Condition activity

Using the Lookup, Web, and Execute Pipeline activities

In this recipe, we shall implement error handling logic for our pipeline – similar to the previous recipe, but with a more sophisticated design: we shall isolate the error handling flow in its own pipeline. Our main **parent** pipeline will then call the **child** pipeline. This recipe also introduces three very useful activities to the user: **Lookup**, **Web**, and **Execute Pipeline**. The recipe will illustrate how to retrieve information from an Azure SQL table and how to invoke other Azure services from the pipeline.

Getting ready

We shall be using all the Azure services that are mentioned in the *Technical requirements* section at the beginning of the chapter. In addition, this recipe requires a table to store the email addresses of the status email recipients. Please refer to the *Technical requirements* section for the table creation scripts and instructions.

We shall be building a pipeline that sends an email in the case of failure. There is no activity in ADF capable of sending emails, so we shall be using the Azure Logic Apps service. Follow these steps to create an instance of this service:

1. In the Azure portal, look for **Logic Apps** in Azure services. Then, use the **Add** button to create a new logic app.

2. Name your logic app ADF-Email-LogicApp and fill in the **Subscription**, **Resource Group**, and **Region information** fields. Click on **Create** and wait until your logic app is deployed. Then, click on **Go to Resource**.

3. In the Logic App Designer, select the **When a HTTP request is received** trigger:

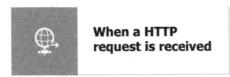

Figure 2.28 – HTTP trigger

4. In the displayed tile, click on **Use sample payload to generate schema**, and use the following code block:

```
{
    "subject": "<subject of the email message>",
    "messageBody": "<body of the email message >",
    "emailAddress": "<email-address>"
}
```

Enter the text in the textbox as shown in the following figure:

Figure 2.29 – Configuring a logic app – the capture message body

5. Click on the **Next Step** button and choose the email service that you want to use to send the notification emails. For the purposes of this tutorial, we shall use Gmail.

> **Note:**
>
> Even though we use Gmail for the purposes of this tutorial, you can also send emails using Office 365 Outlook or Outlook.com. In the *See also* section of this recipe, we included a link to a tutorial on how to send emails using those providers.

6. Select **Gmail** from the list of services and **Send Email** from **Actions**. Log in with your account credentials:

Figure 2.30 – Configuring a logic app – specifying an email service

7. From the **Add new parameter** dropdown, check the **Subject** and **Body** checkboxes:

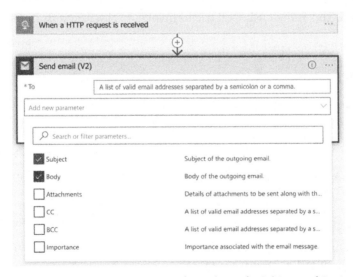

Figure 2.31 – Configuring a logic app – specifying the Body, Subject, and Recipient fields

8.   Place your cursor inside the **To** text field and enter `@{triggerBody()['emailAddress']}`.

9.   In a similar way, enter `@{triggerBody()['subject']}` in the **Subject** text field.

10.   Finally, in the **Body** text box, enter `@{triggerBody()['messageBody']}`:

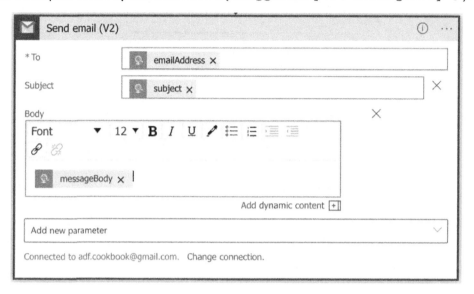

Figure 2.32 – Configuring a logic app – specifying the To, Subject, and Body values

11.   Save your logic app. In the first tile, you should see that **HTTP POST URL** was populated. This is the URL we'll use to invoke this logic app from the Data Factory pipeline.

How to do it...

First, we shall create the child pipeline to retrieve the email addresses of the email recipients and send the status email:

1.   Create a new pipeline and name it `pl_orchestration_recipe_5_child`.

2.   From the **Activities** pane, select a **Lookup** activity and add it to the pipeline canvas. Configure it in the following way:

(a) In the **General** tab, change the activity name to `Get Email Recipients`.

(b) In the **Settings** tab, select **AzureSQLTables** as the value for **Source dataset**, and specify **EmailRecipients** for **tableName**.

(c) Also, in the **Settings** tab, select the **Use Query** radio button and enter SELECT
* FROM EmailRecipients into the text box. Make sure to uncheck the **First
row** only checkbox at the bottom. Your **Settings** tab should look similar to the
following figure:

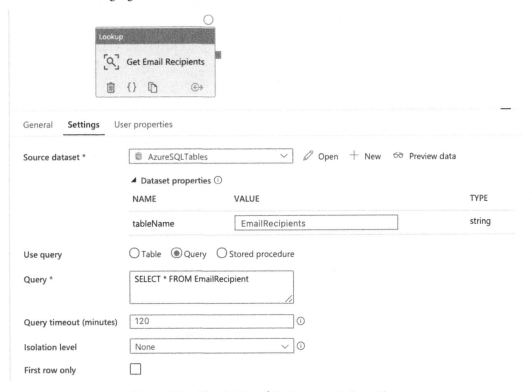

Figure 2.33 – The Get Email Recipients activity settings

3. Next, add a **ForEach** activity to the canvas and configure it in the following way:

    In the **Settings** tab, enter @activity('Get Email Recipients').
    output.value into the **Items** textbox.

4. Click on the pencil icon within the **ForEach** activity. This will open a new canvas.
    Add a Web activity onto this canvas.

    We shall now configure the Web activity. First, go to the **General** tab, and rename
    it Send Email. Then, in the URL text field, paste the URL for the logic app (which
    you created in the *Getting ready* section).

In the **Method** textbox, select **POST**.

In the **Headers** section, click on the **New** button to add a header. Enter `Content-Type` into the **Name** text box and `application/json` into the **Value** textbox.

In the **Body text** box, enter the following text (be sure to copy the quotes accurately):

```
@json(concat('{"emailAddress": "', item().emailAddress,
'", "subject": "ADF Pipeline Failure", "messageBody":
"ADF Pipeline Failed"}'))
```

Your **Settings** tab should look similar to *Figure 2.34*:

Figure 2.34 – The Send Email activity settings

5. Run this pipeline in **Debug** mode and verify that it works. You should have some test email addresses in the `EmailRecipients` table in order to test your pipeline. You can also verify that the email was sent out by going to the **ADF-Email-LogicApp** UI in the Azure portal and examining the run in the **Overview** pane:

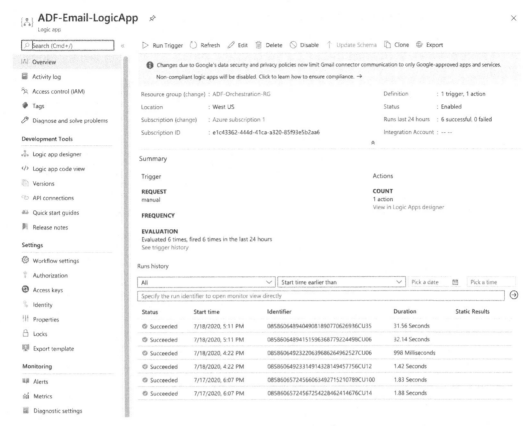

Figure 2.35 – Logic Apps portal view

6. We are ready to design the parent pipeline, which will invoke the child pipeline we just tested. For this, clone the pipeline we designed in the *Chaining and branching activities within your pipeline* recipe. Rename your clone `pl_orchestration_recipe_5_parent`.

7. In this pipeline, delete the **On Failure** Stored Procedure activity, and instead add an **Execute Pipeline** activity to the canvas. Connect it to the red square in the **Copy From Blob to Azure SQL** activity.

8. Configure the **Execute Pipeline** activity:

    In the **General** tab, change the name to **Send Email On Failure**.

    In the **Settings** tab, specify the name of the invoked pipeline as `pl_orchestration_recipe_5_child`.

9. The parent pipeline should already be configured with the incorrect table name in the **Copy** activity sink (we deliberately misconfigured it in order to test the **On Failure** flow). Verify that this is still the case and run the pipeline in **Debug** mode:

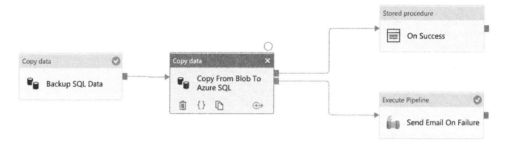

Figure 2.36 – Parent pipeline after execution with an incorrect tableName value

10. Verify that the email was sent to the recipients.

11. Publish your changes to save them.

How it works...

In this recipe, we introduced the concept of parent and child pipelines and used the pipeline hierarchy to incorporate error handling functionality. This technique offers several benefits:

- It allows us to reuse existing pipelines.

- It makes it easier to design/debug parts of the pipeline separately.

- Finally, it allows users to design pipelines that contain more than 40 activities (Microsoft limits the number of activities per pipeline).

To craft the child pipeline, we started by adding a Lookup activity to retrieve a list of email recipients from the database table. This is a very common use for the Lookup activity: fetching a dataset for subsequent processing. In the configuration, we specified a query for the dataset retrieval: `SELECT * from EmailRecipients`. We can also use a more sophisticated query to filter the email recipients, or we can retrieve all the data by selecting the **Table** radio button. The ability to specify a query gives users a lot of choice and flexibility in filtering a dataset or using field projections with very little effort.

The list of email recipients was processed by the ForEach activity. We encountered the ForEach activity in the previous recipe. However, inside the ForEach activity, we introduced a new kind of activity: the Web activity, which we configured to invoke a simple logic app. This illustrates the power of the Web activity: it enables the user to invoke external REST APIs without leaving the Data Factory pipeline.

There's more...

There is another ADF activity that offers the user an option to integrate external APIs into a pipeline: the **Webhook** activity. It has a lot of similarities to the Web activity, with two major differences:

- The Webhook activity always passes an implicit `callBackUri` property to the external service, along with the other parameters you specify in the request body. It expects to receive a response from the invoked web application. If the response is not received within the configurable timeout period, the Webhook activity fails. The Web activity does not have a `callBackUri` property, and, while it does have a timeout period, it is not configurable but limited to 1 minute.

  This feature of the Webhook activity can be used to control the execution flow of the pipeline – for example, to wait for user input into a web form before proceeding with further steps.

- The Web activity allows users to pass linked services and datasets. This can be used for data movement to a remote endpoint. The Webhook activity does not offer this capability.

See also

For more information about the Webhook activity, refer to the Microsoft documentation:

`https://docs.microsoft.com/azure/data-factory/control-flow-webhook-activity`

If you want to learn how to configure a logic app to send emails using providers other than Gmail, follow this tutorial:

`https://docs.microsoft.com/azure/logic-apps/tutorial-process-email-attachments-workflow`

Creating event-based triggers

Often, it is convenient to run a data movement pipeline in response to an event. One of the most common scenarios is triggering a pipeline run in response to the addition or deletion of blobs in a monitored storage account. Azure Data Factory supports this functionality.

In this recipe, we shall create an **event-based trigger** that will invoke a pipeline whenever new backup files are added to a monitored folder. The pipeline will move backup files to another folder.

Getting ready

- To illustrate the trigger in action, we shall use the pipeline in the *Using parameters and built-in functions* recipe. If you did not follow the recipe, do so now.

- We shall be creating a pipeline that is similar to the pipeline in *Using the ForEach and Filter activities* recipe. If you did not follow that recipe, do so now.

- In the storage account (see the *Technical requirements* section), create another folder called `Backups`.

- Following *steps 1 to 3* from the *Using the Copy activity with parameterized datasets* recipe, create a new dataset and point it to the `Backups` folder. Call it `Backups`.

- Register `Event.Grid Provider` with your subscription:

  a. Go to the portal and look for **Subscription**. Click on your subscription name.

  b. In the **Subscription** blade, look for **Resource Provider**.

  c. Find **Microsoft.EventGrid** in the list and hit the **Register** button. Wait until the button turns green (an indication that the registration succeeded).

How to do it...

First, we create the pipeline that will be triggered when a new blob is created:

1. Clone the pipeline from the *Using the ForEach and Filter activities* recipe. Rename the clone `pl_orchestration_recipe_7_trigger`.

2. Rename the **FilterOnCSV** activity `Filter for Backup`. In the **Settings** tab, change **Condition** to `@endswith(item().name, '.backup')`:

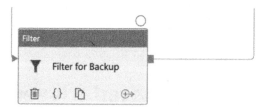

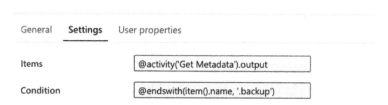

Figure 2.37 – Configuring the Filter for Backup activity

3. In the **ForEach** Activity, change the **Items** value to `@activity('Filter For Backup').output.Value` in the **Settings** tab:

Figure 2.38 – Updating the ForEach activity

4. In the **ForEach** activity canvas, remove the **Metadata** and **Stored Procedure** activities. Add a **Copy** activity to the **ForEach** canvas and configure it the following way:

    Name: `Copy from Data to Backup`

    Source Dataset: `CsvData` (the parameterized dataset created in the first recipe)

    Filename: `@item().name`

    Sink Dataset: The `Backup` dataset

5. In the same **ForEach** canvas, add a **Delete** activity. Leave the default name (`Delete1`). Configure it in the following way:

    In the **Source** tab, specify **Source Dataset** as `CsvData`. In the **Filename** field, enter `@item().name`.

    In the **Logging Settings** tab, uncheck the **Enable Logging** checkbox.

> **Note:**
> In this tutorial, we do not need to keep track of the files we deleted. However, in a production environment, you will want to evaluate your requirements very carefully: it might be necessary to set up a logging store and enable logging for your Delete activity.

6.   Connect the **Copy from Data to Backup** activity to the **Delete1** activity:

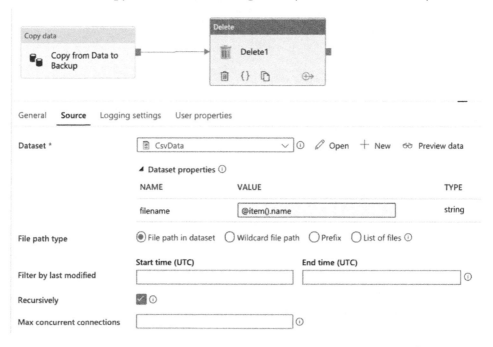

Figure 2.39 – The ForEach activity canvas and configurations for the Delete activity

7.   Configure the event trigger. In the **Manage** tab, select **Triggers** and click on the **New** button to create a new trigger. In the **New trigger** blade, configure it as shown in *Figure 2.39*. Make sure to select the **Yes** radio button in the **Activated** section:

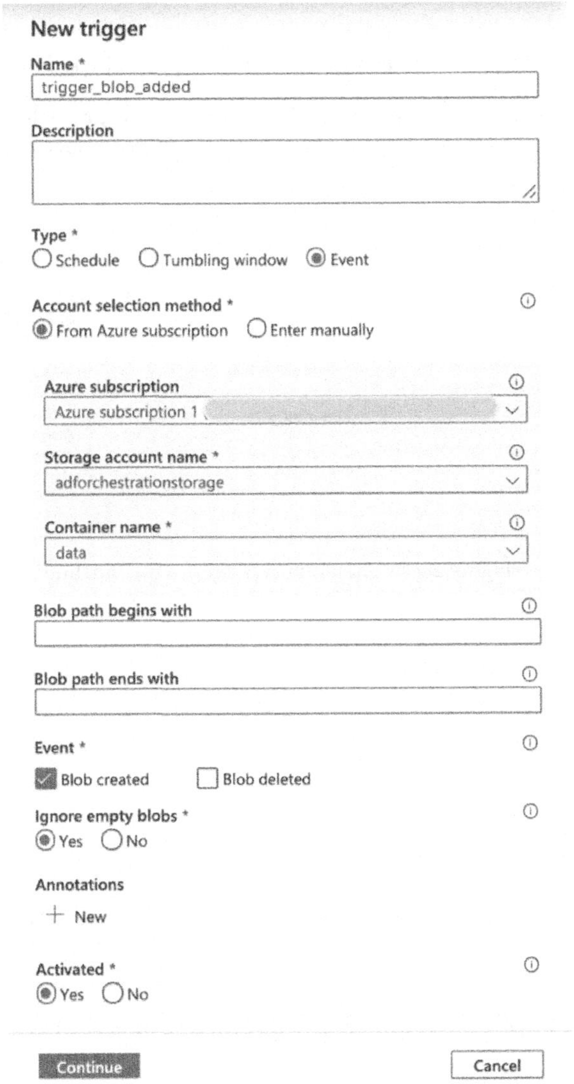

Figure 2.40 – Trigger configuration

After you select **Continue**, you will see the **Data Preview** blade. Click **OK** to finish creating the trigger.

We have created a pipeline and a trigger, but we did not assign the trigger to the pipeline. Let's do so now.

8. In the **Author** tab, select the pipeline we created in *step 1* (`pl_orchestration_recipe_7`). Click the **Add Trigger** button, and select the **New/Edit** option.

In the **Add trigger** blade, select the newly created **trigger_blob_added** trigger. Review the configurations in the **Edit trigger** and **Data preview** blades, and hit **OK** to assign the trigger to the pipeline:

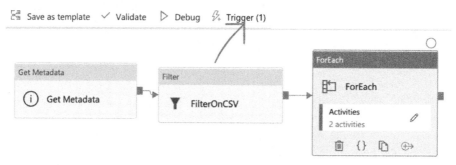

Figure 2.41 – Assigning a trigger to the pipeline

9. Publish all your changes.

10. Run the `pl_orchestration_recipe_1` pipeline. That should create the backup files in the data folder. The trigger we designed will invoke the `pl_orchestration_recipe_7` pipeline and move the files from the `data` folder to the `backups` folder.

How it works...

Under the hood, Azure Data Factory uses a service called Event Grid to detect changes in the blob (that is why we had to register the `Microsoft.EventGrid` provider before starting with the recipe). Event Grid is a Microsoft service that allows you to send events from a source to a destination. Right now, only blob addition and deletion events are integrated.

The trigger configuration options offer us fine-grained control over what files we want to monitor. In the recipe, we specified that the pipeline should be triggered when a new file with the extension `.backup` is created in the data container in our storage account. We can monitor the following, for example:

- **Subfolders within a container**: The trigger will be invoked whenever a file is created within a subfolder. To do this, specify a particular folder within the container by providing values for the container (that is, data) and the folder path(s) in the **blob name begins with** field (that is, `airlines/`).

- `.backup` **files within any container**: To accomplish this, select **all containers** in the container field and leave `.backup` in the **blob name ends with** field.

To find out other ways to configure the trigger to monitor files in a way that fulfills your business needs, please refer to the documentation listed in the *See also* section.

There's more...

In the recipe, we worked with event triggers. The types of events that ADF supports are currently limited blob creation and deletion; however, this selection may be expanded in the future. If you need to have your pipeline triggered by another type of event, the way to do it is by creating and configuring another Azure service (for example, a function app) to monitor your events and start a pipeline run when an event of interest happens. You will learn more about ADF integration with other services in *Chapter 8*, *Working with Azure Services Integration*.

ADF also offers two other kinds of triggers: a **scheduled** trigger and a **tumbling window** trigger.

A scheduled trigger invokes the pipeline at regular intervals. ADF offers rich configuration options: apart from recurrence (number of times a minute, a day, a week, and so on), you can configure start and end dates and more granular controls, for the hour and minute of the run for a daily trigger, the day of the week for weekly triggers, and the day(s) of the month for monthly triggers.

A tumbling window trigger bears many similarities to the scheduled trigger (it will invoke the pipeline at regular intervals), but it has several features that make it well suited to collecting and processing historical data:

- A tumbling window trigger can have a start date in the past.

- A tumbling window trigger allows pipelines to run concurrently (in parallel), which considerably speeds up historical data processing.

- A tumbling window trigger provides access to two variables:

```
trigger().outputs.WindowStartTime
trigger().outputs.WindowEndTime
```

- Those may be used to easily filter the range of the data it is processing, for both past and current data.

A tumbling window trigger also offers the ability to specify a dependency between pipelines. This feature allows users to design complex workflows reusing existing pipelines.

Both event-based and scheduled triggers have a many-to-many relationship with pipelines: one trigger may be assigned to many pipelines, and a pipeline may have more than one trigger. A tumbling window trigger is pipeline-specific: it may only be assigned to one pipeline, and a pipeline may only have one tumbling window trigger.

See also

To learn more about all three types of ADF triggers, start here:

- `https://docs.microsoft.com/azure/data-factory/concepts-pipeline-execution-triggers#trigger-execution`

- `https://docs.microsoft.com/azure/data-factory/how-to-create-event-trigger`

- `https://docs.microsoft.com/azure/data-factory/how-to-create-schedule-trigger`

- `https://docs.microsoft.com/azure/data-factory/how-to-create-tumbling-window-trigger`

3
Setting Up a Cloud Data Warehouse

This chapter will cover the key features and benefits of cloud data warehousing and **Azure Synapse Analytics**. You will learn how to connect and configure Azure Synapse Analytics, load data, build transformation processes, and operate pipelines.

You will navigate Azure Synapse Analytics and learn about its key components and benefits.

You will also learn how to create an **Azure Synapse Analytics workspace**, to load and transform data in Azure Synapse Analytics.

Then, you will learn how to develop, execute, and monitor pipelines using Azure Synapse.

Here is a list of recipes that will be covered in this chapter:

- Connecting to Azure Synapse Analytics
- Loading data to Azure Synapse Analytics using SSMS
- Loading data to Azure Synapse Analytics using Azure Data Factory
- Pausing/resuming an Azure SQL pool from Azure Data Factory
- Creating an Azure Synapse workspace

- Loading data to Azure Synapse Analytics using bulk load
- Copying data in Azure Synapse Orchestrate
- Using SQL on-demand

> **Note**
>
> Currently, Azure Synapse Analytics is in beta version, and some of its tools and features may change after its release to general availability (that is, the Orchestrate tool is going to be renamed to Integrate).

Technical requirements

For this chapter, you'll need the following:

- **An active Azure account**: This could be either your business account or a personal account. If you don't have an Azure account yet, you can activate an Azure free-trial license through Microsoft's main website: `https://azure.microsoft.com/en-us/free/`.

- **Microsoft SQL Server Management Studio (SSMS)**: The latest version can be found at `https://docs.microsoft.com/en-us/sql/ssms/download-sql-server-management-studio-ssms`.

- **GitHub repository**: You can download the dataset from the book's GitHub repository or you may use your own one: `https://github.com/PacktPublishing/Azure-Data-Factory-Cookbook/tree/master/data`.

Connecting to Azure Synapse Analytics

In this recipe, we are going to create and set up a new Azure resource called **Azure Synapse Analytics** (formerly Azure SQL DW).

Getting ready

Before we start, please ensure that you have an Azure license and are familiar with the basics of Azure resources, such as the following:

- The Azure portal
- Creating and deleting Azure resources

- Managing subscriptions

- Managing costs and budgets in Azure

Let's get started!

How to do it...

1. To create a new resource, search for `Azure Synapse Analytics (formerly SQL DW)` and press **Create**.

2. Choose an existing subscription.

3. Choose a resource group in which you want your new resource to be located:

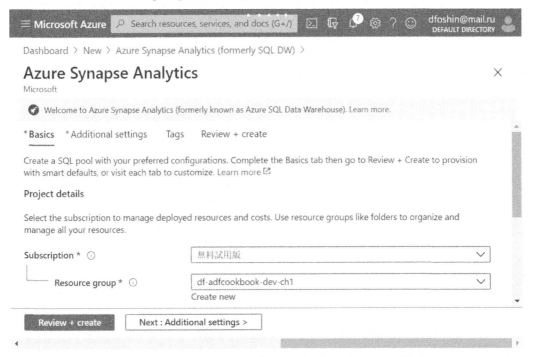

Figure 3.1 – Creating an Azure Synapse Analytics instance – basics

4.   Enter a SQL pool name – for example, `adfcookbookch1devsqldb`:

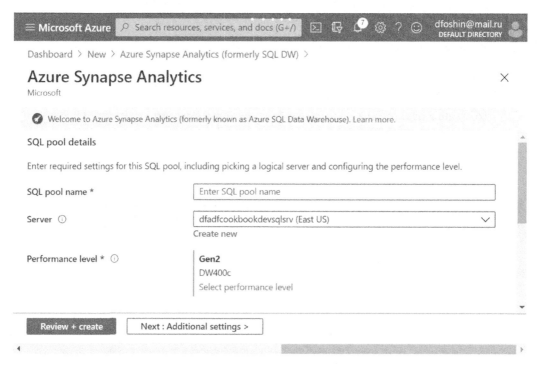

Figure 3.2 – Creating an Azure Synapse Analytics instance – SQL pool

5.   Choose a server (or create a new one). If you are creating a new server, you also need to create a server admin login and server admin password. As we are going to use a SQL pool with Data Factory, we should create this in the same region; otherwise, you could incur data transfer charges.

6.   Choose a performance level (set this to the lowest possible level for this recipe to save costs).

7.   In **Additional settings**, you can click on the **Sample in Use** existing data options, and **AdventureWorksDW** will be created in your data warehouse. In this use case, we don't need sample data as we will upload our own data in Synapse Analytics.

8. Your Azure Synapse Analytics account is billed hourly according to the chosen performance level. So, the best practice is to pause your Azure Synapse Analytics resource when it is not used to avoid unwanted charges. To do this, simply go to the resource and click **Pause**:

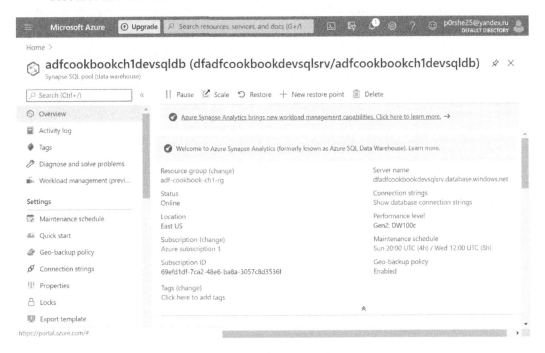

Figure 3.3 – Creating Azure Synapse Analytics – Pause

9. As we are going to connect to a SQL pool via Data Factory, you need to go to **Firewalls and virtual networks** of the **Security** section and set **Allow Azure services and resources to access this server** to **Yes**.

How it works...

When you create a new Azure Synapse Analytics resource, the new SQL Server data warehouse is created in the cloud within an Azure resource group and in a logical SQL server. It can store massive amounts of data, up to 4 PB, scale up and down, and is fully managed. Azure Synapse Analytics has features for working with big data and serving it for further analysis and visualization, such as PolyBase T-SQL queries, **massive parallel processing** (**MPP**), and the ability to pause and resume the service.

There's more...

To prevent external applications and users from connecting to your databases, it is recommended to create a server-level firewall rule:

1. To do this, simply go to the Synapse SQL pool created and choose **Firewalls and virtual networks**.

2. You can leave all the fields as the default and click **Add client IP**. Your IP address will appear in the rules table as follows:

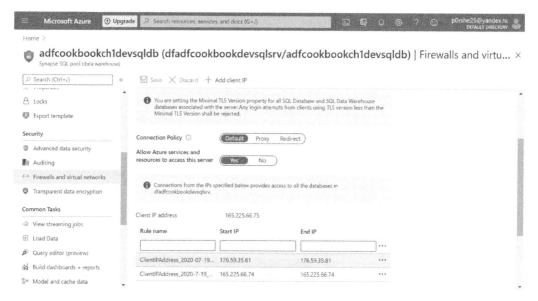

Figure 3.4 – Creating Azure Synapse Analytics – firewall and virtual networks

In this table, you can manage your firewall rules, create new ones, and delete existing ones.

Loading data to Azure Synapse Analytics using SSMS

In this recipe, we are going to configure Azure Synapse Analytics, add a new user, and load data into Azure Synapse Analytics from an external resource, such as Azure Blob storage.

Getting ready

Before we start, please ensure that you have created an Azure storage account and uploaded data into a Blob storage container. Please refer to *Chapter 2, Orchestration and Control Flow*, for guidelines on how to do that.

You need to upload the dataset from this book's GitHub repository to the container. Then, you need to generate shared access signatures to connect blobs via Azure Synapse Analytics.

You can download the dataset from the book's GitHub repository, or you can use your own: `https://github.com/PacktPublishing/Azure-Data-Factory-Cookbook/tree/master/data`.

In this section, we will use the following link to an Azure Blob storage container: `https://adfcookbookch3adls.blob.core.windows.net/flightscontainer`. You need to replace this with the link referring to a storage account you've already created in *Chapter 2, Orchestration and Control Flow*.

How to do it...

To configure Azure Synapse Analytics, use the following steps:

1. Run SSMS and connect as an administrator using the database information you created in the previous recipe:

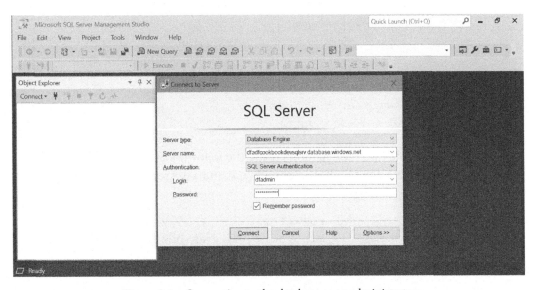

Figure 3.5 – Connecting to the database as an administrator

2. Loading data into Azure Synapse Analytics is a rather memory-consuming operation. The best practice is to create a new user that will be used for loading data as you can also configure the resource class for maximum memory allocation. You need to select **New Query**, enter the following script, and click **Execute**:

```
CREATE LOGIN adfuser WITH PASSWORD = 'ADF3password';
CREATE USER adfuser FOR LOGIN adfuser;
GRANT CONTROL ON DATABASE::[adfcookbookch1devsqldb] to
adfuser;
EXEC sp_addrolemember 'staticrc10', 'adfuser';
```

3. Reconnect to SSMS as `adfuser` using the password created in the previous step. Before loading data into Azure Synapse Analytics, you need to create the table schema. This is the SQL script for table creation:

```
CREATE TABLE [dbo].[Countries]
([Name] varchar(50) NOT NULL,
[iso_code] varchar(50) NULL,
[dafif_code] varchar(50) NULL)


CREATE TABLE [dbo].[Airlines]
([Airline_ID] varchar(50) NOT NULL,
[Name] varchar(50) NULL,
[Alias] varchar(50) NULL,
[IATA] varchar(10) NULL,
[ICAO] varchar(10) NULL,
[Callsign] varchar(50) NULL,
[Country] varchar(50) NULL,
[Active] varchar(1) NULL)
```

4. You can load data into created tables using the following SQL script. Please ensure that you've replaced the Blob storage path and **Shared Access Signature** (**SAS**) secret with your own ones:

```
COPY INTO dbo.[Countries] FROM 'https://
adfcookbookch3adls.blob.core.windows.net/
flightsblobstorage/countries.csv'
WITH
    (
    CREDENTIAL=(IDENTITY= 'Shared Access Signature',
```

```
SECRET='sp=r&st=2020-07-19T15:29:25Z&se=2020-07-
19T23:29:25Z&spr=https&sv=2019-10-10&sr=b&sig=dJ2WrdoraHL
RL3L1QJNdh51z6TdzEVi3DDh8GdxZDmo%3D'),
    FIELDTERMINATOR=';'
    )

COPY INTO dbo.[Airlines] FROM 'https://adfcookbookch3adls.
blob.core.windows.net/flightsblobstorage/airlines.csv'
WITH
    (
    CREDENTIAL=(IDENTITY= 'Shared Access Signature',
SECRET='sp=r&st=2020-07-31T18:39:02Z&se=2020-08-
01T02:39:02Z&spr=https&sv=2019-12-12&sr=b&sig=4J%2Fk9M6DB
UzGUc51d%2FRCsDLndUMRn0sN6%2FZxlyNQ9SU%3D'),
    FIELDTERMINATOR=';'
    )
```

Let's see how it works in the next section.

How it works...

The CREATE LOGIN command allows you to create a login with a specified password.
The CREATE USER command allows you to create a new user for the created login.
The GRANT CONTROL ON DATABASE command allows you to provide access to the
database for a specified user. sp_addrolemember is a stored procedure that adds
a user to a particular role. CREATE TABLE is a command for creating a new table in the
SQL database with specified fields. The COPY INTO command allows you to copy data
from the specified file into the created table. You also need to specify the credentials for
accessing the file. In this case, the blob is accessed via **Shared Access Signature** with
a generated secret.

There's more...

If you are loading huge amounts of data, that is, migrating your database into the cloud,
it would be helpful to use a clustered columnstore index in your tables. Even when
using that operation, the load could take a lot of time. One more tip is to show the status
of the load using the following script:

```
SELECT  t1.[request_id]
,       t1.[status]
,       t1.resource_class
```

```
,          t1.command
,          sum(bytes_processed) AS bytes_processed
,          sum(rows_processed) AS rows_processed
FROM       sys.dm_pdw_exec_requests t1
                JOIN sys.dm_pdw_dms_workers t2
                     ON t1.[request_id] = t2.request_id
WHERE [label] = 'COPY : Load [dbo].[Countries] - Flights
dataset' OR
     [label] = 'COPY : Load [dbo].[Airlines] - Flights dataset'
and session_id <> session_id() and type = 'WRITER'
GROUP BY t1.[request_id]
,          t1.[status]
,          t1.resource_class
,          t1.command;
```

This query returns a table that shows the status of each current `WRITER` request to the database from the system tables.

Loading data to Azure Synapse Analytics using Azure Data Factory

In this recipe, we will look further at how to load data into **Azure Synapse Analytics** using **Azure Data Factory**.

Getting ready

Before we start, please ensure that you have created a linked service to a Blob storage container and know how to create a Copy Data statement in **Azure Data Factory**. Please refer to *Chapter 2, Orchestration and Control Flow*, for guidelines on how to do that.

How to do it...

To load data into Azure Synapse Analytics using Azure Data Factory, use the following steps:

1. Before we create a Copy Data statement in Azure Data Factory, we need to create a new table in Azure Synapse Analytics:

```
CREATE TABLE [dbo].[Planes]
([Name] varchar(100) NOT NULL,
[IATA_code] varchar(10) NULL,
[ICAO_code] varchar(10) NULL)
```

2. Open Azure Data Factory and launch the **Copy data** tool (as seen in the following screenshot), then select the linked service to **Azure Blob storage** or create a new one (refer to *Chapter 2, Orchestration and Control Flow*, if you're facing issues with doing this):

Figure 3.6 – Launching the Copy data tool

3. In the **Source** section, choose the file or folder in Azure Blob storage:

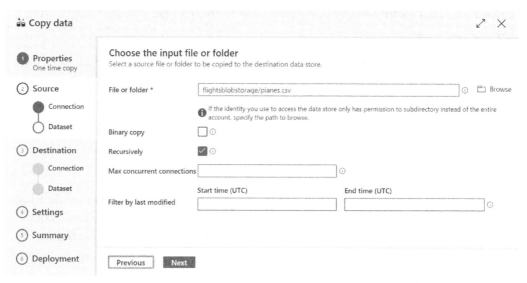

Figure 3.7 – Azure Data Factory Copy Data – Choose the input file

4. Usually, file format settings are detected automatically but you can alter these settings:

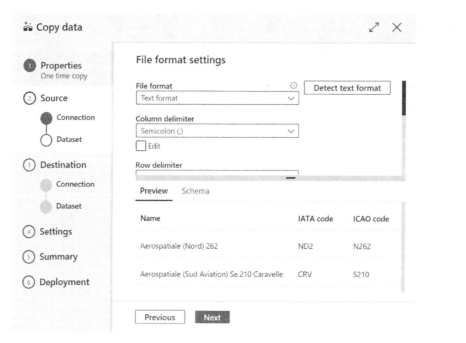

Figure 3.8 – Azure Data Factory Copy Data – File format settings

5. In the **Destination** section, you need to choose the linked service to Azure Synapse Analytics or create a new one. You can choose **SQL authentication** for **Authentication type** and enter the username and password created in the previous recipe:

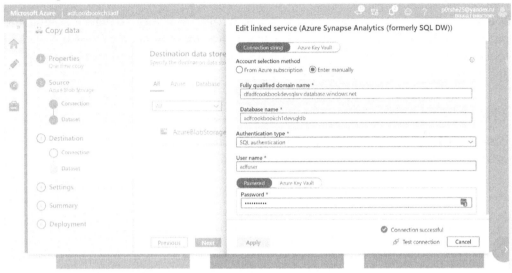

Figure 3.9 – Azure Data Factory Copy Data – linked service

6. In **Destination**, choose the table in Azure Synapse Analytics and choose how the source and destination columns are mapped. Click **Next**. Using the Azure Data Factory Copy Data tool doesn't require you to have equally named fields in your dataset. In **Additional settings**, uncheck **Enable staging**, then click **Next | Next | Finish**.

7. When the pipeline is finished, you can debug it and see that the data appears in Azure Synapse Analytics:

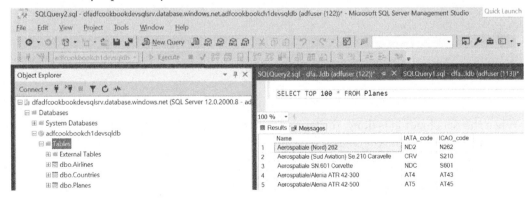

Figure 3.10 – Checking data has appeared in Azure Synapse Analytics

With that, you have successfully loaded data into Azure Synapse Analytics using Azure Data Factory.

How it works...

While migrating your data warehouse to Azure Synapse Analytics, configuring automatic pipelines in Azure Data Factory to copy data will save you a lot of time. The Copy Data tool can connect to various dataset types using a service principal or managed identity and push the data into Azure Synapse Analytics.

There's more...

For loading huge amounts of data, it is better to enable staging. To do this, you need to specify the staging account linked service and storage path:

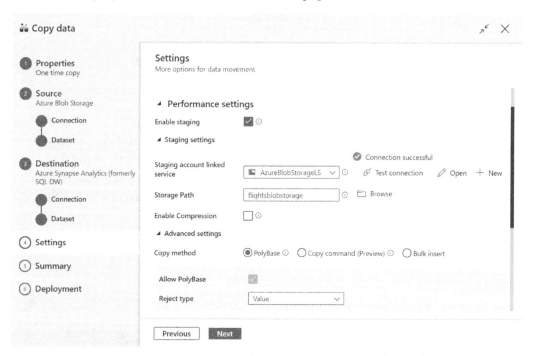

Figure 3.11 – Azure Data Factory Copy data – enabling staging

When the data loading is done, the temporary data in Blob storage will be automatically deleted, as shown in the previous screenshot.

Pausing/resuming an Azure SQL pool from Azure Data Factory

In this recipe, you will create a new Azure Data Factory pipeline that allows you to automatically pause and resume your Azure SQL data warehouse.

Getting ready

Pause your Azure SQL pool before starting this recipe as you are going to resume it automatically using Azure Data Factory.

How to do it...

To pause or resume an Azure SQL pool with Azure Data Factory, use the following steps:

1. Open the **Author** section of Azure Data Factory, create a new pipeline, and in the **Activities** section, choose **Web**. Rename the activity and the pipeline:

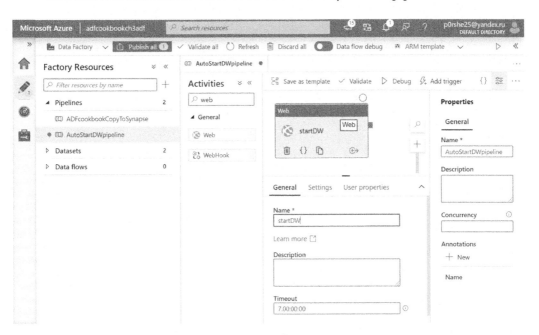

Figure 3.12 – Azure Data Factory – web activity

Go to the settings, then copy and paste the following text into **URL**:

```
https://management.azure.com/subscriptions/
{subscription-id}/resourceGroups/{resource-group-name}/
providers/Microsoft.Sql/servers/{server-name}/databases/
{database-name}/resume?api-version=2019-06-01-preview
```

2. As you can see, there are some parameters that you need to change for your values: `{subscription-id}`, `{resource-group-name}`, `{server-name}`, and `{database-name}`. You can find these values in the **Overview** section of your **SQL pool**:

    a. `{subscription-id}` for **Subscription ID**.

    b. `{resource-group-name}` for **Resource group**.

    c. `{server-name}` for **Workspace name** if you're using an Azure Synapse workspace; if you're using Azure Synapse Analytics, this is *only* the name of server, not the `.database.windows.net` part (which is almost always needed in other cases).

    d. `{database-name}` is the name of the SQL pool:

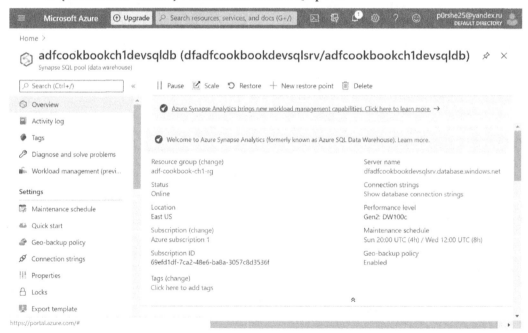

Figure 3.13 – SQL pool overview

If you have the same names as in the preceding screenshot, the text should look like this:

```
https://management.azure.com/subscriptions/69efd1df-
7ca2-48e6-ba8a-3057c8d3536f/resourceGroups/
adf-cookbook-ch1-rg/providers/Microsoft.Sql/servers/
dfadfcookbookdevsqlsrv/databases/adfcookbookch1devsqldb/
resume?api-version=2019-06-01-preview
```

3. For **Method**, choose **POST**, for **Body**, type { }, expand the **Advanced** section, change the authentication to **MSI**, and for **Resource**, type `https://management.core.windows.net`:

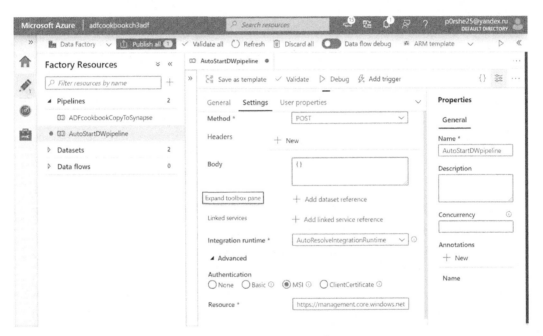

Figure 3.14 – Azure Data Factory – web activity settings

4. The next thing to do is to grant permissions to Data Factory. To do this, you need to go to the **Access control (IAM)** area of SQL Server and click on the plus sign to add a new role assignment. In the opened dialog box, make the following selections:

a. **Role**: **Contributor**.

b. **Assign access to**: **Data Factory**.

   c. **Subscription**: Choose your subscription.

   d. **Select**: Choose the needed Data Factory.

   e. Click on **Save**:

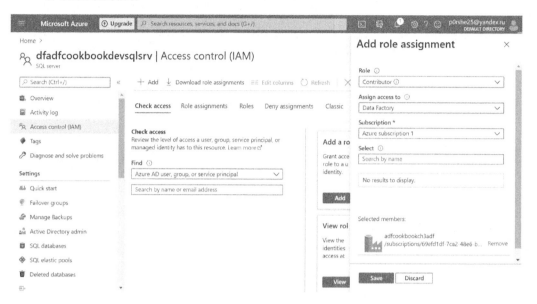

Figure 3.15 – New role assignment for SQL Server

5. Now, you can switch back to Azure Data Factory, click **Publish all** to save all the changes to your pipeline, and click **Debug**.

6. If you go to your Azure SQL pool resource page, you'll see that the status has changed to **Resuming**.

7. Now, you can easily create a pipeline for auto-pausing your SQL pool. You just need to clone the created pipeline and change a word in the URL text from `resume` to `pause`:

```
https://management.azure.com/subscriptions/
{subscription-id}/resourceGroups/{resource-group-name}/
providers/Microsoft.Sql/servers/{server-name}/databases/
{database-name}/pause?api-version=2019-06-01-preview
```

In our use case, the URL text will look like this:

```
https://management.azure.com/subscriptions/69efd1df-
7ca2-48e6-ba8a-3057c8d3536f/resourceGroups/
adf-cookbook-ch1-rg/providers/Microsoft.Sql/servers/
dfadfcookbookdevsqlsrv/databases/adfcookbookch1devsqldb/
pause?api-version=2019-06-01-preview
```

8. Rename the pipeline and leave all the other settings in the pipeline the same as in the previous one. Click **Publish all** to save the new pipeline:

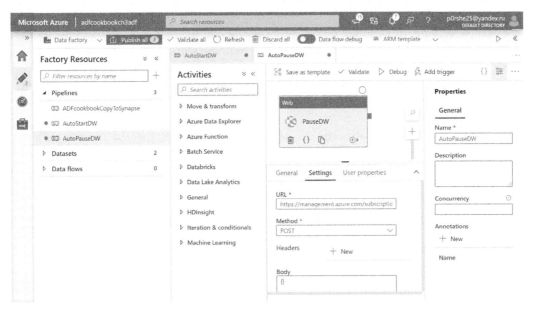

Figure 3.16 – Azure Data Factory – publishing the pipeline

9. Ensure that your Azure SQL pool is running now and debug the **AutoPauseDW** pipeline. While debugging is in progress, go to the Azure SQL pool and see that the status has changed to **Pausing**.

How it works...

Azure Data Factory connects to the Azure SQL pool using the Contributor role that is assigned in the Azure portal settings and pushes the URL text that allows automatically pausing or resuming your databases.

There's more...

The text in the URLs of this recipe is hardcoded in the pipelines, but you can also use dynamic content to parametrize the pipelines if you have several Azure Synapse Analytics instances in your organization. Also, it's a useful scenario to run these pipelines using different triggers. For example, you can keep your databases paused outside of working hours if you don't need them (to save costs on running your Azure SQL pool). You can create similar pipelines to automate your SQL pool in the Azure Synapse workspace Orchestrate tool (which is going to be covered in the following recipes).

Creating an Azure Synapse workspace

Azure Synapse is a combination of capabilities that brings together data integration, SQL analytics that you frequently pair with something such as Power BI, and also Spark for big data processing into a single service for building enterprise analytics solutions. In this recipe, you will learn how to create a new Azure Synapse workspace and migrate your Azure SQL data warehouse into it.

Getting ready

You need to have an Azure subscription, an Azure resource group, and a Synapse SQL pool created.

How to do it...

To create an Azure Synapse workspace, use the following steps:

1. In the Azure portal, click on **Create new resource** and select **Azure Synapse Analytics (workspaces preview)**.

2. Select your subscription and resource group:

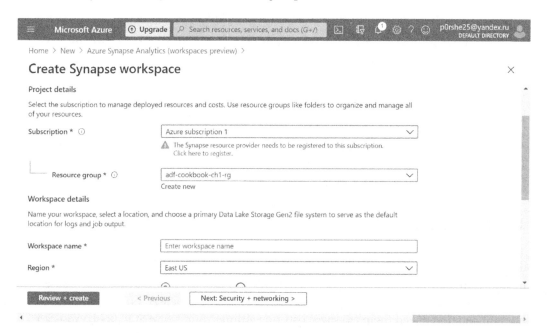

Figure 3.17 – Creating an Azure Synapse workspace

3. Enter a new workspace name and select a region. You can either create a new **Azure Data Lake Storage Gen2** account and filename or use existing ones. If you choose to create a new storage account, data access will be automatically granted using the Storage Blob Data Contributor role:

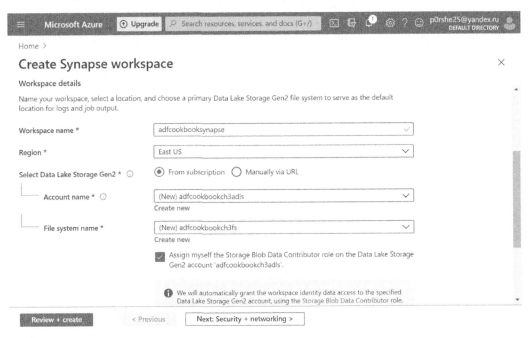

Figure 3.18 – Creating an Azure Synapse workspace – new storage account

4.   Enter an admin username and password for the Synapse workspace. This could be used to connect to a SQL pool and a SQL on-demand endpoint:

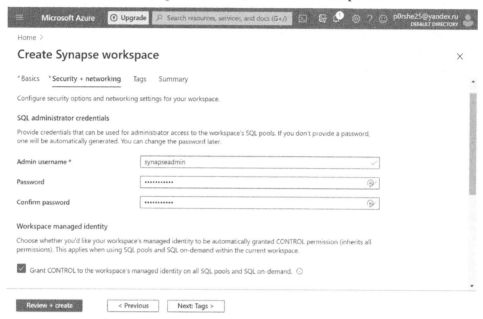

Figure 3.19 – Creating an Azure Synapse workspace – security

Click **Review + create**, then **Create**.

The deployment process will take some time, but after it has succeeded, you will get a notification:

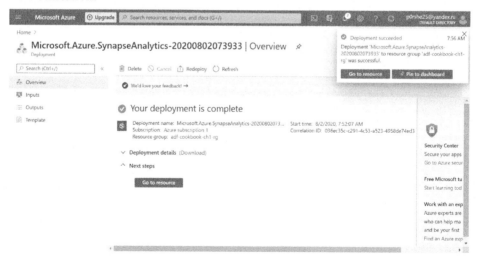

Figure 3.20 – Creating an Azure Synapse workspace – notification on successful deployment

Once you receive the notification, you have successfully created an Azure Synapse workspace.

There's more...

If you open the resource and go to your SQL pools, you will only see **SQL on-demand**. This is created automatically with the Azure Synapse workspace. But you can migrate your existing Azure Synapse Analytics pool into the workspace to have all the needed resources in one place:

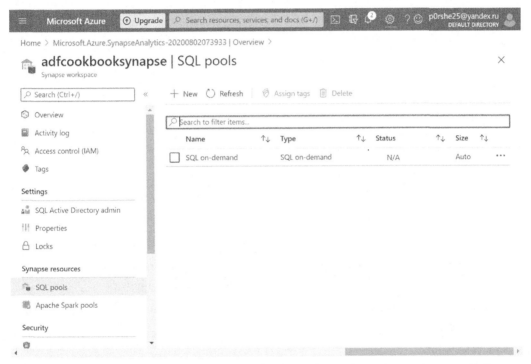

Figure 3.21 – Creating an Azure Synapse workspace – SQL on-demand created automatically

Here is a list of steps that you can follow to migrate your existing Azure Synapse Analytics pool into the workspace:

1. Ensure that the instance is now running and go to your Synapse SQL pool (data warehouse) and create a new restore point. You need to provide a name for this and click **Apply**:

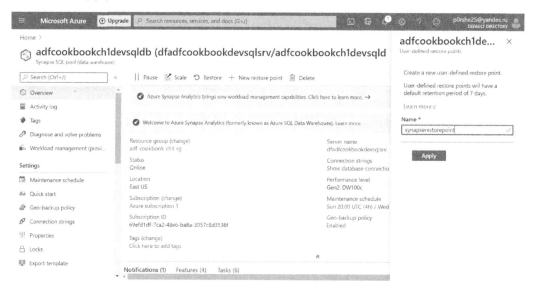

Figure 3.22 – Creating a new restore point for the Synapse SQL pool

2. After you receive the notification that the restore point is created, go to your Synapse workspace, click **SQL pools**, and choose to create a new one.

3. Enter your new SQL pool name and choose the performance level, but do not click **Create**.

4. Go to **Additional settings** and for the **Use existing data** setting, choose **Restore point**. Enter the necessary information about your existing Azure SQL pool – server, SQL pool name, and the name of your user-defined restore point – and click **Create**:

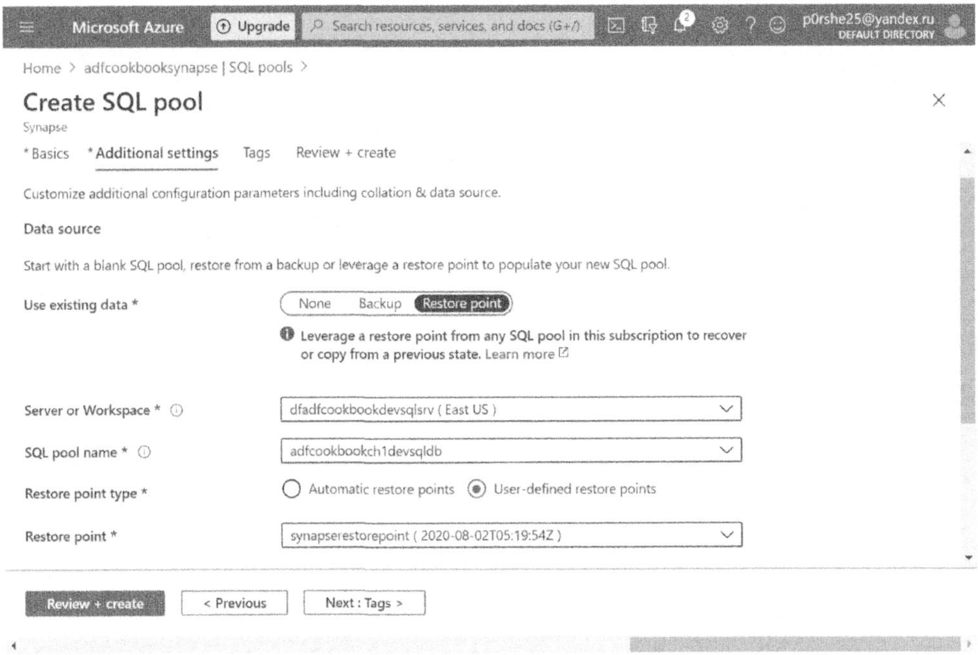

Figure 3.23 – Creating a new SQL pool from the user-defined restore point

5.   After the deployment has succeeded, you can find the new SQL pool in your Synapse workspace:

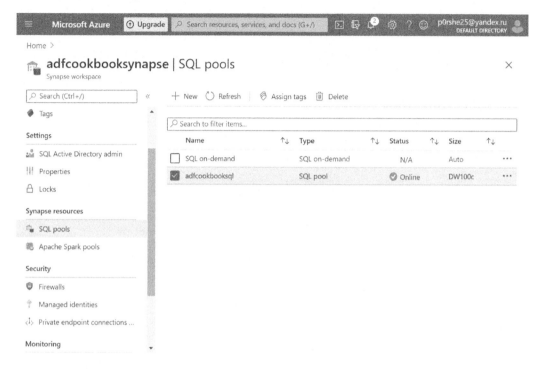

Figure 3.24 – Azure Synapse workspace SQL pools

Let's learn about loading data to Azure Synapse Analytics using bulk load in the next recipe.

Loading data to Azure Synapse Analytics using bulk load

Azure Synapse workspaces allow users to simply load data into a SQL pool with minimum mouse clicks. In this recipe, you will learn how to do this.

Getting ready

You need to have created an Azure Synapse workspace and a SQL pool, and Azure Data Lake Storage Gen2 should be linked to that workspace. The Flights dataset (or any other dataset) should be uploaded to your storage.

How to do it...

1. Open the Azure Synapse workspace (also known as **Synapse Studio**).

2. Click on the **Data** tab on the left side of your screen.

3. Expand your SQL pool and click on **Actions** to the right of **Tables**. Select **New SQL script | New table**:

Figure 3.25 – Creating a new SQL script table in the Synapse Analytics workspace

4. An automatically generated SQL query for a new table will be shown in the canvas. Replace it with the following script:

```
CREATE TABLE [dbo].[Routes]
(
    Airline VARCHAR(10) NOT NULL,
    Airline_ID VARCHAR(20) NULL,
    Source_airport VARCHAR(20) NOT NULL,
    Source_airport_ID VARCHAR(50) NULL,
    Destination_airport VARCHAR(20) NOT NULL,
    Destination_airport_ID VARCHAR(50) NULL,
    Codeshare VARCHAR(10) NULL,
    Stops int NOT NULL,
```

```
        Equipment VARCHAR(50) NULL
)
WITH
(

        CLUSTERED COLUMNSTORE INDEX
)
GO
```

5. Click on **Run**. If you click on **Actions** to the right of **Tables** and choose **Refresh**, you can ensure that a new table has been created:

Figure 3.26 – Refreshing the list of tables in an Azure Synapse SQL pool

6. Click on **Linked** and you'll see all the storage accounts and datasets that are linked to your Synapse workspace.

7. Choose the storage in which you uploaded the needed dataset (the storage account should have a hierarchy set in order to be linked).

8. Right-click on the file you are going to load into the Azure SQL pool and select **New SQL script | Bulk load**:

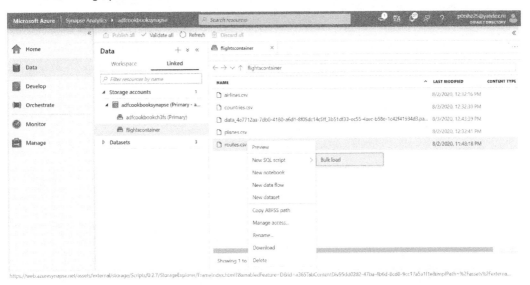

Figure 3.27 – Creating a new SQL script bulk load in the Synapse Analytics workspace

9. In the opened **Bulk load** menu, click **Continue**:

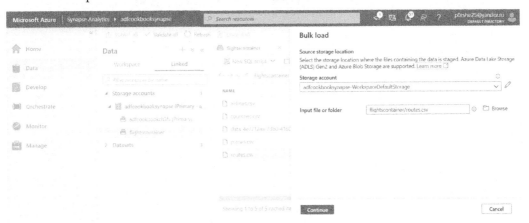

Figure 3.28 – Bulk load settings in the Synapse Analytics workspace

10. For **Field terminator**, choose **Semicolon (;)**.

11. Click on **Preview data** to see the schema detected by Azure Synapse. If you're happy with the schema, click **Continue**:

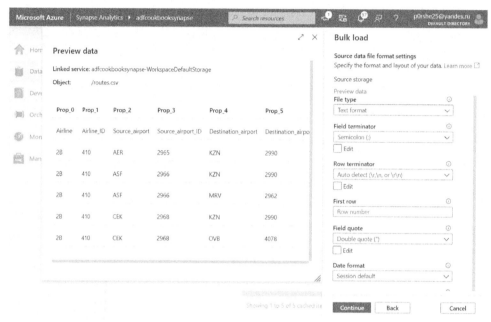

Figure 3.29 – Bulk load preview data in the Synapse Analytics workspace

12. Specify the target SQL pool and select the name of the table in which you are going to upload data:

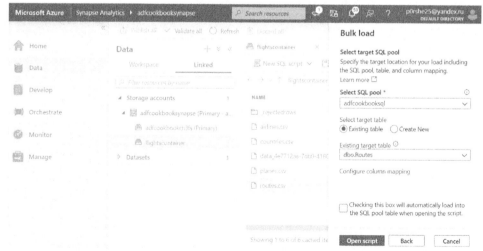

Figure 3.30 – Specifying the target SQL pool in the Synapse Analytics workspace

13. It is useful to click **Configure column mapping** and make sure that columns in the file and SQL pool table are mapped correctly.

14. Click **Open script** and the COPY INTO script will be generated to enrich the target SQL pool table:

```
--Uncomment the 4 lines below to create a stored
procedure for data pipeline orchestration
--CREATE PROC bulk_load_Routes
--AS
--BEGIN
COPY INTO dbo.Routes
(Airline 1, Airline_ID 2, Source_airport 3, Source_
airport_ID 4, Destination_airport 5, Destination_airport_
ID 6, Codeshare 7, Stops 8, Equipment 9)
FROM 'https://adfcookbookch3adls.dfs.core.windows.net/
flightscontainer/routes.csv'
WITH
(
      FILE_TYPE = 'CSV'
      ,MAXERRORS = 0
      ,FIELDQUOTE = '"'
      ,FIELDTERMINATOR = ';'
      ,ERRORFILE = 'https://adfcookbookch3adls.dfs.core.
windows.net/flightscontainer/'
      ,IDENTITY_INSERT = 'OFF'
)
--END
GO


SELECT TOP 100 * FROM Routes
GO
```

15. Run the script and you'll see the first 100 rows of the copied data.

How it works...

The Orchestrate tool in the Azure Synapse workspace works like Azure Data Factory but it is built into the workspace and gives users some advantages over Data Factory. You don't need to set up connections and linked services as they are already configured within one Synapse workspace. Furthermore, the Synapse Orchestration tool has the ability to generate automatic SQL queries for basic operations, such as creating tables, dropping tables, and copying and loading data. Note that using the bulk load capability, you can load data not only from CSV but also from Parquet file formats, which is rather useful in dealing with data lakes.

Copying data in Azure Synapse Orchestrate

In this recipe, you will create a Copy Data pipeline using Azure Synapse Orchestrate.

Getting ready

You need to have an **Azure Synapse workspace** created and the Flights database loaded into an **Azure Synapse SQL pool**.

How to do it...

To copy data in Azure Synapse Orchestrate, use the following steps:

1. Open the Azure Synapse workspace and go to **Orchestrate**.

2. Add a new resource, select **Pipeline**, then select the **Copy data** activity, and rename it:

Figure 3.31 – Creating a new pipeline with the Orchestrate tool of the Synapse Analytics workspace

3. In the **Source** section, create a new source with a connection to Azure Synapse Analytics. Select **Linked service**, then enter the database name and the name of the table: dbo.Routes. Test the connection. You can also click **Preview data** to ensure that the table is loading correctly:

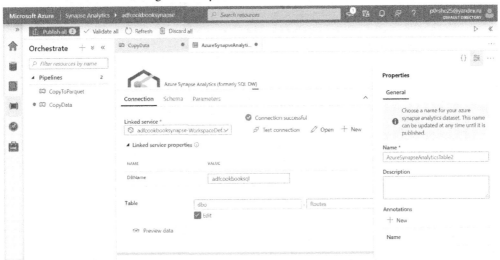

Figure 3.32 – Specifying a connection in the Orchestrate tool of the Synapse Analytics workspace

4. In the sink section, create a new sink dataset. Select **Azure Data Lake Storage Gen2** and choose the Parquet format. Choose an existing linked service and specify the target file path:

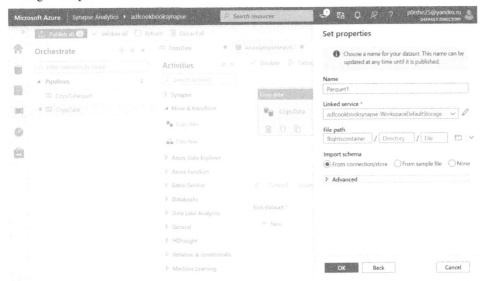

Figure 3.33 – Setting target dataset properties in the Orchestrate tool of the Synapse Analytics workspace

5. Publish all your changes. Note that debugging before publishing may fail your pipeline. Currently, this is a Synapse bug, but it is going to be resolved soon:

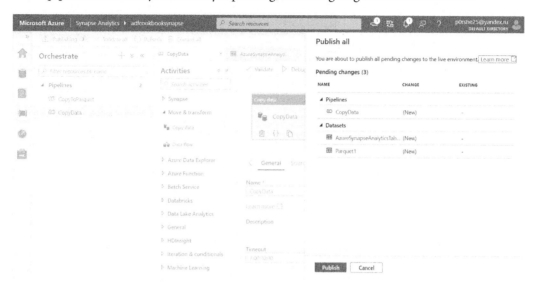

Figure 3.34 – Publishing changes in the Orchestrate tool of the Synapse Analytics workspace

6. If you go to the **Monitor** tool of the Synapse workspace, and then to the **Orchestration** section, you will see the status of your pipeline as **Succeeded**:

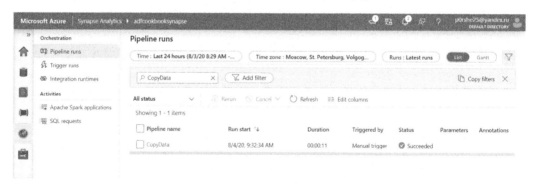

Figure 3.35 – Monitoring runs in the Synapse Analytics workspace

7. If you go to the **Data** tool of the Synapse workspace, and then the **Linked** section, you'll see the created datasets and the copied Parquet file:

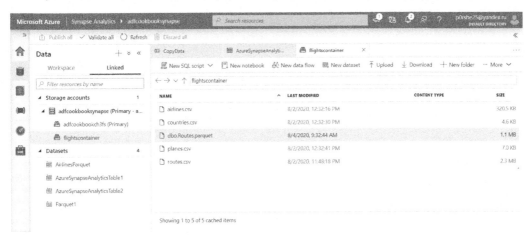

Figure 3.36 – The result of pipeline execution

How it works...

The Orchestrate tool in the Azure Synapse workspace allows you to perform common data processing operations. Creating pipelines and monitoring them works pretty much the same as in Azure Data Factory (see *Chapter 2, Orchestration and Control Flow*). Copying data in this recipe requires a data warehouse to be running. But connecting to an Azure SQL database will only require SQL on-demand, which is serverless.

Using SQL on-demand

In this recipe, you will learn how to use SQL on-demand in an Azure Synapse workspace.

Getting ready

You need to have an Azure Synapse workspace created and the file in Parquet format kept in your Azure Synapse storage account.

How to do it...

1. Open the Azure Synapse workspace, go to **Data**, and open the folder that contents the **Parquet** format file.

2. Right-click on the file and choose **New SQL script | Select TOP 100 rows**:

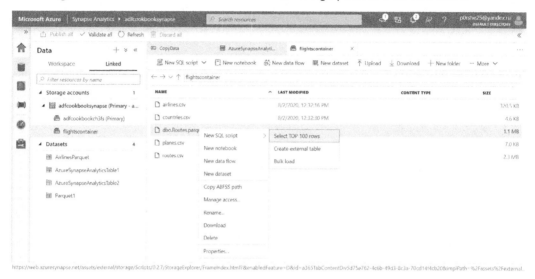

Figure 3.37 – Creating a new SQL script for a file in a storage account

A new script is created for connecting to the file using SQL on-demand:

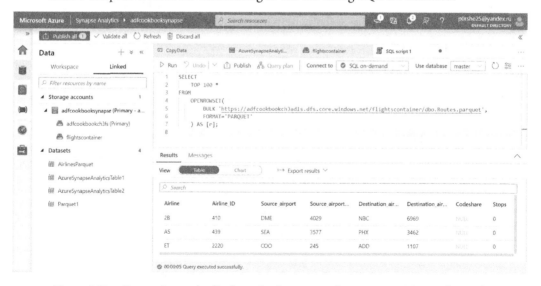

Figure 3.38 – Connecting to the file from the Synapse workspace using SQL on-demand

> **Note**
> The query executes within several seconds; you don't need to wait several minutes for the cluster to start. You can copy this script and then paste it into SSMS.

3. You can also use SQL on-demand to connect from SSMS or a visualization tool (such as Power BI or Tableau). For this, you need to use a SQL on-demand endpoint as the server name. This can be copied from the Synapse workspace overview:

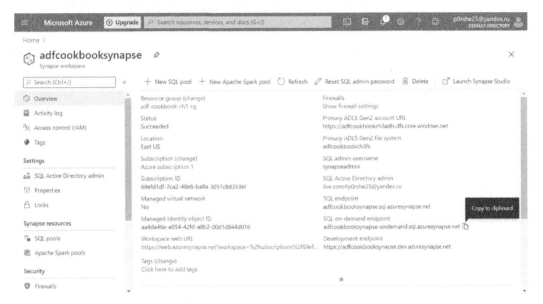

Figure 3.39 – Synapse workspace overview

4. Open SSMS and paste the SQL on-demand endpoint as the server name. You can use your admin credentials for the Synapse workspace as the login and password:

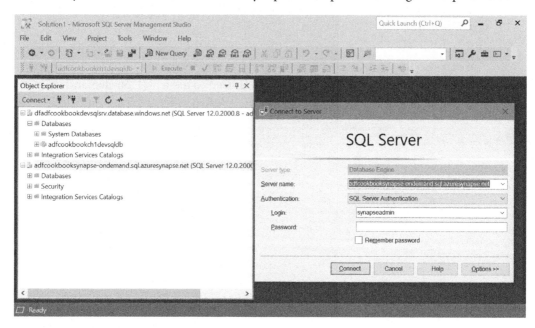

Figure 3.40 – Connecting to a SQL on-demand endpoint from SSMS

5. Here's the script to connect to Parquet format file (you can copy the script returning the file from your storage account in *step 3*):

```
SELECT
    TOP 100 *
FROM
    OPENROWSET(
        BULK 'https://adfcookbookch3adls.dfs.core.
windows.net/flightscontainer/dbo.Routes.parquet',
        FORMAT='PARQUET'
    ) AS [r];
```

The query will return the top 100 rows of the table from the Parquet file. Apart from SSMS, you can also use the same query to connect to this file from BI systems such as Power BI or Tableau. So, it gives you extra opportunities in analyzing data stored in your Azure storage:

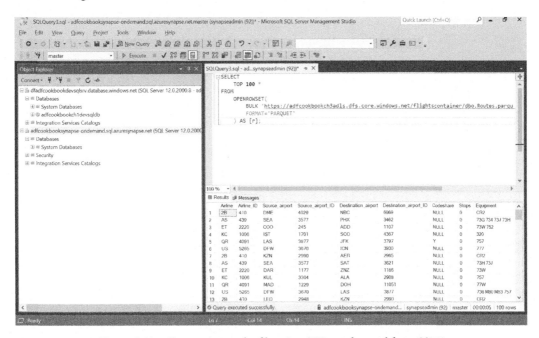

Figure 3.41 – Connecting to the file using SQL on-demand from SSMS

How it works...

SQL on-demand is a new capability allowing you to query the contents of your data lake with SQL without the need to spin up a Spark cluster or SQL warehouse. This is how we can take advantage of serverless capabilities using Azure Synapse.

4
Working with Azure Data Lake

A **data lake** is a central storage system that stores data in its raw format. It is used to collect huge amounts of data that are yet to be analyzed by analysts and data scientists or for regulatory purposes. As the amount of information and the variety of data that a company operates with increases, it gets increasingly difficult to preprocess and store it in a traditional data warehouse. By design, data lakes are built to handle unstructured and semi-structured data with no pre-defined schema.

On-premise data lakes are difficult to scale and require thorough requirements and cost estimations. Cloud data lakes are often considered an easier-to-use and -scale alternative. In this chapter, we will go through a set of recipes that will help you to launch a data lake, load data from external storage, and build ETL/ELT pipelines around it.

Azure Data Lake Gen2 can store both structured and unstructured data. In this chapter, we will load and manage our datasets in Azure Data Lake Gen2. These datasets will then be used for analytics in the next chapter.

In this chapter, we are going to cover the following recipes:

- Setting up Azure Data Lake Storage Gen2
- Connecting Azure Data Lake to Azure Data Factory and loading data
- Creating big data pipelines using Azure Data Lake and Azure Data Factory

Technical requirements

You need to have access to Microsoft Azure. An Azure free account is sufficient for all recipes in this chapter. To create an account use the following link: `https://azure.microsoft.com/free/`.

Setting up Azure Data Lake Storage Gen2

Azure Data Lake Storage Gen2 is a versatile solution that can be used as a single storage platform.

It is Hadoop compatible, so you can use it with **HDInsights** and **Databricks**, which we will cover in the next chapter.

Setting up properly configured storage is a critical operation for developers and data engineers. In this section, we will set up and configure a scalable Azure data lake to be used with Azure Data Factory.

Getting ready

To get started with your recipe, log in to your Microsoft Azure account.

How to do it...

Azure Data Lake Gen2 uses hierarchical namespaces. Unless you already have a storage account with hierarchical namespaces, you will have to create a new one.

Now that we have set up the resource group, let's create a storage account:

1. Search for `Storage accounts` in the Azure search bar and click on it.
2. To add a new storage account, click **+ Add**.
3. Select **Azure Subscription** and **Resource Group**.

4. Add a Storage account name. This needs to be globally unique. See `https://docs.microsoft.com/en-us/azure/azure-resource-manager/management/resource-name-rules`, and set a data center location as shown in the following screenshot. In order to minimize latency, pick a region close to the location of your servers:

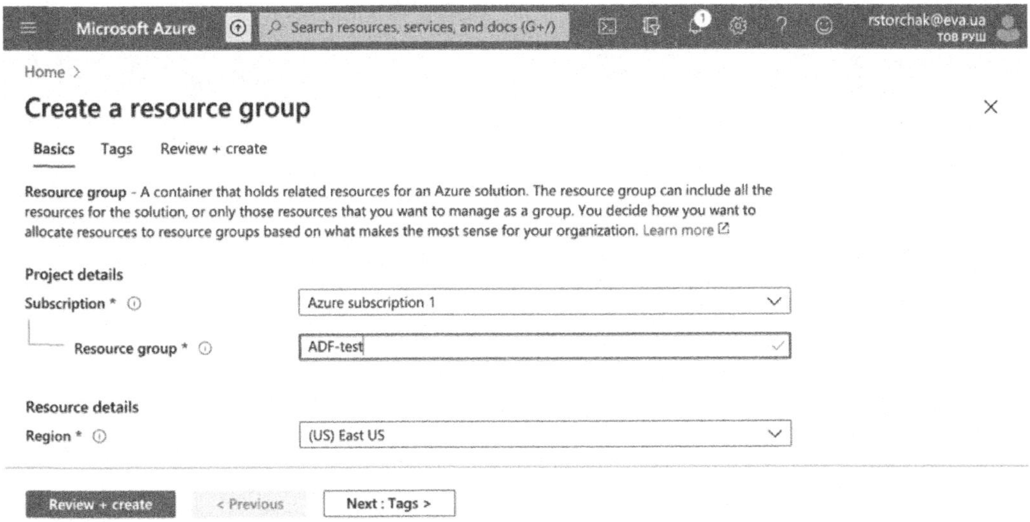

Figure 4.1 – Creating a storage account

5. Pick **Standard** or **Premium** performance. Use the **Standard** option for cheaper and slower hard drive-based storage.

6. Select **StorageV2 (general purpose v2)** for **Account kind**.

> **Important note**
>
> Note that **StorageV1 (general purpose v1)** is deprecated. **BlobStorage** is a specialized type that stores only blobs and can also be considered outdated.

7. Select **Replication** of **Locally-redundant storage (LRS)**.

8. Set **Access tier(default)** to **Cool** and click **Next: Networking**.

9. Let's configure network connectivity for our new storage account. You can connect to your storage account either publicly or privately. Select **Public endpoint (all networks)** and **Microsoft network routing (default)** as shown in the following screenshot:

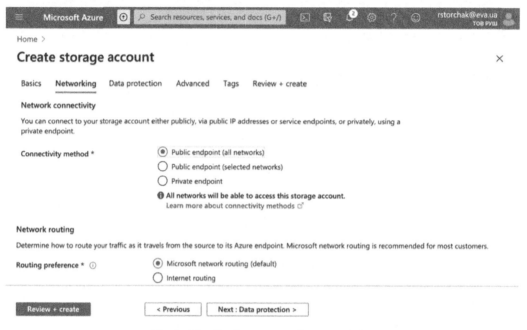

Figure 4.2 – Configure network connectivity

10. Click **Next: Data protection**. On this tab, we have to set up policies for soft delete and blob versioning, which can help us recover files after overwrites and file share data. We are not going to track changes, so we will keep the default settings:

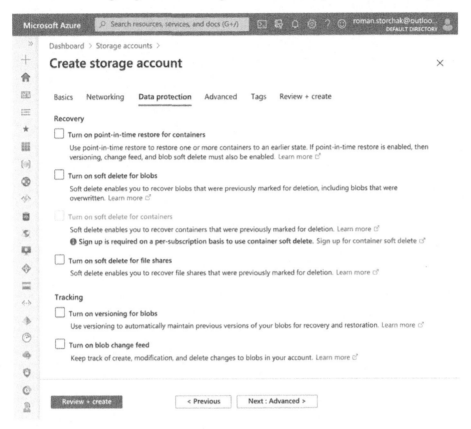

Figure 4.3 – Setting up data protection

11. Let's set everything to disabled and click **Next: Advanced** to move to the next tab, shown in the following screenshot:

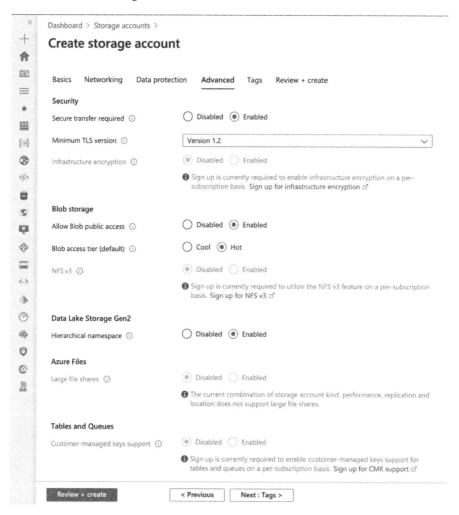

Figure 4.4 – Setting advanced features

12. Set up the following parameters on the **Advanced** tab:

   (a) Set **Secure transfer required** to **Enabled**.

   (b) Set an appropriate **Minimum TLS version**. (The default version is fine for this recipe and most cases of production usage.)

   (c) Leave **Infrastructure encryption** as **Disabled**.

   (d) Set **Allow Blob public access** to **Enabled**.

(e) Set **Blob access tier (default)** to **Hot**.

(f) Leave **NFS v3** as **Disabled**.

(g) Set **Hierarchical namespace** to **Enabled**. Please note that **Hierarchical namespace** is a feature of Data Lake Storage Gen2 and has to be enabled.

(h) Leave **Large file shares** as **Disabled**. If you are planning to use files bigger than 5 TiB, then you will need to reconfigure storage options.

(j) Leave **Customer-managed keys support** as **Disabled**.

13. Proceed to the **Tags** tab. Fill tags and add appropriate tags as per your requirements.

14. After checking all inputs on the **Review + create** tab, click **Create**.

15. After a short wait, we will have our storage account created and ready for use with Azure Data Factory. Don't forget to delete unused storage accounts.

Connecting Azure Data Lake to Azure Data Factory and loading data

Moving data is one of the typical tasks done by data engineers. In this recipe, we will be connecting Azure Data Factory to external storage (**Azure Blob Storage**) and moving the `Chicago Safety Data` dataset to **Azure Data Lake Gen2** that we set up in the previous recipe.

Getting ready

Make sure you have set up Azure Data Lake Gen2 in the *Setting up Azure Data Lake Storage Gen 2* recipe.

The dataset that we are going to use in this recipe, `Chicago Safety Data`, is stored here: `https://azure.microsoft.com/en-us/services/open-datasets/catalog/chicago-safety-data/`. This dataset is published as a part of Azure Open Datasets, which is built to distribute data.

How to do it...

To transfer the dataset from **Azure Blob storage** to **Azure Data Lake Gen2** with Data Factory, first, let's go to the Azure Data Factory UI:

1. Click **+** and select **Copy Data tool** as shown in the following screenshot:

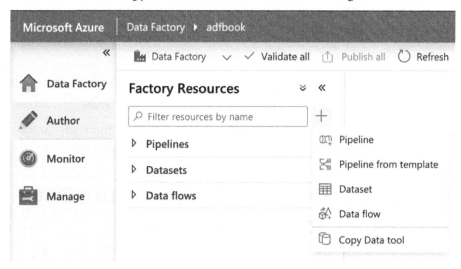

Figure 4.5 – Set up the copy data tool

Data Factory will open a wizard window that looks as follows:

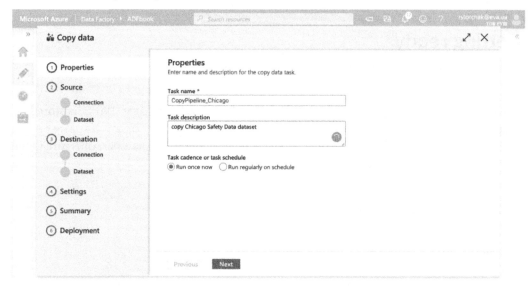

Figure 4.6 – Creating a Data Factory activity

2. Fill in **Task name** and **Task description** and select the appropriate task schedule. In our case, we will download the whole dataset once.

3. To connect to the Azure Blob storage where our dataset is stored, select the **Azure** tab, click **+ Create new connection** and **Azure Blob Storage**. Click **Continue**.

4. Create or select a linked service. You can treat a linked service as a connection string that contains addresses and credentials for external resources. (See *Chapter 2, Orchestration and Control Flow.*):

Figure 4.7 – Creating a linked service

5. Name the new linked service and add an appropriate description.

6. Select an integration runtime. In this case, the default
    AutoResolveIntegrationRuntime will be the right option.

7. Select an **SAS URI** authentication method and paste in the SAS URL,
    `https://azureopendatastorage.blob.core.windows.net/`
    `citydatacontainer/Safety/Release/city=Chicago?""`, which
    contains the address of our dataset of interest and an empty password string.

8. Test the connection by clicking **Test connection**. If **Connection successful** is
    displayed, click the **Create** button as shown in the following screenshot:

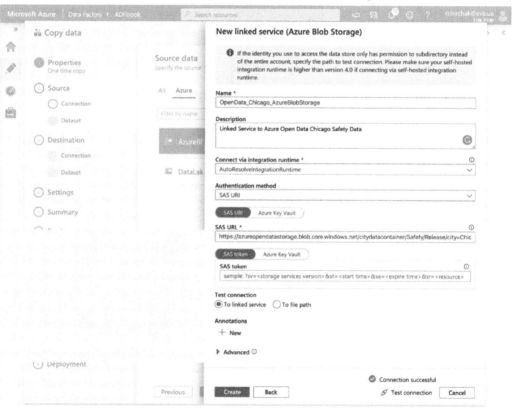

Figure 4.8 – Setting up a new linked service

9. Go back to the **Source data store** page, select our newly created linked service, and click **Next**.

10. Choose an input folder. In our case, it is **citydatacontainer/Safety/Release/ city=Chicago** as shown in *Figure 4.12*.

11. Fill in the appropriate fields according to whether you need a binary or recursive copy. We don't know the structure of the input folder, so a **Recursive** copy is more appropriate.

12. Filter by the last modified field. In our case, we will copy the whole dataset.

13. Click **Next**:

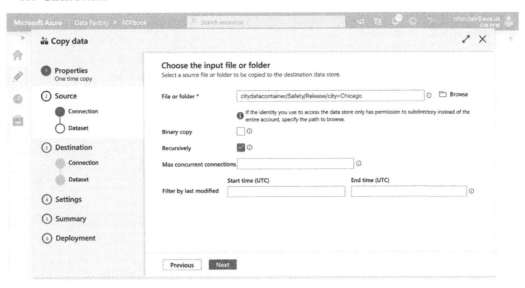

Figure 4.9 – Choosing the input folder

14. Select an appropriate file format. In this case, it is **Parquet format** and the **snappy** compression type. You will see a valid **Preview** of the data and **Schema**. If the preview is unreadable or absent, pick an appropriate file format and compression type, as shown in the following figure:

Figure 4.10 – Setting the file format

Now that we have set up the properties of the **Copy data** activity and **Source**, we have to set an output destination:

1. Create or select a linked service for Azure Data Lake Storage Gen2 (*Figure 4.11*).

2. Add a **Name** and **Description**.

3. Select an integration runtime. Since we are working on a fully managed cloud solution, **AutoResolveIntegrationRuntime** is a good choice.

4. Set **Authentication method** to **Account key** and select an **Account selection method**. The **From Azure subscription** selection should be your choice, but you can use the manual method too.

5. Click **Test connection** and if the test is successful, click **Apply**:

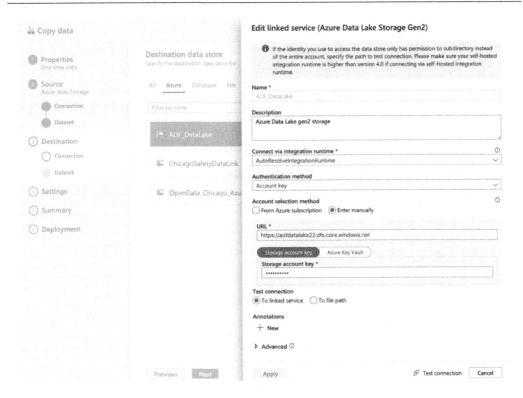

Figure 4.11 – Creating a linked service

6. Choose the output folder as shown in the following figure:

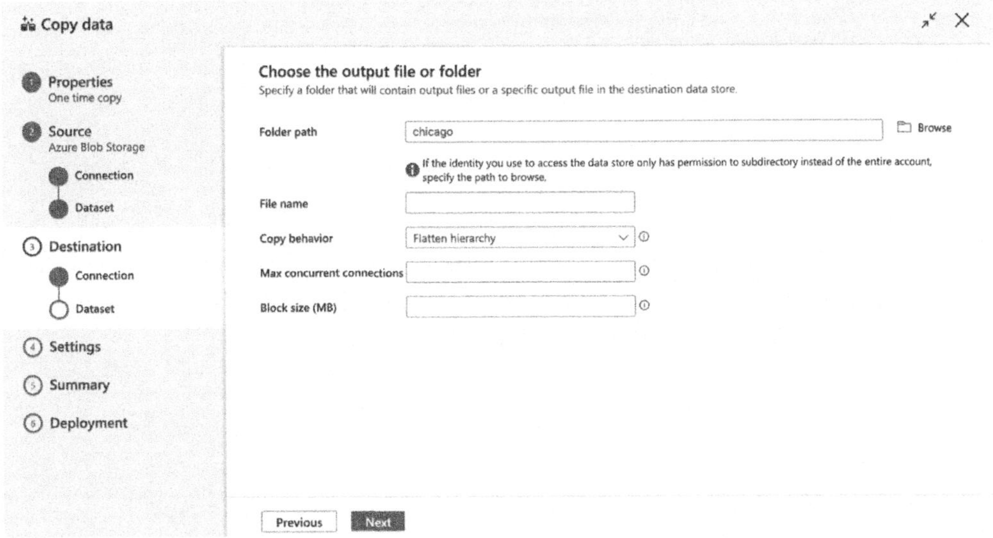

Figure 4.12 – Setting up a destination

> **Important note**
> You can't create a new folder from Azure Data Factory. If you want to create a new folder, you can create it from the Azure Data Lake UI.

7. In this recipe, we can leave **Block size (MB)** and **Max concurrent connections** as the default.

8. Click **Next**.

9. Set **File format** and **Compression type**. We are copying this dataset, so let's leave the same format as the original dataset, as shown in the following screenshot:

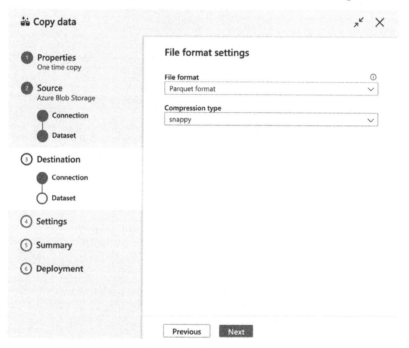

Figure 4.13 – Setting the file format and compression type

10. Let's check the final settings. Set **Fault tolerance** to **Skip incompatible rows**. Add a **Folder path** for logging and enable or disable staging. For this recipe, staging should be disabled, as shown in the following screenshot:

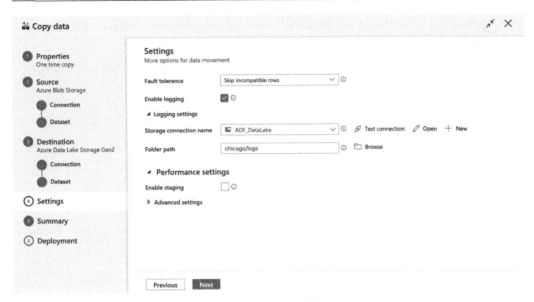

Figure 4.14 – Setting the properties of the Copy data activity

11.   As a final step, check all the settings in **Summary** and click **Next** if everything seems right:

Figure 4.15 – Verifying the copy activity

The pipeline will be deployed immediately. After a short delay, you will see a **Deployment complete** message as shown in the following screenshot:

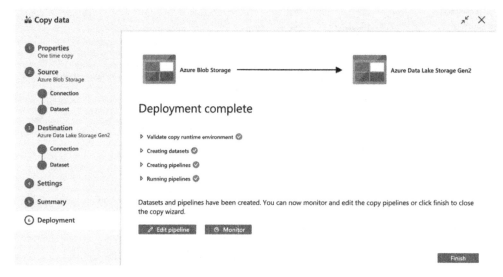

Figure 4.16 – Successful deployment

Congratulations, we have copied our dataset to Azure Data Lake.

How it works...

An Azure Data Factory instance was created to execute and orchestrate ETL/ELT activities. Copying data is one of the most frequent activities that Azure Data Factory executes. In order to get access to the data, Azure Data Factory needs linked services, which govern the connections to various services.

A linked service to Azure Blob storage allows us to connect to the Azure Open Datasets service, which stores the dataset. Another linked service (to Azure Data Lake Gen2) is used to write the dataset of interest in our data lake.

While setting up this activity, we have to specify the parameters of the source and destination, and a copy activity itself.

Creating big data pipelines using Azure Data Lake and Azure Data Factory

Running big data pipelines is an essential feature of Azure Data Factory. They allow you to ingest and preprocess data at any scale. You can program and test any ELT/ETL processes out of the web UI. This is one of the core tasks of the data engineer in your company.

Getting ready

Let's load and preprocess the `MovieLens` dataset (F. Maxwell Harper and Joseph A. Konstan. 2015. *The MovieLens Datasets: History and Context*. ACM Transactions on Interactive Intelligent Systems (TiiS) 5, 4: 19:1–19:19. `https://doi.org/10.1145/2827872`). It contains ratings and free-text tagging activity from a movie recommendation service.

The `MovieLens` dataset exists in a few sizes, which have the same structure. The smallest one has 100,000 ratings, 600 users, and 9,000 movies. The biggest one can be as big as 1.2 billion reviews, 2.2 million users, and 855,000 items.

`MovieLens` is distributed as a set of `.csv` files. Go to `https://grouplens.org/datasets/movielens/` and download a dataset that seems to be appropriate for your practice and Azure budget.

Make sure you have set up Azure Data Lake Gen2. You can use the *Setting up Azure Data Lake Storage Gen 2* recipe:

1. Log in to your Azure Data Lake Storage account and create a new container and name it `movielens` as shown in the following screenshot:

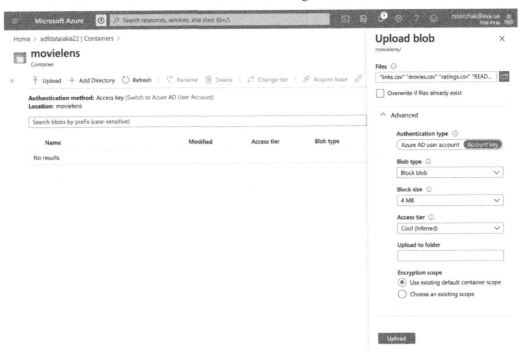

Figure 4.17 – Uploading the dataset

2. Upload files to the `movielens` container via the Azure Data Lake UI. See the following screenshot:

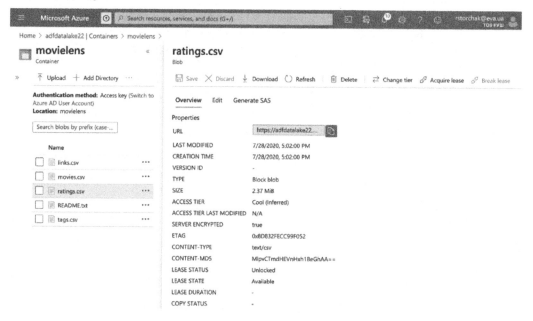

Figure 4.18 – Verifying the dataset

How to do it...

To create your first Data Factory pipeline, go to the Data Factory UI and create a dataset:

1. Select **Azure Data Lake Storage Gen2** and click **Next**.

2. Set the **Format** type of the data to **DelimitedText(csv)**.

3. Enter the dataset name and select a linked service. Use the linked service that we created in the second recipe of this chapter.

4. Set up the proper file path and check **First row as a header**.

5. Lucky us – row and column delimiters, encoding, the escape character, quote character, and so on are set up correctly even by default. If you need to change them, you can click on the dataset name in `Datasets` and modify parameters on the **Connections** tab:

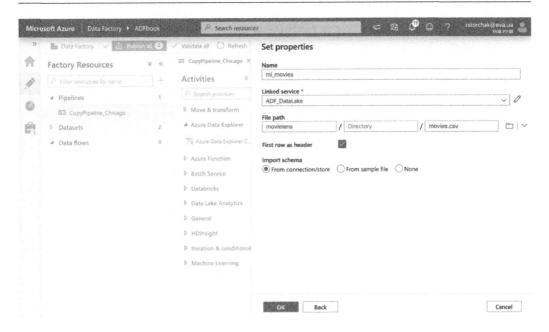

Figure 4.19 – Connecting datasets

6.   Repeat *Step 3* for each file, and click **Publish All**.

Now we have all the datasets required to process **Movie Rankings** data. Let's build a 'data flow' that preprocesses data from the **MovieLens** dataset:

1.   Click + and **Pipeline**.

2.   Go to **Move & Transform** and drag **Data Flow** into your workspace.

3.   Select **Create new data flow** and click on **Data Flow** and **OK**.

4.   Name your data flow. In the production environment, write a description of your data flow.

5.   Click **Add Source**, which you can find in the top-left corner of your workspace.

6. Fill in **Output stream name** and **Source type**. Select a dataset from the drop-down menu or add a new one. In our case, we have already prepared our datasets. So, select the **ml_ratings** dataset, as shown in the following figure:

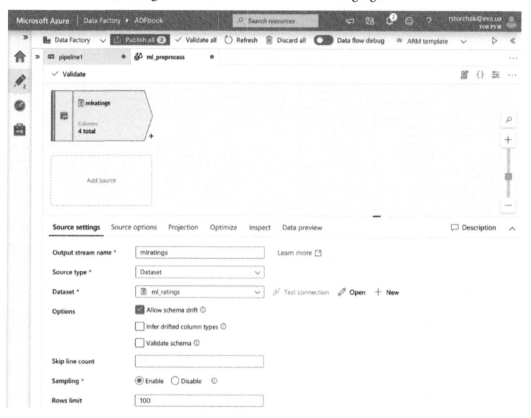

Figure 4.20 – Creating a data flow

7. Classical ETL/ELT patterns often fail when the schema of input data changes. Azure Data Factory can handle schema drift. So, your process can handle changes in upstream data source changes.

8. Set up **Infer drifted column types** and **Validate schema** according to the expectations of the behavior of your ETL/ELT procedure.

9. When working with massive datasets, enable **Sampling** and select an appropriate **Rows limit**. Usually, it falls between 100 and 1,000 rows. For this recipe, let's enable **Sampling**.

10. If your dataset consists of multiple files, fill in the **Source options** tab. In this case, we don't need to fill in anything.

11. Keep in mind that the contents of **Data preview** and **Projection** have to be fetched from the dataset. Hence, you have to launch **Data flow debug**. Select **AutoResolveIntegrationRuntime**. Be aware that starting **Data flow debug** requires some time to start a compute instance or cluster and start billing (*Figure 4.24*).

12. Go to the **Projection** tab and check if the column names and data types are correct. If not, fix it by clicking **Import projection** or do it manually. Please note that Azure Data Factory does not automatically parse timestamps in **UNIX** or **POSIX** time format. So, we should set **Type** to integer and we will fix it during preprocessing:

Figure 4.21 – Setting up the projection of the source

13. Go to the **Optimize** tab. Setting the **Optimal partition** option is critical for performance. If the whole dataset fits one worker, use **Single partition**. You can use custom partitioning logic by selecting **Set Partitioning**.

14. Check the column types on the **Inspect** tab and check data on the **Data preview** tab.

15. Repeat *steps 11-20* for the **ml_movies** dataset. Make sure that the **movieId** column has the same type as the **movieId** column from the **mlratings** dataset.

16. Let's transform a timestamp column from the **mlratings** output stream. Click + and select **Derived Column** as shown in the following figure:

Figure 4.22 – Adding derived columns

17. Fill in the derived column's name. We will name it `Date`. Check if the incoming stream is right, and add transformation logic in **Columns**. In this case, we have to add `toDate(seconds(timestamp), 'yyyy-MM-dd')` in a pop-up window.

18. Store the dataset by selecting **Sink** for the next step.

19. Let's add the average ranking and count of rankings to each movie in the `mlmovies` stream.

(a) First, we have to group **ml_ratings** by **movieID** and add aggregation logic: **Count()** and **mean(raring)**, shown in the following figure:

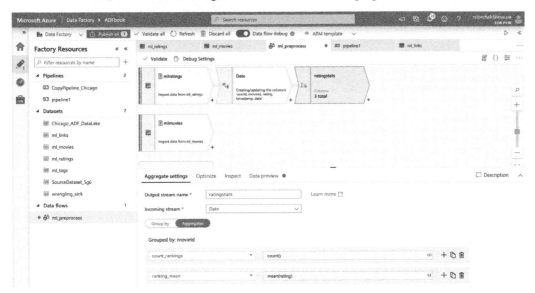

Figure 4.23 – Aggergating data

(b) Then join the **ratingstats** output stream with **mlmovies**. Click + and **Join**. Select **Left stream** and **Right Stream**, then **Join type**. Select columns and join logic in **Join conditions**. During this exercise, we will use **Left outer join** and the `movieId` column (*Figure 4.23*).

(c) Go to the **Optimize** tab and set the **Broadcast** option to **Auto** and **Partition option**. As usual, select a single partition if your dataset is small. Otherwise, choose another option. You can check for the details here: `https://docs.microsoft.com/azure/data-factory/concepts-data-flow-performance`.

(d) Inspect the column names and check out **Data preview**.

(e) We can drop redundant columns by clicking **Remove** and **Confirm** on the **Data preview** tab. It will automatically generate the next step and the appropriate output stream.

(f) Add the appropriate name of the step. You can modify the column mapping manually.

(g) Add the sink dataset, where we will store our preprocessed data. Please note that a dataset can be created in Azure Data Factory.

(h) If you need to store your dataset in a separate folder, you have to go to the Azure Data Lake admin page and create it. Then, specify the desired path for the sink dataset:

Figure 4.24 – Joins in the data flow

20. To save your data flow, click **Publish all**.

21. Close your **Data flow** tab and switch to the pipeline that we created in *Step 1* of this recipe.

22. Rename your mapping data flow. The default properties on the **General** tab are fine for our task, as shown in the following figure:

Figure 4.25 – Cleaning up your data flow

23. Go to the **Settings** tab. Check the **Data flow** name and integration runtime and select properties of the instances that will execute your data flow. **Compute type** and **Core count** have to be selected based on your dataset size and preprocessing in the pipeline, as shown in the following figure:

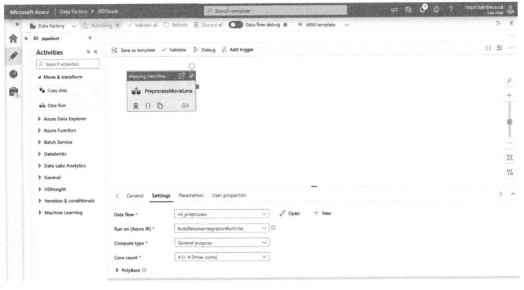

Figure 4.26 – Setting up data flow properties

24. Click **Debug** to run a pipeline.

25. In a few minutes, you can check the outcome of the pipeline execution. Please note that we have used sampling in the **Add source** steps for **mlmovies** and **mlratings**:

Figure 4.27 – Data flow debug

26. Remove sampling in each source and rerun the data flow.

Congratulations, you have built and debugged a code-free big data pipeline that processes the **MovieLens** dataset.

How it works

Data flows are one of the core features of Azure Data Factory. You can ingest data, process it, and sink it to a predefined location.

Specifically, a data flow connects to one or more source datasets using linked services. Then, data is put through processing, which you coded via the Azure Data Factory web GUI. Processing is scalable and is implemented with Spark. Consequently, you can work with billions of records in your data flows without noticing.

Processed data can be stored in one of a few storage options available for Azure Data Factory.

5
Working with Big Data – HDInsight and Databricks

Azure Data Factory (ADF) is known for its efficient utilization of big data tools. This allows building fast and scalable ETL/ELT pipelines and easily managing the storage of petabytes of data. Often, setting up a production-ready cluster used for data engineering jobs is a daunting task. On top of this, estimating loads and planning for an autoscaling capacity can be tricky. Azure with HDInsight clusters and Databricks make these tasks obsolete. Now, any Azure practitioner can set up an Apache Hive, Apache Spark, or Apache Kafka cluster in minutes.

In this chapter, we are going to cover the following recipes that will help build your ETL infrastructure:

- Setting up an HDInsight cluster
- Processing data from Azure Data Lake with HDInsight and Hive
- Processing big data with Apache Spark
- Building a machine learning app with Databricks and Azure Data Lake Storage

Technical requirements

You need to have access to Microsoft Azure. You will be able to run HDInsight clusters with Azure credits, but running Databricks requires a pay-as-you-go account. Also, you can use the code from `https://github.com/PacktPublishing/Azure-Data-Factory-Cookbook/`.

Setting up an HDInsight cluster

HDInsight is a comprehensive solution based on a diverse list of open source platforms. It includes Apache Hadoop, Apache Spark, Apache Kafka, Apache HBase, Apache Hive, Apache Storm, and so on. Solutions based on HDInsight can be integrated with ADF, Azure Data Lake, Cosmos DB, and so on.

In this section, we will set up the HDInsight service, build a basic pipeline, and deploy it to ADF.

Getting ready

Before getting started with the recipe, log in to your Microsoft Azure account.

We assume you have a pre-configured resource group and storage account with Azure Data Lake Gen2.

How to do it...

We will go through the process of creating an HDInsight cluster using the Azure portal and its web interface. Follow these instructions:

1. Create a user-assigned managed identity. We will need it in the next step, to set up HDInsight cluster access to Data Lake v2. Find **Managed Identities** in Azure and click **+Add**.

2. Fill in the appropriate details, such as **Resource group**, **Region**, and **Name**, as shown in the following screenshot:

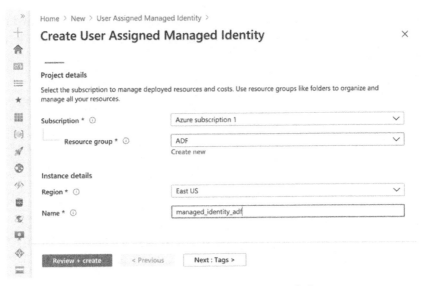

Figure 5.1 – Create User Assigned Managed Identity

3. Click on **Next : Tags >** and fill in tags that will help you with tracking this managed identity.

4. Now, click **Create** and wait for a few seconds while the identity is created.

5. Once the managed identity is created, go to **Storage accounts** and select an appropriate storage account that you will use with the HDInsight cluster.

6. Click **Access Control (IAM) | + Add | Add role assignment**, as shown in the following screenshot:

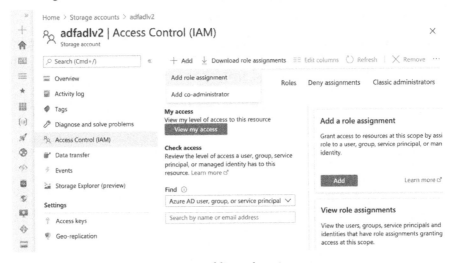

Figure 5.2 – Adding role assignment

7. Select the **Storage Blob Data Owner** role, assign access to **User assigned managed identity**, which is in the following dropdown, and select your subscription, as shown in *Figure 5.3*.

8. Click **Save** to finalize the role assignment:

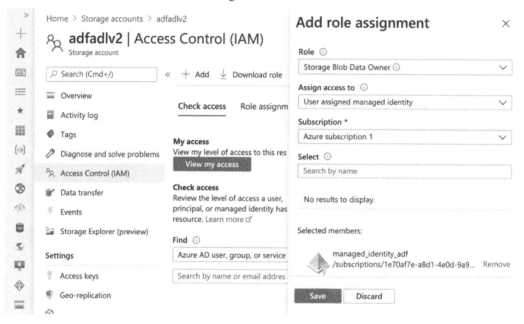

Figure 5.3 – Setting up a role assignment

9. Go to **HD Insight clusters** and click **+ Add.**

10. Select your subscription and resource group.

11. Name your cluster, select the region, and select a cluster type, as shown in the following screenshot. For this recipe, we will select Hadoop version 2.7.3, which is the default choice as of September 2020:

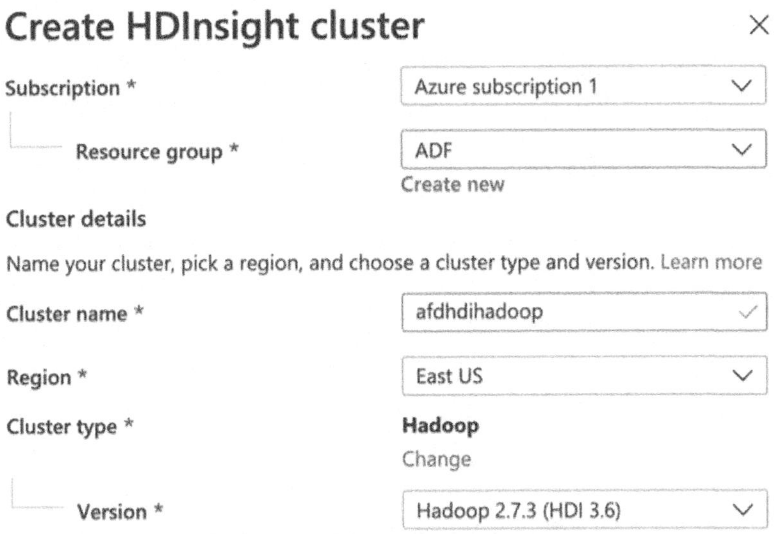

Figure 5.4 – Creating an HDInsight cluster

12. Set your details for the **Cluster login username** and **Cluster login password fields** and confirm the password (*Figure 5.5*).

13. Fill in the **Secure Shell (SSH) username** field and allow usage of the cluster login password for SSH:

Figure 5.5 – Adding HDInsight cluster credentials

14. Click **Next: Storage** to set up the storage options.

15. Select **Primary storage type**. Be aware that Azure Data Lake Storage Gen2 is not yet the default choice despite all of its advantages, as shown in the following screenshot:

Create HDInsight cluster   ✕

Primary storage

Select or create a storage account that will be the default location for cluster logs and other output.

Primary storage type *	Azure Data Lake Storage Gen2 ⌄
Primary storage account *	adfadlv2 ⌄
Filesystem * ⓘ	afdhdihadoop-2020-09-14t15-18-43-322z ✓

Identity

Select a user-assigned managed identity to represent the cluster for Azure Data Lake Gen2 Storage account access. Only identities with access to the selected storage account are listed. Assign the managed identity to the 'Storage Blob Data Owner' role on the storage account. Learn more

User-assigned managed identity * ⓘ	managed_identity_adf ⌄

Figure 5.6 – Setting up storage for an HDInsight cluster

16. Select a primary storage account, which is our Data Lake Gen2 storage, and its filesystem. The HDInsight cluster will use this storage and filesystem as its main storage. Even if you decide to delete your cluster, the data will stay intact.

17. Select the user-assigned managed identity that we created during *steps 1–4* and granted necessary rights to during *steps 5–8* of this recipe.

18. You can add additional Azure storage, an external Ambari database, and external metadata stores for Hive and Oozie. For our setup, those fields should be blank.

19. Click **Next: Security + networking**.

20. Leave **Enable enterprise security package** not selected.

21. Set **Minimum TLS version** to its default: 1.2.

22. In our setup, we do not need to connect our cluster to a virtual network and provide our own disc encryption settings. Select **User-assigned managed identity** to represent our cluster for the enterprise security package.

23. Click **Next: Configuration + pricing**.

24. Select appropriate node types and the price for the task you are intending to use this cluster for, as shown in the following screenshot:

Create HDInsight cluster

×

ⓘ This configuration will use 40 of 40 available cores in the East US region.
View cores usage

+ Add application

Node type	Node size		Number of ...	Estimated cost/h...
Head node	D12 v2 (4 Cores, 28 GB RAM), 0.37 USD/hour	∨	2	0.75 USD
Worker node	D4 v2 (8 Cores, 28 GB RAM), 0.59 USD/hour	∨	4	2.36 USD

☐ Enable autoscale
Learn More

Total estimated cost/hour   3.11 USD

Figure 5.7 – Configuring hardware

25. Click **Next** and add appropriate tags that will help you to track your resources.

26. Click the **Review + create** button to finalize cluster creation. Check whether everything is correct.

27. The Azure portal will forward you to the **Deployment** page. After a short wait, you will see that your cluster is created and functional, as seen in the following screenshot. You can use it with ADF or directly:

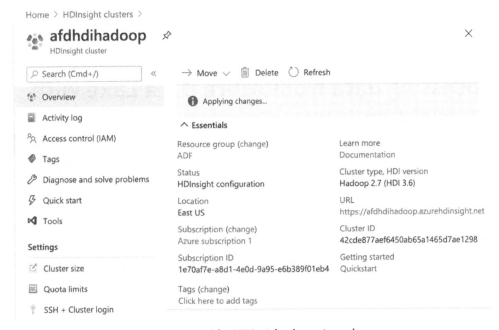

Figure 5.8 – The HDInsight cluster is ready

> **Important note**
> Azure charges for the HDInsight cluster even if it is not used. So, you have to programmatically create clusters, execute jobs, and delete clusters.

How it works...

HDInsight clusters are a versatile service that allow the easy deployment of various open source technologies. They allow running the following:

- Hadoop

- Spark

- Kafka

- HBase

- Interactive Query (Hive)

- Storm

- Machine learning services (R server)

In this recipe, we built a managed Hadoop cluster that is ready to be used with ADF. Hadoop requires permissions to access storage accounts. In our case, it is Azure Data Lake Storage (Gen2). To grant this access, we have to create a user-assigned managed identity and grant the appropriate rights (Storage Blob Data Owner for our storage). Then, the Hadoop cluster uses this managed identity to access the storage.

Processing data from Azure Data Lake with HDInsight and Hive

HDInsight clusters are versatile open source tools that can handle ETL/ELT and data analytical and scientific tasks at scale. Unfortunately, usage of Azure HDInsight is chargeable even when the cluster is inactive or not loaded. But ADF can create and manage short-lived HDInsight clusters. Let's build one.

Getting ready

Ensure that you have a pre-configured resource group and storage account with Azure Data Lake Gen2. Now, log in to your Microsoft Azure account.

How to do it...

For processing data from Azure Data Lake with HDInsight and Hive, use the following steps.

1. Go to the Azure portal and find **Azure Active Directory**.

2. Click **App registrations**, as shown in the following screenshot:

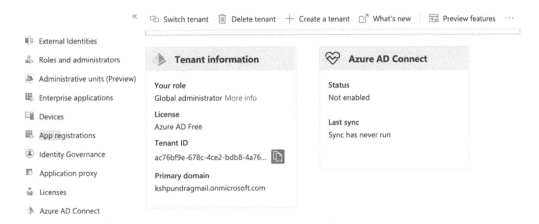

Figure 5.9 – App registrations

3. Then, click **+ New registration** and fill in the name of your app, as shown in the following screenshot:

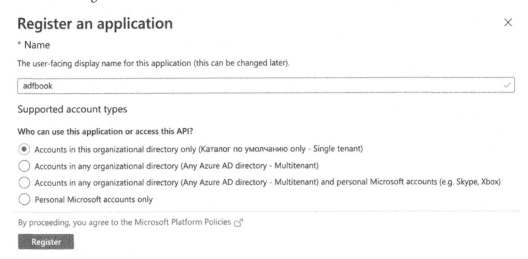

Figure 5.10 – Registering an app

4.   Leave the default answer to **Who can use this application or access this API?** and click **Register**.

5.   Go to the Azure portal and then to **Subscriptions**. Select a subscription that you will use to run your app, as shown in the following screenshot:

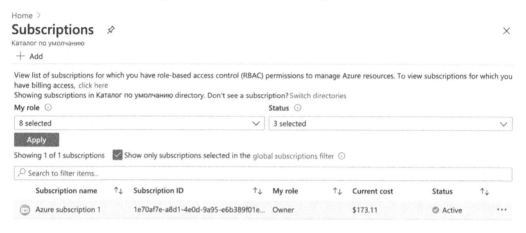

Figure 5.11 – Selecting subscriptions

6.   Click **Access control (IAM) | + Add role**, as shown in the following screenshot:

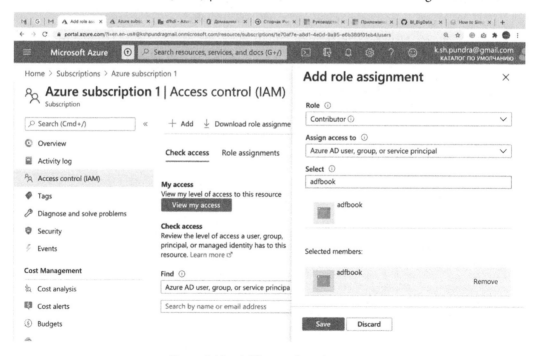

Figure 5.12 – Adding a role assignment

7. Assign the **Contributor** role to the app that you have created. Select **Azure AD user, group, or service principal** for **Assign access to** and select your app by its name.

   Congratulations, you have registered an app and added the necessary role to use it with an on-demand HDInsight cluster in ADF!

8. Go to the ADF interface. Click **Create Pipeline**. Add a name and description. Set **Concurrency** to 1 since we don't need simultaneous pipeline runs, as shown in the following screenshot:

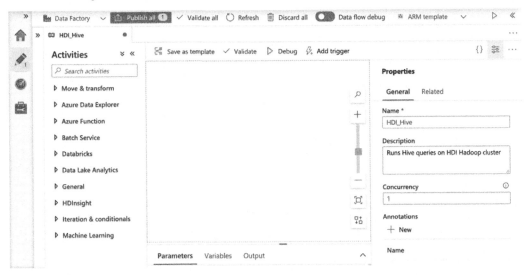

Figure 5.13 – Creating a Hive pipeline

9. Click on **HDInsight** and drag and drop **Hive** to the workspace.

10. Set the name as HiveJob, add a description, and set **Timeout**, the number of retries, and **Retry interval** (*Figure 5.14*).

11. Leave **Secure input** and **Secure output** unchecked:

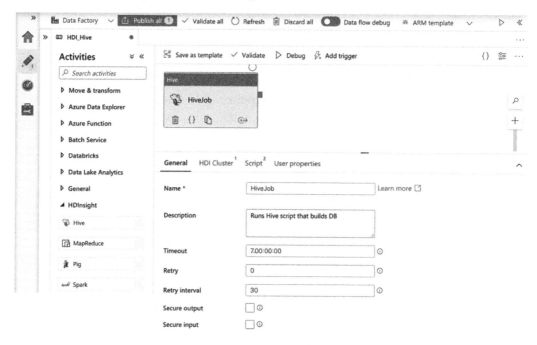

Figure 5.14 – Setting up a Hive job

12. Go to the **HDI Cluster** tab. Click to create a new HDInsight linked service.

13. Add a name and description for the linked service, as shown in the following screenshot:

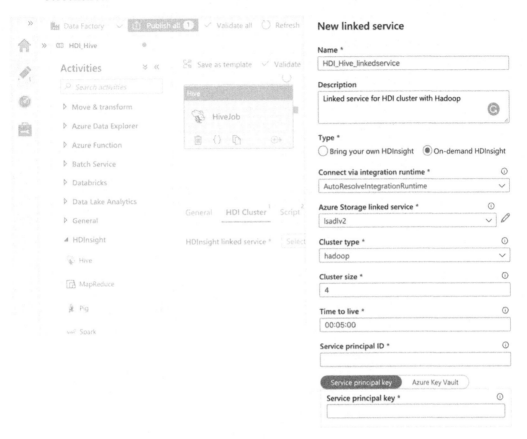

Figure 5.15 – Setting up a Hive linked service

14. Select **On-demand HDInsight**.

15. Leave the default **Connection via integration runtime** setting (**AutoResolveIntegrationRuntime**).

16. Select an existing or create a new Azure Storage linked service (we created linked services in *Chapter 4, Working with Azure Data Lake*).

17. Set **Cluster type** to hadoop and **Cluster size** to 1. The smallest cluster size will be enough for testing purposes.

18. **Time to live** specifies the amount of time that a cluster can be inactive for. Then, it will be deleted. Please note that data is stored separately in Azure Storage, so it will be available after cluster deletion.

19. Switch to **Active Directory | App Registrations |** the app page. Copy the **Application (client) ID** value, as shown on the following screenshot, and insert it into the **Service principal ID** field (that you can see in *Figure 5.15*):

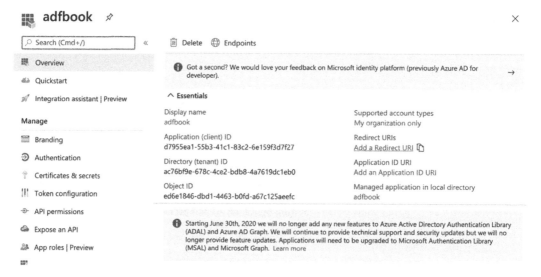

Figure 5.16 – Getting the application ID

20. Go to **Certificates & secrets** and click **+ New client secret**. Set the password time and copy the password value.

21. Paste the password into **Service principal key** on the **New linked service** interface in ADF, as shown in the following screenshot:

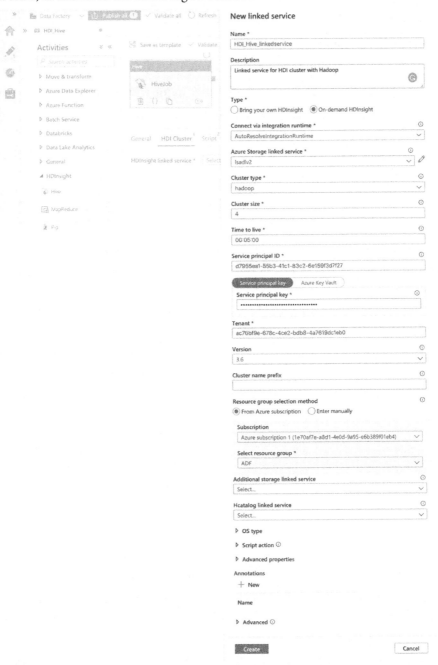

Figure 5.17 – Creating an HDInsight Hive cluster linked service

22. The **Tenant** field should be generated automatically. Otherwise, copy-paste it from **Active Directory | App Registrations |** the app page.

23. Leave the default version of the HDInsight cluster.

24. Leave **Cluster name prefix** blank.

25. Select your subscription and resource group.

26. Click on **OS type** and fill **Cluster SSH user name** with `sshuser` and a password.

27. Add details for the Cluster user name and **Cluster password** fields. They will be useful for cluster monitoring and troubleshooting.

28. Click `Create`.

29. Switch to the **Script** tab.

30. Add a script linked service. This is a linked service that allows access to the storage where the Hive script is stored.

31. Copy or clone the `query.hql` file from `https://github.com/PacktPublishing/Azure-Data-Factory-Cookbook/`. It contains a toy query that we will run.

32. Upload `query.hql` to Azure Data Lake Storage (Gen2) to the same folder where the MovieLens dataset files are stored.

33. Fill in placeholders for the Azure storage account name and container name where you store a dataset. Then, specify the location of the `movies.csv` file.

34. Add a Hive script file path that will be executed, as shown in the following screenshot:

Figure 5.18 – Adding a Hive script to ADF

35. Don't forget to save a pipeline by clicking **Publish all** and confirming it. Please be aware that ADF does not allow publishing pipelines with activities that contain empty fields.

36. Manually trigger a pipeline to run it. Please note that launching a cluster takes about 10+ minutes.

37. After some time, you can check that your job was successful, as seen in the following screenshot. Keep in mind that Hive stores its data in your Azure Data Lake (Gen2) area, so you can log in to your storage account and visually inspect tables and so on. So, when the HDInsight cluster is deleted, you still have access to its data:

Details   ○ Refresh   ⤢ ✕

Name	Value
Duration	00:07:14
Integration runtime	DefaultIntegrationRuntime (East US)
Log location	abfss://adfjobs@adfadlv2.dfs.core.windows.net/HiveQueryJobs/f1c65e62-c14b-4d2f-a74c-986105d7a13b/15_09_2020_07_38_49_335/Status
Compute information	https://hi-742f6925-b633-4d7c-ac9d-3c1049017c47.azurehdinsight.net:443/
Job ID	job_1600198594805_0001
Execution progress	Succeeded
YarnApplicationUri	https://hi-742f6925-b633-4d7c-ac9d-3c1049017c47.azurehdinsight.net//yarnui/hn/cluster/app/application_16001985948...
JobStatusDetailsFromHDI	application_1600198594805_0001
Duration in queue	{"integrationRuntimeQueue":10}
billingReference	{"activityType":"ExternalActivity","billableDuration":[{}]}

Figure 5.19 – Hive job details

How it works...

Apache Hive is a piece of data warehouse software that can run SQL queries. The HDInsight Hive cluster stores the data in Azure Data Lake Storage (Gen2). ADF can create a temporary HDInsight Hive cluster, run queries, and delete unused clusters.

In order to allow ADF to create and kill HDInsight Hive clusters, we need to create an Azure Active Directory app. Then, we assign a Contributor role to the app, allowing it to manage resources in Azure. Later, when we use Hive jobs from ADF, an application with proper permissions is needed to automatically create a cluster.

During the execution, these ADF pipelines create a cluster, run Hive scripts, store Hive query outputs, and kill the cluster.

Processing big data with Apache Spark

Apache Spark is a well-known big data framework that is often used for big data ETL/ELT jobs and machine learning tasks. ADF allows us to utilize its capabilities in two different ways:

- Running Spark in an HDInsight cluster
- Running Databricks notebooks and JAR and Python files

Running Spark in an HDInsight cluster is very similar to the previous recipe. So, we will concentrate on the Databricks service. It also allows running interactive notebooks, which significantly simplifies the development of the ETL/ELT pipelines and machine learning tasks.

Getting ready

Assuming you have a preconfigured resource group and storage account with Azure Data Lake Gen2, log in to your Microsoft Azure account. To run Databricks notebooks, you have to switch to a pay-as-you-go subscription.

How to do it...

1. Go to the Azure portal and find **Databricks**.
2. Click **+ Add** and fill in the project details.
3. Select your subscription and resource group, as shown in the following screenshot:

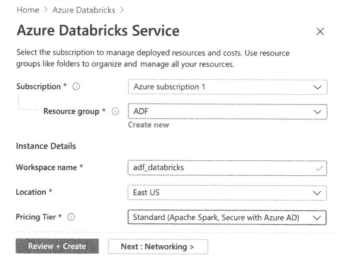

Figure 5.20 – Setting up Azure Databricks

4. Name your Databricks workspace and select a location.

5. Pick **Standard** for **Pricing Tier** as it is more than enough for our application.

6. Click **Next: Networking**.

7. Now, select **No** for **Deploy Azure Databricks workspace in your own Virtual Network (VNet)**.

8. Click **Next: Tags** and add appropriate tags to simplify recourse tracking and management.

9. Click **Review + Create**, and then **Create**.

    After a short deployment process, Databricks will be operational.

10. Go to the ADF UI, then click on **Manage | Linked services | + New**.

11. Select the **Compute** tab and click on **Azure Databricks** and **Continue**, as shown in the following screenshot:

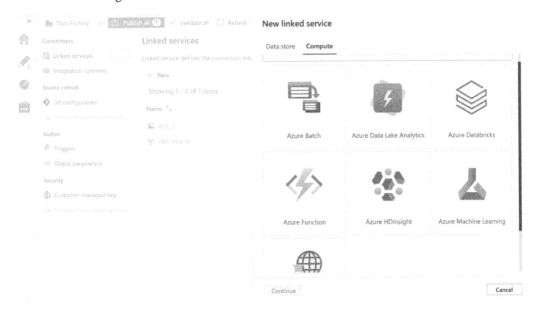

Figure 5.21 – Selecting Azure Databricks

12. Fill in the **Name** and **Description** fields for the linked service.

13. Select **AutoRevolveIntegrationRuntime** for the **Connect via integration runtime** field.

14. Select your subscription from the **Azure subscription** drop-down menu in the Databricks workspace that we created in *steps 1–9* of this recipe.

15. In **Select cluster**, pick **New job cluster**. This option will allow you to start Spark clusters, process the data, and stop them.

16. Log in to your Databricks workspace. If you're logging in to the **Azure Databricks Service** for the first time, click on your service and click **Launch Workspace**.

17. Click on the user icon in the top-right corner and select **User Settings**, as shown in the following screenshot:

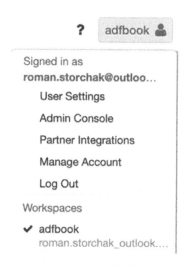

Figure 5.22 – Setting up storage for the HDInsight cluster

18. Click **Generate New** Token and enter an appropriate lifetime and a comment.

19. Copy the token and paste it into the **Access token** field in **New Linked Service (Azure Databricks)**.

20. Check the default cluster version in the Databricks interface and select it. At the time of writing, it is **Runtime 7.0 (Scala 2.12,** Spark 3.0.0**)**. Select it in the Current version field.

21. Pick **Standard_D3_v2**, **Cluster node type**, and **Python Version 3**.

22. For this recipe, **Worker options** should be set to **Fixed** since we will not need both autoscaling and two workers.

23. Click **Create**. Congratulations, you have created a linked service to a Databricks cluster!

24. Go to **Author | Pipelines | Create new pipeline**. Name it and drag and drop the **Databricks: Notebook** activity to the workspace.

25. In the **General** tab, fill in the **Name** and **Description** fields.

26. For this recipe, leave **Timeout**, **Retry**, **Retry interval**, **Secure output**, and **Secure input** at their default values.

27. Go to the **Azure Databricks** tab. Select your linked service and test the connection.

28. Go to the **Settings** tab and select your notebook. We will go through the process of creating a Databricks notebook in the *Building a machine learning app with Databricks and Azure Data Lake Storage* recipe later in this chapter.

> **Note**
>
> Databricks clusters can only access files stored in the **Databricks Filesystem (DBFS)**. We can mount any Azure storage to DBFS. Also, files can be loaded manually via the Databricks web interface, the Databricks CLI, the DBFS API, and so on.

29. Add parameters that the Databricks notebook might require in **Base parameters**.

30. Save your pipeline by clicking **Publish all**.

31. Now you can run or debug your notebook activity within ADF.

How it works...

ADF can create new Databricks clusters or utilize existing ones. Leveraging a linked service, ADF connects to the external service and programmatically triggers the execution of Databricks notebooks and JAR and Python files.

You can create extremely complex pipelines using AFD and Databricks.

Building a machine learning app with Databricks and Azure Data Lake Storage

In addition to ETL/ELT jobs, data engineers often help data scientists to productionize machine learning applications. Using Databricks is an excellent way to simplify the work of the data scientist as well as create data preprocessing pipelines.

As we have seen in the previous recipe, ADF can trigger the execution of notebooks and JAR and Python files. So, parts of the app logic have to be encoded there.

A Databricks cluster uses its own filesystem (**DBFS**). So, we need to mount Azure Data Lake Storage to DBFS to access input data and the resulting files.

In this recipe, we will connect Azure Data Lake Storage to Databricks, ingest the MovieLens dataset, train a basic model for a recommender system, and store the model in Azure Data Lake Storage.

Getting ready

First, log in to your Microsoft Azure account.

We assume you have a pre-configured resource group and storage account with Azure Data Lake Gen2 and the Azure Databricks service from the previous recipe.

Hence, we assume the following:

- ADF has a linked service for Azure Data Lake Storage.
- The MovieLens dataset (used in *Chapter 4, Working with Azure Data Lake*) is loaded in Azure Data Lake Storage (Gen2).

Create or use the Azure Active Directory application that we created in the *Processing data from Azure Data Lake with HDInsight and Hive* recipe.

How to do it...

Use the following steps to build a machine learning app with Databricks and Azure Data Lake Storage

1. Log in to your Databricks web UI. Click on **New Cluster**, as shown in the following screenshot:

Figure 5.23 – Home of the Databricks UI

2. Add a cluster name and set **Cluster Mode** to **Single Node**. Leave the **Pool** setting as **None**. Select the default Databricks runtime version. At the time of writing, it is **Runtime 7.0 (Scala 2.12, Spark 3.0.0)**.

Check **Terminate after** and set 10 minutes of inactivity. Select an appropriate node type. We are testing Databricks with a small dataset, so the **Standard_F4s** node fits our recipe, as shown in the following screenshot:

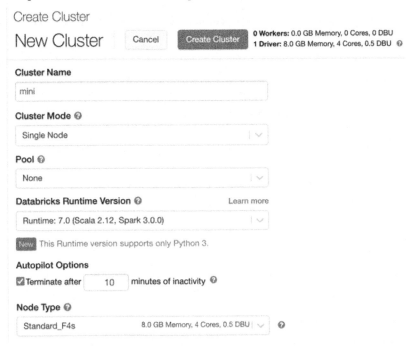

Figure 5.24 – Creating a new cluster

3. Click **Create Cluster**.

4. Go to the Databricks main page and click on **New Notebook**.

5. Fill in the notebook name, set **Default Language** to **Python**, and click **Create**.

Preparing access credentials and code

Let's prepare the credentials and the code that will mount Azure Data Lake Storage (Gen2) to a Databricks cluster. Please follow these instructions:

1. Our Azure Data Lake Storage already contains data, so we do not need to initialize it.

2. Go to Azure Active Directory.

3. Click **App registrations** and create a new app following the steps from the *Processing data from Azure Data Lake with HDInsight and Hive* recipe.

4. Go to your application page. Copy the **Application (client) ID** value and the directory (tenant) ID.

5. Go to **Certificates & secrets** and click **+ New client secret**. Set the password time to live and copy the password value.

6. Insert the data that we have prepared in the following config and paste it into your Databricks notebook:

```
configs={"fs.azure.account.auth.type": "OAuth",

"fs.azure.account.oauth.provider.type": "org.apache.
hadoop.fs.azurebfs.oauth2.ClientCredsTokenProvider",

"fs.azure.account.oauth2.client.id": "<Application
(Client) ID>",

"fs.azure.account.oauth2.client.secret":"<Client
Secret>",

"fs.azure.account.oauth2.client.endpoint": "https://
login.microsoftonline.com/<Directory (tenant) ID>/oauth2/
token"}
```

> **Important note**
>
> It is unsafe to store a client secret as plain text. Here, it is done only for demonstrational purposes. Databricks has secrets (`https://docs.databricks.com/security/secrets/secrets.html`), which should be used to store secret material.

7. Check that your app has the Contributor role set up in the Azure portal **Subscriptions** area.

8. If your app does not have a proper role, add it by following the instructions from the *Processing data from Azure Data Lake with HDInsight and Hive* recipe.

9. Make sure that your application has the **Storage Blob Data Owner** or **Storage Blob Data Contributor** role. If not, use the instructions from the *Setting up an HDInsight cluster* recipe.

10. Let's configure and use a Databricks secret to ensure safe storage of the client secret. First, we need to set up the Databricks CLI, which will be used to manage secrets.

    Go to the Azure portal and click the Azure Cloud Shell icon, as shown in the following screenshot:

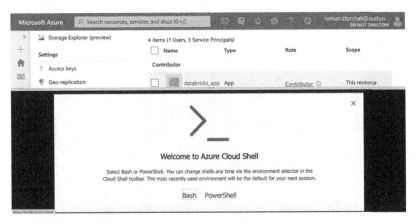

Figure 5.25 – Selecting the type of Azure Cloud Shell instance

11. Click on **Bash**.

12. Select your subscription and click **Show advanced settings**, as shown in the following screenshot:

Figure 5.26 – Selecting your subscription

13. Fill **Cloud Shell region**, then select one of the existing resource groups. In our case, it is called adf-databricks. **Click on Create new under Storage account** and add a name. Click on **Create new** under **File share** and add a name, as shown in the following screenshot:

Figure 5.27 – Advanced settings for the Azure CLI

14. Click **Create storage**. In a few seconds, you will see a working terminal, as shown in the following screenshot:

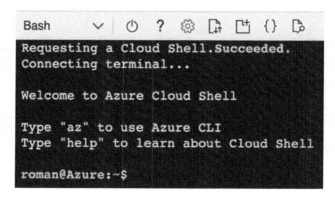

Figure 5.28 – Running the Azure CLI

15. Let's install the Databricks CLI by running `pip install databricks-cli`.

16. Now, we have to set up authentication with Databricks. In this recipe, we will use an access token from Databricks. Generate an access token as we did in the previous recipe.

17. Execute `databricks configure --token` in the Azure CLI (*Figure 5.29*).

18. Go to the Azure Databricks service UI. On the overview page, copy the URL:

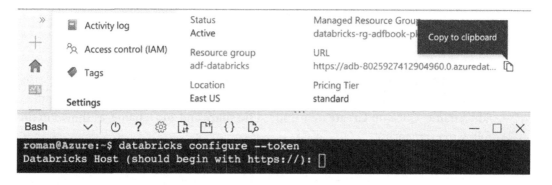

Figure 5.29 – Configuring the Databricks CLI

19. Paste it into the prompt of the Databricks host in the Azure CLI. Press *Enter*. Then, paste the Databricks access token.

20. We can get a list of Databricks clusters by executing `databricks clusters list`.

21. Then, we have to create a secret scope. This is a named collection of secrets that can store up to 100 secrets, up to 128 KB each.

22. Run the following command to create a scope:

```
databricks secrets create-scope --scope <scope-name>
--initial-manage-principal users
```

23. Now, let's add a secret to this scope. Execute the following:

```
databricks secrets put --scope <scope-name> --key
<key-name>
```

24. After running this command for the first time, you will be asked to choose a text editor. Pick any editor that you are familiar with. Usually, I use the Nano editor, which is already preinstalled in the Azure CLI.

25. Paste your client secret that we will use to access Azure Data Lake Storage (Gen2). Save the file (press *Ctrl + O*) and exit to the Azure CLI.

26. We can check secrets given a scope by running the following:

```
databricks secrets list --scope <scope-name>
```

27. You can see the output in the following figure:

```
Bash        ∨    ⏻   ?   ⚙   ⎘   ⎗   {}   ⎚

 3. /usr/bin/vim.basic

/usr/bin/select-editor: 32: /usr/bin/select-editor: gettext: not found
 1-3 [1]: 1
Use "fg" to return to nano.

[1]+  Stopped                    databricks secrets put --scope adf-book --key adls
roman@Azure:~$ databricks secrets put --scope adf-book --key adls
roman@Azure:~$ databricks secrets list --scope adf-book
Key name        Last updated
----------      ------------
adls            1603208672111
roman@Azure:~$ █
```

Figure 5.30 – Setting up a secret

28. Now, instead of leaving sensitive information in code, we can use the following:

```
dbutils.secrets.get(scope="<scope-name>", key="<service-
credential-key-name>")
```

29. We can rewrite a config using Databricks secrets:

```
configs={"fs.azure.account.auth.type": "OAuth",
"fs.azure.account.oauth.provider.type": "org.apache.
hadoop.fs.azurebfs.oauth2.ClientCredsTokenProvider",
"fs.azure.account.oauth2.client.id": "<Application
(Client) ID>",
"fs.azure.account.oauth2.client.secret": dbutils.secrets.
get(scope="<scope-name>", key="<service-credential-key-
name>"),
"fs.azure.account.oauth2.client.endpoint": "https://
login.microsoftonline.com/<Directory (tenant) ID>/oauth2/
token"}
```

30. Go to Databricks, then to your notebook. Paste the config from the previous
    step with **Application (Client) ID**, **Directory (tenant) ID**, **scope-name**, and
    service-credential-key-name filled in.

31. Add the following code with your credentials inserted:

```
dbutils.fs.mount(
    source = "abfss://<file-system-name>@<storage-account-
name>.dfs.core.windows.net/",
    mount_point = "/mnt/<mount-name>",
    extra_configs = configs)


dbutils.fs.ls("/mnt/<mount-name>")
```

In this recipe, I have used `adfs` for `mount-name`. As a rule of thumb, give an
easily recognizable and simple-to-type mount path name.

32. Then, run it. Booting up a cluster will take a few minutes. After Databricks starts
    the cluster, it will execute the first snippets of code. You can see this in the following
    screenshot:

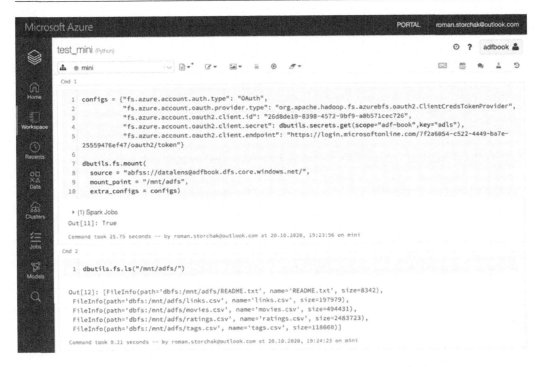

Figure 5.31 – Databricks notebook with mounted Azure Data Lake Storage

External storage will be mounted until you execute the following in a Databricks notebook:

```
dbutils.fs.unmount("/mnt/adfs")
```

Creating a basic recommender model

Let's train a basic model-based recommender system. As a toy example, we will use the **Alternating Least Squares (ALS)** factorization technique implemented in PySpark. We will skip hyperparameter tuning, cross-validation, and model evaluation. This recipe will, however, give an example of building workflows.

Here is a code snippet that reads the data into a DataFrame and prints the first five lines:

```
ratings_df_schema = "userId integer, movieId integer, rating
float"
ratingsDF = spark.read.csv("/mnt/adfs/ratings.csv",
header=True, schema=ratings_df_schema).cache()
ratingsDF.head(5)
```

It splits the dataset into two parts for model training and evaluation:

```
(trainingDF, testDF) = ratingsDF.randomSplit([0.8, 0.2],
seed=1)
```

Then, it initializes the model and trains it with a training subset of the data:

```
from pyspark.ml.recommendation import ALS
als = (ALS()
        .setUserCol("userId")
        .setItemCol("movieId")
        .setRatingCol("rating")
        .setPredictionCol("predictions")
        .setMaxIter(2)
        .setSeed(1)
        .setRegParam(0.1)
        .setColdStartStrategy("drop")
        .setRank(12))
alsModel = als.fit(trainingDF)
```

The following code evaluates the model by predicting rankings for the subset of the data that we left aside. It also calculates the mean squared error between the ground truth and the predicted values:

```
from pyspark.ml.evaluation import RegressionEvaluator

regEval = RegressionEvaluator(predictionCol="predictions",
labelCol="rating", metricName="mse")
predictedTestDF = alsModel.transform(testDF)
testMse = regEval.evaluate(predictedTestDF)

print('MSE on the test set is {0}'.format(testMse))
```

It saves the model to the mounted Azure Data Lake Storage:

```
alsModel.save("/mnt/adfs/models/")
```

To run the notebook that we have walked through in this chapter, follow these steps:

1. Go to the Databricks UI, then **Clusters**, then click your cluster name. Click **Start** to launch a cluster, as shown in the following screenshot:

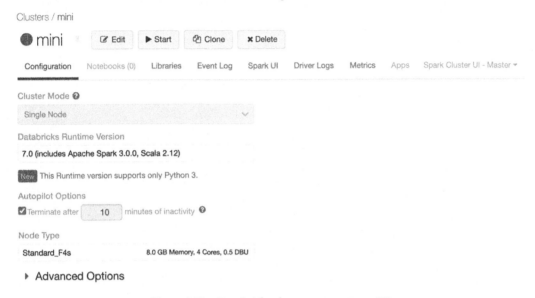

Figure 5.32 – Databricks cluster management UI

2. Go to your notebook and attach your cluster to the notebook.

3. Then, run each block by pressing *Shift + Enter*.

4. Our cluster is fully functional and executes Spark jobs that ingest the data and train and save the recommender model. In the following screenshot, you can see a list of the jobs and their IDs, as well as stages, statuses, and durations:

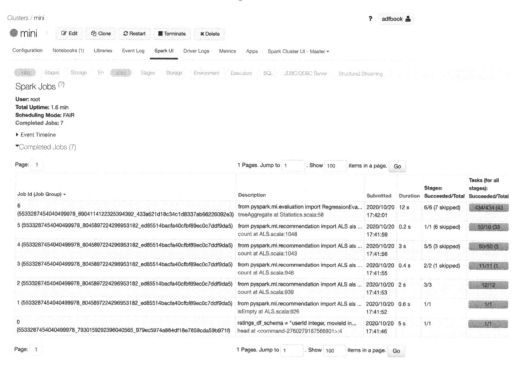

Figure 5.33 – Spark UI and jobs list

5. You can go to **Clusters**, click on your cluster, then **Metrics**, and download a snapshot of the cluster overview, which includes load statistics, memory, network, CPU usage in the last hour, and so on. A partial view of this snapshot is presented in the following screenshot:

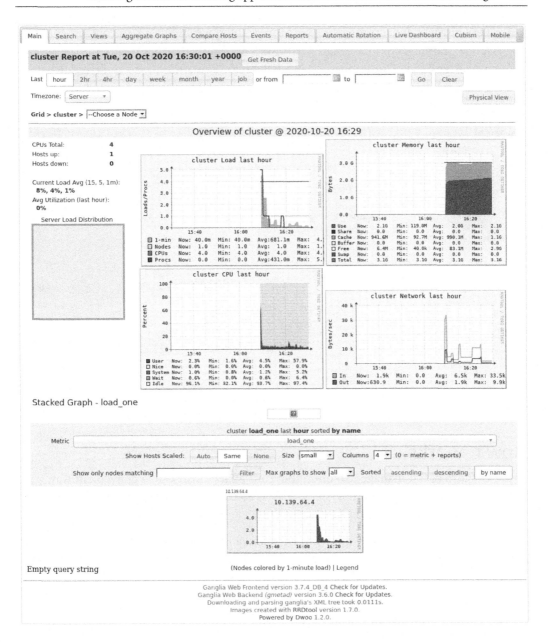

Figure 5.34 – Cluster metrics snapshot

6. Let's move to our Azure Data Lake Storage interface and check the outcomes of the model training. Go to **Storage Accounts**, click on your account with the data and model, and then **Containers**. Then, click on the container name and check what is inside. We can see that Databricks stored the model in the pre-defined location, as shown in the following screenshot:

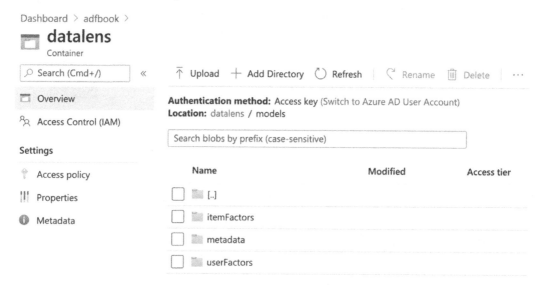

Figure 5.35 – Checking out outputs to Azure Data Lake Storage

How it works...

Azure Databricks is a managed solution that runs Spark clusters in a convenient way. These clusters use an internal filesystem. ADF is able to forward parameters and credentials and trigger the execution of notebooks and JAR and Python files.

In order to organize a data flow between ADF and a Databricks cluster, we need to mount storage that both services use. In this recipe, we mounted Azure Data Lake Storage (Gen2) to DBFS.

This requires quite a few preparations, as listed here:

- We need to use an Azure Active Directory app with permissions to use Azure Data Lake Storage (the Storage Blob Data Owner role).

- Generate application secrets.

- Store secrets securely in a Databricks cluster (using Databricks secrets and the Databricks CLI).

Later, when we run Spark jobs, we can securely mount Azure Data Lake Storage and both read data that we process and write process outputs.

Databricks is known not only for its simplicity of big data ETL/ELT jobs but also for its machine learning capabilities. As an example, we can leverage a PySpark machine learning package and train a simple recommender model based on the ALS algorithm of matrix factorization and store it in Azure Data Lake Storage (Gen2).

6
Integration with MS SSIS

SQL Server Integration Services is a highly capable ETL/ELT tool that is built into Microsoft SQL Server. Often, it is used to move and transform data on-premises and in cloud environments. Its features somewhat resemble the main features of **Azure Data Factory** (**ADF**). At the same time, ADF has high availability and is massively scalable.

ADF adds convenience as it allows the execution of SSIS packages in Azure-SSIS integration or on-premises runtimes. With this tool, you can leverage existing SSIS packages and use familiar development tools.

Running SSIS packages is an essential feature in ADF. In this recipe, we will create a basic SSIS package, deploy it to a managed Azure SQL database, and then trigger its execution in ADF.

In this chapter, we will cover the following topics:

- Creating a SQL server database
- Building an SSIS package
- Running SSIS packages from ADF

By the end of the chapter, you will be able to build a scalable ETL/ELT job using SQL Server, SSIS, and ADF, with its Azure-SSIS integration runtime. This will allow you to move the execution of conventional SSIS packages to the cloud.

Technical requirements

You need to have access to Microsoft Azure. An Azure free account is sufficient for all recipes in this chapter. Also, you have to download and install Visual Studio 2019. During installation, check the **Data storage and processing** and **SQL Server Data Tools** fields. You can use the following tutorial: `https://docs.microsoft.com/en-us/sql/ssdt/download-sql-server-data-tools-ssdt?view=sql-server-ver15#ssdt-for-visual-studio-2019`.

Creating a SQL Server database

SSIS is part of the SQL Server ecosystem. Hence, we need to create a SQL Server and a database and fill it with the data that will be used in the following recipes to deploy and run SSIS packages.

Getting ready

To get started with your recipe, log in to your Microsoft Azure account.

We assume that you have pre-configured a resource group and storage account with Azure Data Lake Gen2.

How to do it...

Let's prepare a SQL Server database. Later, it will be used to run the SQL Server Integration Service package. Perform the following steps:

1. Go to **SQL databases** on Azure, as shown in the following screenshot:

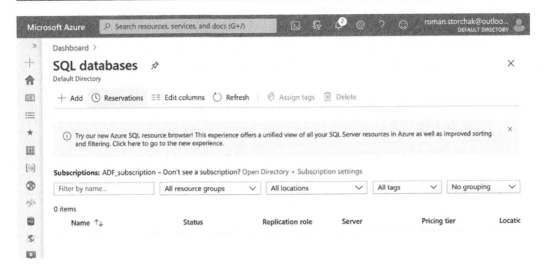

Figure 6.1 – Adding a SQL database

Next, click **+ Add** and then fill in the **Database name** field and click **Create new**, as shown in the following screenshot:

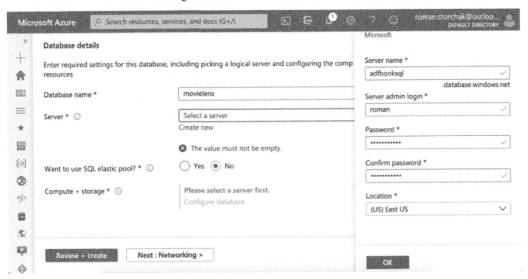

Figure 6.2 – Setting a SQL Server

2. Fill in the **Server name**, **Server admin login**, **Password**, and **Confirm password** fields. Select a **Location**. Preferably, it should be the same as the location of your data factory. Then, click **OK**.

3. Let's configure our SQL server. ADF and Azure-SSIS IR are resilient and scalable. But for convenience purposes, we will use the smallest dataset and smallest server. Click on **Basic** and set 1 GB as the **Data max size**, as shown in the following screenshot:

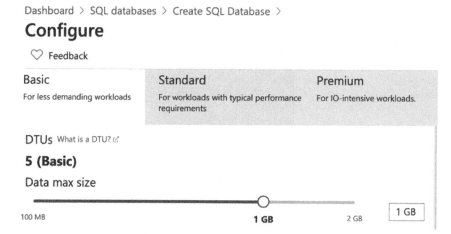

Figure 6.3 – Configuring a SQL server

4. Congratulations! You have prepared a SQL server for our databases!

5. Leave the default settings of **Networking** for a SQL database. Click **Next: Additional settings**, as shown in the following screenshot:

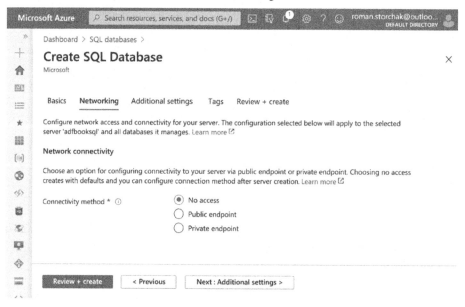

Figure 6.4 – Setting up networking for a SQL database

6. Leave **Use existing data** and **Collation** as their default settings. You can set **Not now** for **Enable Azure Defender for SQL**, as shown in the following screenshot:

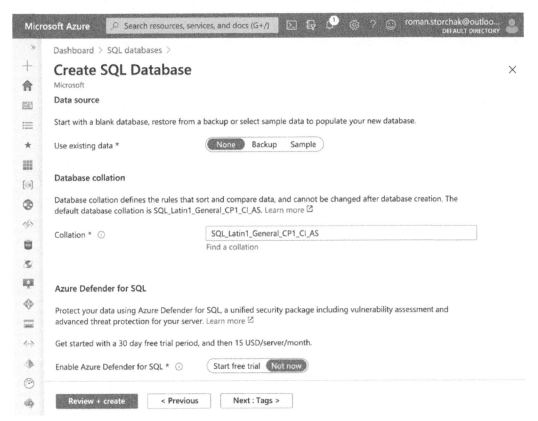

Figure 6.5 – Setting up additional settings for a SQL database

7. Click **Review + create**. If everything is fine, click **Create**.

Let's populate the movielens database with data. This will require a minor modification to the *Connecting Azure Data Lake to Azure Data Factory and loading data* recipe from *Chapter 4, Working with Azure Data Lake*. Please make sure that you understand it before proceeding, as we will just discuss the differences.

8. Go to **Azure Data Factory UI | Manage | Linked Services**.

9. Click **+ New** and then select **Azure SQL Database**.

10. Fill in all the required fields and then click **Test connection**. You will probably see a **Connection failed** message. Expand it and you'll see the following:

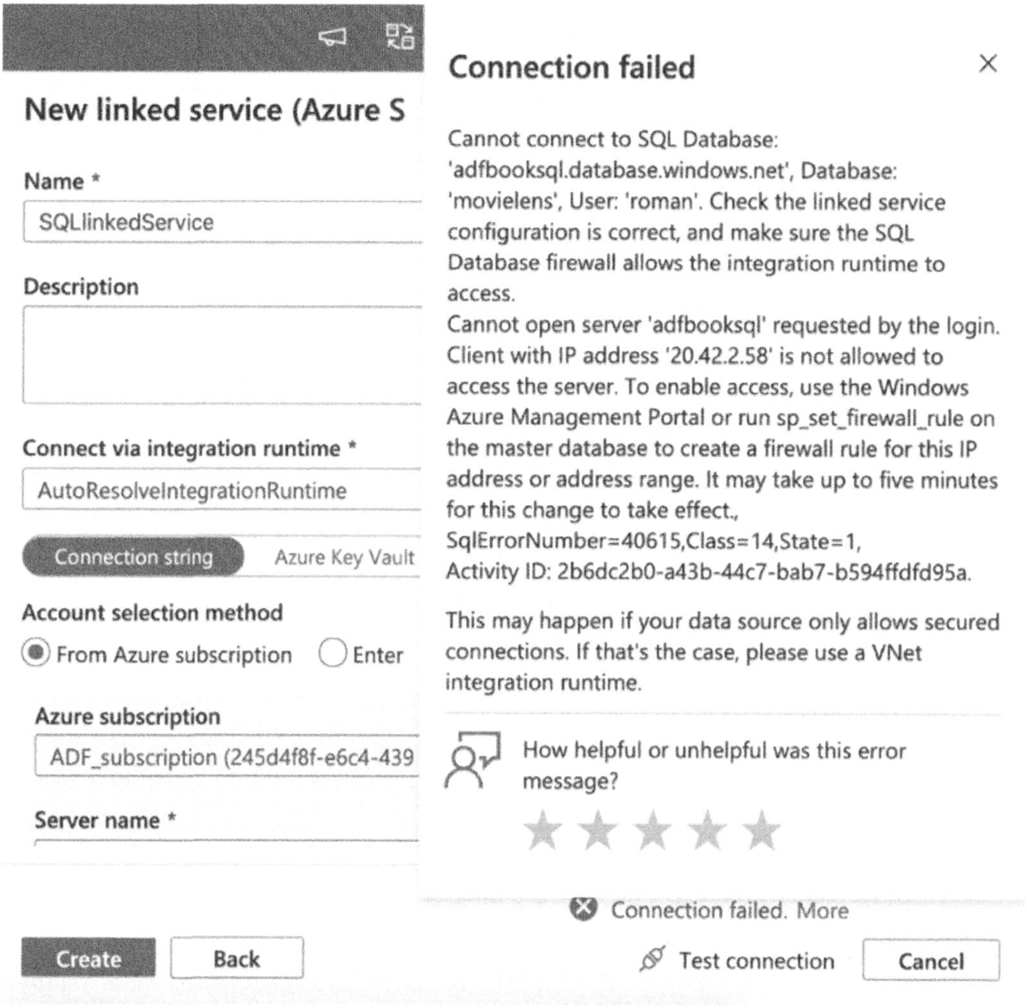

New linked service (Azure S

Name *

SQLlinkedService

Description

Connect via integration runtime *

AutoResolveIntegrationRuntime

Connection string   Azure Key Vault

Account selection method

⦿ From Azure subscription   ◯ Enter

Azure subscription

ADF_subscription (245d4f8f-e6c4-439

Server name *

Create   **Back**

Connection failed   ✕

Cannot connect to SQL Database: 'adfbooksql.database.windows.net', Database: 'movielens', User: 'roman'. Check the linked service configuration is correct, and make sure the SQL Database firewall allows the integration runtime to access.
Cannot open server 'adfbooksql' requested by the login. Client with IP address '20.42.2.58' is not allowed to access the server. To enable access, use the Windows Azure Management Portal or run sp_set_firewall_rule on the master database to create a firewall rule for this IP address or address range. It may take up to five minutes for this change to take effect., SqlErrorNumber=40615,Class=14,State=1, Activity ID: 2b6dc2b0-a43b-44c7-bab7-b594ffdfd95a.

This may happen if your data source only allows secured connections. If that's the case, please use a VNet integration runtime.

How helpful or unhelpful was this error message?

★ ★ ★ ★ ★

❌ Connection failed. More

🖉 Test connection   **Cancel**

Figure 6.6 – Connection failed due to a default firewall setting

11. SQL databases are placed behind a firewall, so we need to configure it. In this recipe, we will allow access from the particular IP range. Go to **SQL Databases**, select your database, and then click on **Set firewall settings**. Now, set **Allow Azure services and resources to access this server** to **Yes**, as shown in the following screenshot. As an option, you can add an IP address or a range of IP addresses, but it is not recommended:

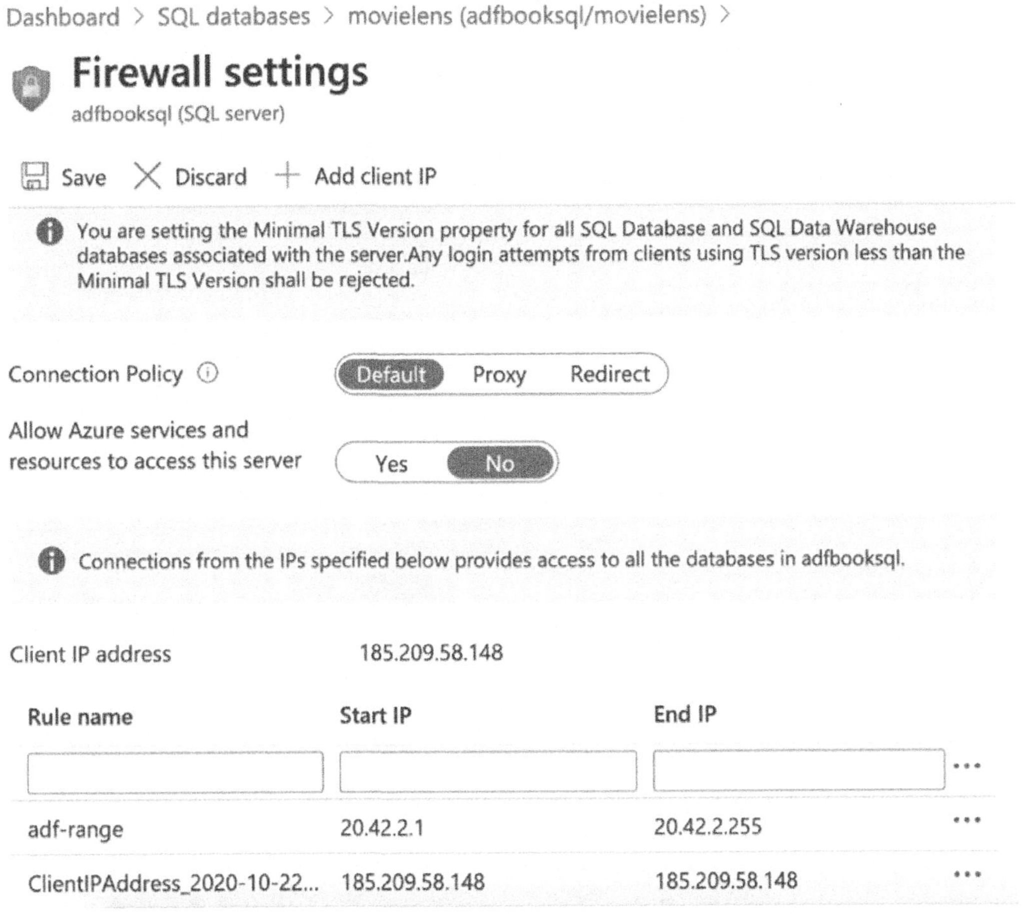

Dashboard > SQL databases > movielens (adfbooksql/movielens) >

Firewall settings
adfbooksql (SQL server)

🔲 Save   ✕ Discard   + Add client IP

> ℹ You are setting the Minimal TLS Version property for all SQL Database and SQL Data Warehouse databases associated with the server.Any login attempts from clients using TLS version less than the Minimal TLS Version shall be rejected.

Connection Policy ⓘ   (Default   Proxy   Redirect)

Allow Azure services and
resources to access this server   (Yes   No)

> ℹ Connections from the IPs specified below provides access to all the databases in adfbooksql.

Client IP address   185.209.58.148

Rule name	Start IP	End IP	
			•••
adf-range	20.42.2.1	20.42.2.255	•••
ClientIPAddress_2020-10-22...	185.209.58.148	185.209.58.148	•••

Figure 6.7 – Setting up a firewall for the SQL database

12. Now, ADF Linked Service will work. Click on **Test connection** and, if you see **Connection successful**, click **Create**, as shown in the following screenshot:

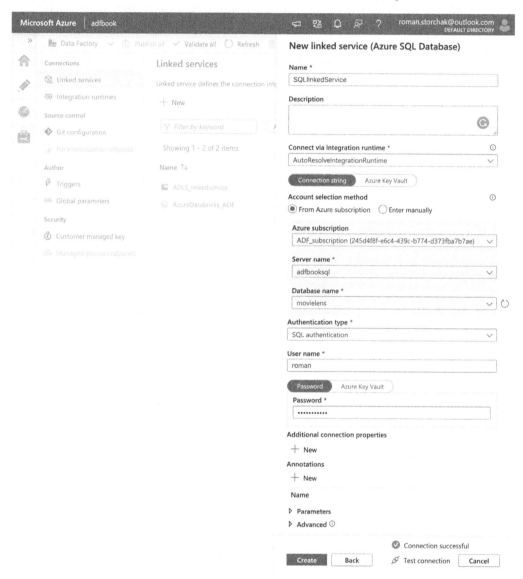

Figure 6.8 – Creating a linked service

13. Let's populate our database by creating a copy activity between Azure Data Lake Storage (gen 2) and the SQL Server database for `ratings.csv` and `movies.csv`. You can use the *Connecting Azure Data Lake to Azure Data Factory and loading data* recipe from *Chapter 4, Working with Azure Data Lake*.

How it works...

SQL Server Integration Service requires an active SQL Server database to run and deploy its packages. So, we have created a minimalistic SQL server, a database, and populated it with data for further use.

Building an SSIS package

SSIS packages are a great way to build ETL/ELT processes with SQL Server. Packages (or projects) store the sequence of steps that are performed to execute an activity. Let's build a package that will connect to the SQL Server database, which stores the `movielens` dataset, preprocess it, and store the output in a new table.

Getting ready

In order to follow this recipe, you need to finish the *Creating a SQL Server database* recipe, as we will build an SSIS package that will use both a database and data that we have prepared previously.

Then, you have to install the most recent version of Visual Studio and log in to Azure via Visual Studio. Visual Studio Community edition fully supports all the features that we will use in the following recipes.

How to do it...

Let's build an SSIS package that joins two tables and deploy it to SSISDB in Azure:

1. Open **Visual Studio** and create a new project.
2. Select **Integration Services Project (Azure Enabled)**.

3. Name your project, check the **Place solution and project in the same directory** checkbox, and then click **Create**, as shown in the following screenshot:

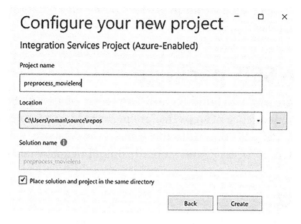

Figure 6.9 – Creating a new project in Visual Studio

4. Let's now set up our working environment and connect to the SQL Server database. Go to **SQL Server Object Explorer** and click on the **Add SQL Server** button. Fill in the **Server Name** field and select the authentication method. In our recipe, we use **SQL Server Authentication**. Type in UserName and Password and select **Database Name** from the drop-down menu, as shown in the following screenshot:

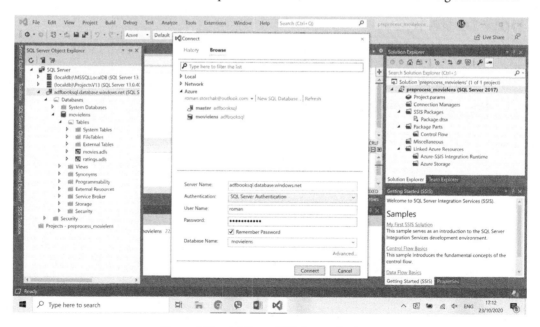

Figure 6.10 – Adding a SQL Server database

5. Right-click on **SSIS Packages** and choose **New SSIS package**, as shown in the following screenshot:

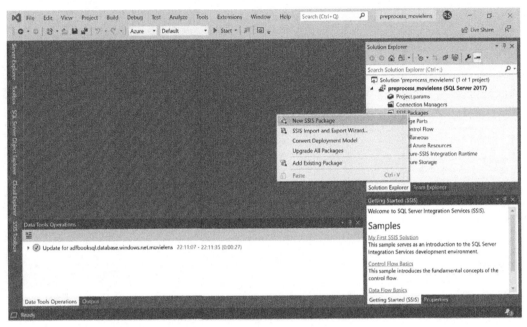

Figure 6.11 – Creating an SSIS package

6. Click **Data Flow** and follow the instructions on screen to create a data flow.

7. Double-click **ADO.NET Source** from **SSIS Toolbox**. Then, double-click on the rectangle with **ADO.NET Source**, which appears in the workspace.

8. Click on **ADO.NET Source** and then click **New…**, as shown in the following screenshot:

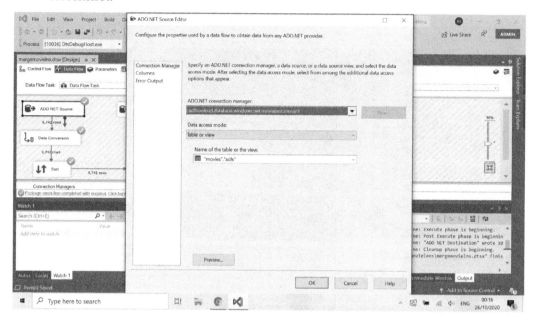

Figure 6.12 – ADO.NET Source Editor

9. If you do not see your server and database here, click **New…**:

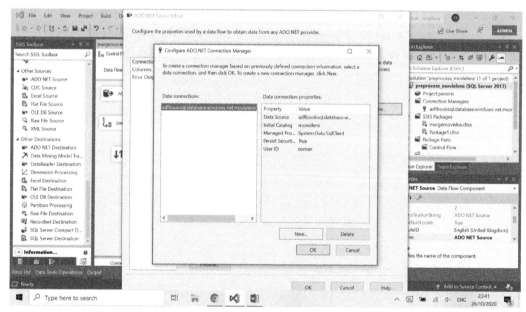

Figure 6.13 – Configuring ADO.NET Connection Manager

10. Fill in the server name with the SQL Server address. Now, set the **Authentication** method. Fill in the Username and Password fields. Check the **Save my password** checkbox. Then, select your database of interest from the **Select or enter a database name** drop-down menu, as shown in the following screenshot:

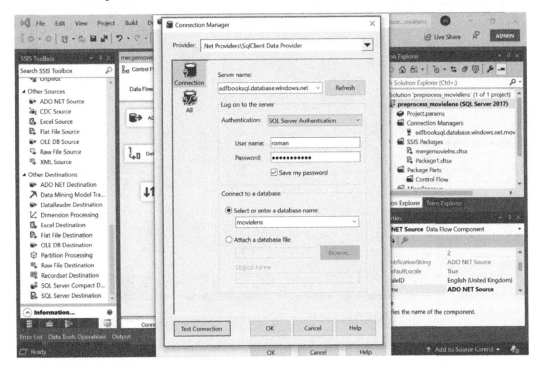

Figure 6.14 – Adding a new connection in Connection Manager

11. Click on **Test Connection**, and if the connection is successful, click **OK**.

12. Select your server in **Configure ADO.NET Connection Manager**, as shown in *Figure 6.13*, and then click **OK**.

13. Select **Data access mode: Table or view**. Then, in the drop-down menu, pick a table of interest, as shown in *Figure 6.12*.

14. Click on **Columns**, visually check the contents, and then click **OK**, as shown in the following screenshot:

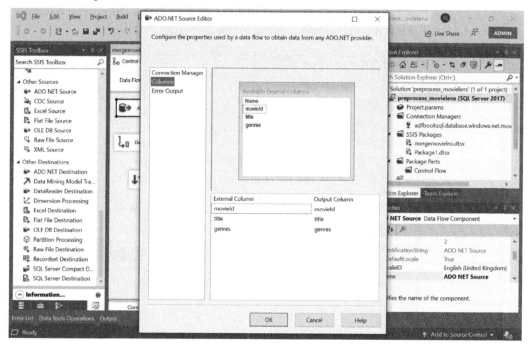

Figure 6.15 – Columns in ADO.NET Source Editor

15. We will skip setting up error output in order to simplify this recipe.

16. Repeat *steps 7-15* to set up ADO.NET Source for the ratings table.

17. SSIS can only perform a merge join operation on sorted data. So, we have to sort join key columns on both tables before executing a merge join.

18. Depending on the data type, you might need to use **Data Conversion**. For example, SQL Server and SSIS cannot process Unicode [DT_NTEXT] columns. Click on **Data Conversion**, and then connect ADO.NET Source and **Data Conversion** with blue arrows. Click on **Data Conversion** to start **Data Conversion Transformation Editor**, as shown in the following screenshot:

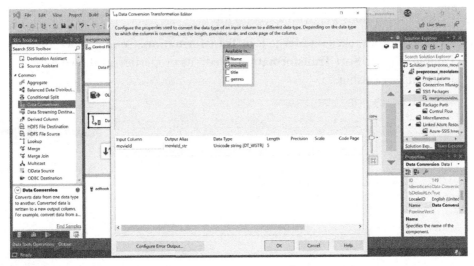

Figure 6.16 – Data Conversion Transformation Editor

19. Type in `Output Alias`, set **Data Type** to `Unicode string [DT_WSTR]`, **Length** equal to 5, and then click **OK**.

20. Apply the same transformation to both data sources.

21. In **SSIS Toolbox**, click on **Sort Transformation**. Connect it to **Data Conversion** by means of the blue line. Double-click on **Sort Transformation** to edit its properties, as shown in the following screenshot:

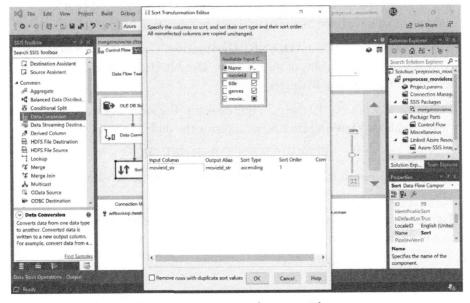

Figure 6.17 – Sort Transformation Editor

22. Repeat the previous step with a second input.

23. In **SSIS Toolbox**, click on **Merge Join Transformation**. Connect it to both inputs. Double-click on **Sort Transformation** to edit its properties, as shown in the following screenshot:

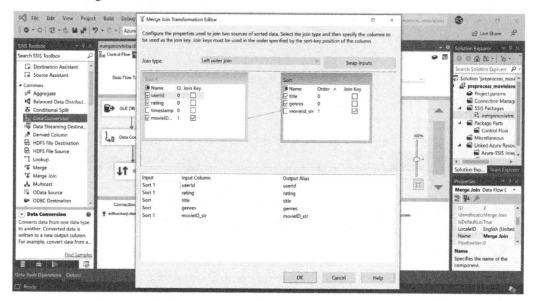

Figure 6.18 – Merge Join Transformation Editor

24. Select **Join Type** (in this recipe, we will use **Left Outer Join** and **Join Key,** and add columns that have to be included in the transformation output.

25. In **SSIS Toolbox**, click on **ADO.NET Destination**. Connect it to **Merge Join Transformation** by means of the blue line. Double-click on **ADO.NET Destination** and select **Connection Manager**.

26. Select the appropriate database. In our case, it is the same as we are reading the data. Select **Table or View** and click **New….** Name the table or the view.

27. Fix the name in the pop-up window, and then click **OK**.

28. Check **Mappings** in the tab, as shown in the following screenshot, and then click **OK**.

29. Let's now review the contents of the package. You have to get the same process as shown in the following screenshot:

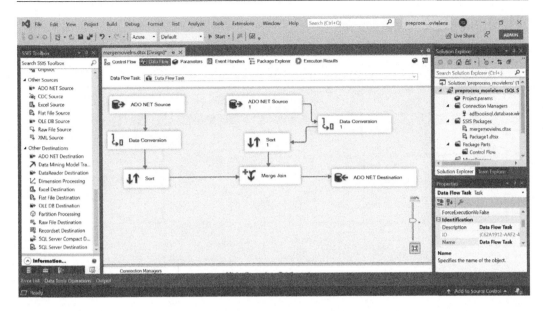

Figure 6.19 – Package contents

30. Click **Project | SSIS in Azure Data Factory | Assess Project for Executions in Azure**.

31. Fix the issues shown in **Assessment Report**, if anything appears as shown in the following screenshot:

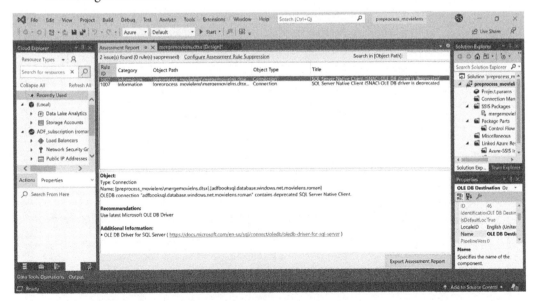

Figure 6.20 – Assessment Report example of using a deprecated SQL Server Native Client

32. Don't forget to save your project.

33. Click **Build** followed by **Build Solution**. In a few seconds, examine the logs. If everything is OK, move to the next step:

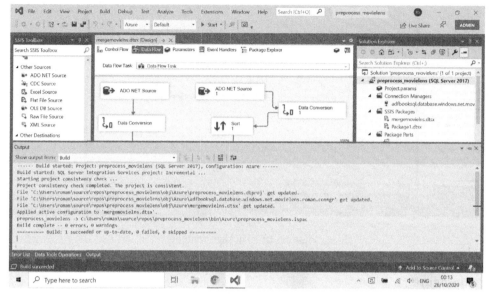

Figure 6.21 – Building an SSIS package

34. **Click Debug** and **Start Debugging**. This will trigger a test run in debug mode. You can see a visual representation of how data is processed in the following screenshot:

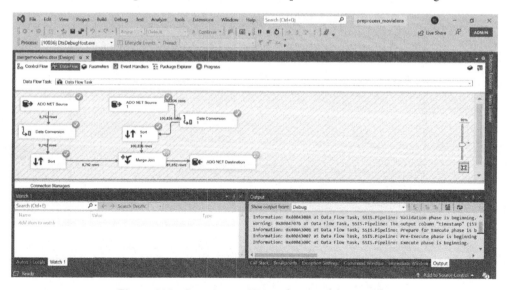

Figure 6.22 – Running an SSIS package in debug mode

How it works...

We use Data Flow tasks in SQL Server Integration Services. First, we configure data sources. We appoint a specific table to read and process the data. Then we preprocess the data so that it can be joined. Following data conversion and sorting, we invoke a merge join task and obtain a preprocessed dataset. As a final step, we store our processed data in a separate table.

Running SSIS packages from ADF

SSIS packages are commonly used in on-premises tasks. In order to leverage existing infrastructure and scale up operations, SSIS packages can be run in the cloud. Let's prepare a cloud infrastructure, deploy a package that we created in a previous recipe to the Azure Cloud, and then trigger its execution via ADF.

Getting ready

Log in to your Microsoft Azure account.

We assume that you have followed all the previous recipes from this chapter. We will use the outcomes of all of them.

How to do it...

Let's create a SQL database that we will need to store data and host SSIS packages:

1. Go to the **Azure Data Factory** interface that you use for learning on the **Author & Monitor**, **Manage**, **Integration runtimes** page (see *Figure 6.26*).

2. To add a new integration runtime, click **+ New**:

Integration runtimes

The integration runtime (IR) is the compute infrastructure to provide the following data integration capabilities across different network environment. Learn more ☐

+ New   ○ Refresh

▽ *Filter by keyword*

Showing 1 - 2 of 2 items

Name ↑↓	Type ↑↓	Sub-type ↑↓	Status ↑↓	Region ↑↓	Version ↑↓
AutoResolveIn...	Azure	Public	● Running	Auto Resolve	---
● ▷	Azure-SSIS	---	● Stopped	East US	---

Figure 6.23 – Integration runtimes in Azure Data Factory

3. Select **Azure-SSIS (Lift-and-shift existing SSIS packages to execute in Azure)**. Then, click **Continue**.

4. Fill in the **Name** and **Description** fields. Select **Location**. Preferably, this should be the same as the location of your data factory. Pick **Node size** and **Node number** that are appropriate for your task. We are working with a relatively small toy dataset. As you can see in the following screenshot, we have selected the smallest node size. Pick **Standard Edition/license**:

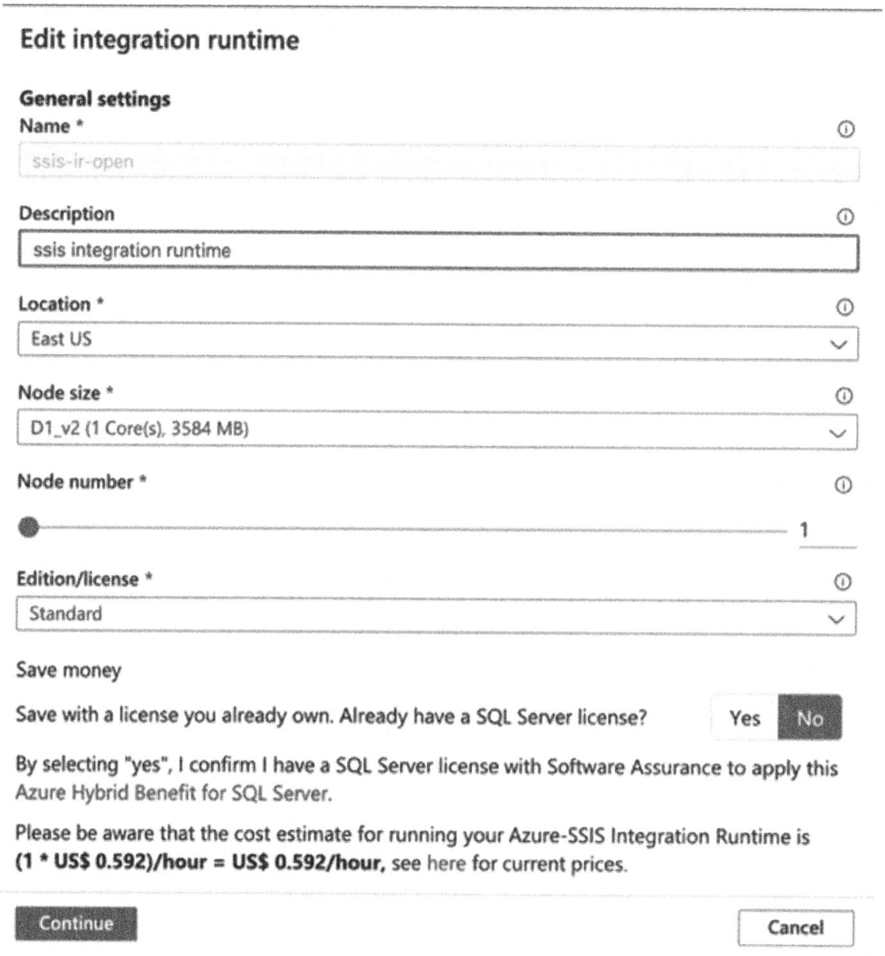

Edit integration runtime

General settings

Name *

ssis-ir-open

Description

ssis integration runtime

Location *

East US

Node size *

D1_v2 (1 Core(s), 3584 MB)

Node number *

●―― 1

Edition/license *

Standard

Save money

Save with a license you already own. Already have a SQL Server license?   Yes   No

By selecting "yes", I confirm I have a SQL Server license with Software Assurance to apply this Azure Hybrid Benefit for SQL Server.

Please be aware that the cost estimate for running your Azure-SSIS Integration Runtime is **(1 * US$ 0.592)/hour = US$ 0.592/hour**, see here for current prices.

Continue   Cancel

Figure 6.24 – Adding an integration runtime

5. If your company is eligible for Azure Hybrid benefits for SQL Server, set **Already have a SQL Server license?** to **Yes**. Click **Continue**.

6. Check the **Create SSIS catalog (SSISDB) hosted by Azure SQL Database server/ Managed Instance to store your projects/packages/environments/execution logs** checkbox.

7. Paste your SQL database address in the **Catalog database server endpoint** field.

8. Leave the **Use AAD authentication with the managed identity for your Data Factory** field unchecked.

9. Fill in the **Admin username** and **Admin password** fields, and then select **Basic** for the **Catalog database service tier** field, as shown in the following screenshot. Then, click **Continue**:

Edit integration runtime

Deployment settings

☑ Create SSIS catalog (SSISDB) hosted by Azure SQL Database server/Managed Instance to store your projects/packages/environments/execution logs   ⓘ
(See more info here)

Catalog database server endpoint *   ⓘ

    adfbooksql.database.windows.net

☐ Use AAD authentication with the managed identity for your Data Factory ⓘ
    (See how to enable it here)

Admin username *   ⓘ

    roman

Admin password *   ⓘ

    ••••••••••

Catalog database service tier *   ⓘ

    Basic

☐ Create package stores to manage your packages that are deployed into file system/Azure   ⓘ
    Files/SQL Server database (MSDB) hosted by Azure SQL Database Managed Instance
    (See more info here)

Continue	Back		Cancel

Figure 6.25 – Creating an SSIS catalog

10. For our recipe, we do not require parallel execution, so set **Maximum parallel executions per node** to 1. Leave the other options unchecked, as can be seen in the following screenshot. Then, click **Continue**:

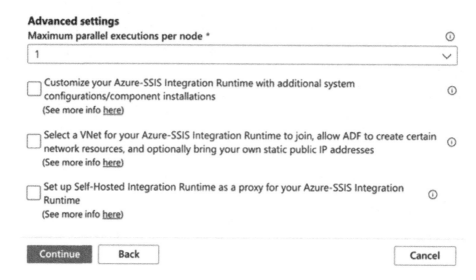

Figure 6.26 – Setting up advanced settings

11. Check the summary and all the settings. If everything is OK, click **Create**.

12. Launch SSIS integration runtime, as can be seen in the following screenshot. It will take a few minutes to start.

13. Please note that launching SSIS-IR in **Virtual Network** requires a significantly longer amount of time:

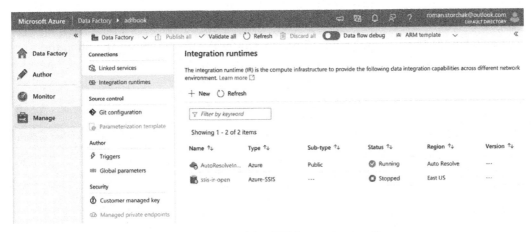

Figure 6.27 – Launching SSIS integration runtime

14. Let's now deploy the SSIS package that we prepared in a previous recipe. Go to Visual Studio, select your project, and then click **Deploy**. Then, click **Next >**:

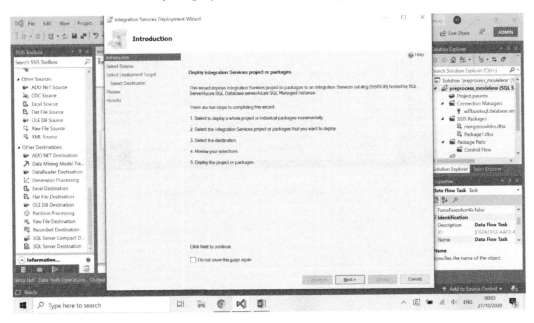

Figure 6.28 – Introduction to the deployment wizard

15. Select **SSIS in Azure Data Factory** and then click **Next**.

16. Fill in the **Server name** field, select the **Authentication** method, and fill in the
    Login and **Password** fields, as shown in the following screenshot:

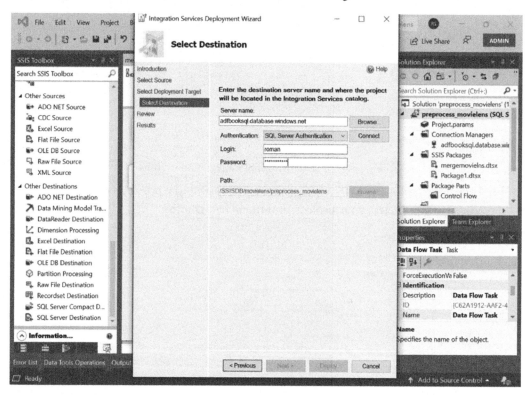

Figure 6.29 – Selecting a destination for deployment

17. Click **Deploy** and then wait a short while for deployment:

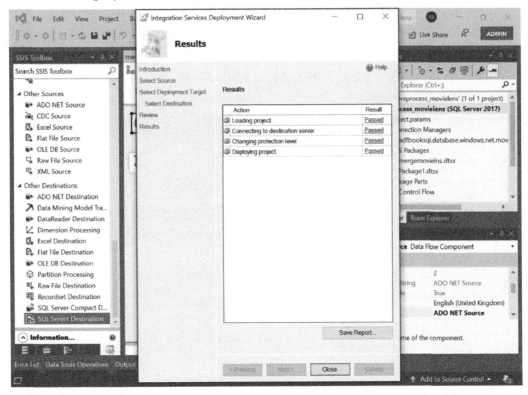

Figure 6.30 – Deploying an SSIS package

Integration Services Deployment Wizard successfully deploys an SSIS package to the remote database. Later, we will trigger the execution of this package with ADF.

18. Go to the **Azure Data Factory** UI, **Create new pipeline**. Then, go to **Activities**, **General**, **Execute SSIS package**, and drag it to the workspace.

19. Modify the name of the activity and then add a description, as shown in the following screenshot:

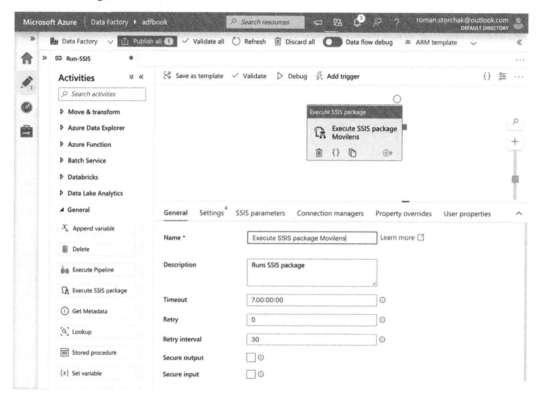

Figure 6.31 – Executing an SSIS package activity

20. Click on the **Settings** tab, as shown in the following screenshot. Select an active **Azure-SSIS IR** package, and set the **Package location**, **Folder**, **Project**, and **Package** fields to be executed. Then, as shown in the following screenshot, set the **Logging level** to **Basic**:

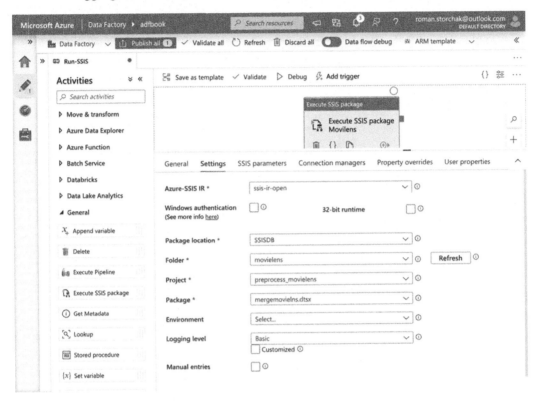

Figure 6.32 – Setting up an activity

21. Let's now check the SSIS connection managers under the **Connection managers** tab, as shown in the following screenshot:

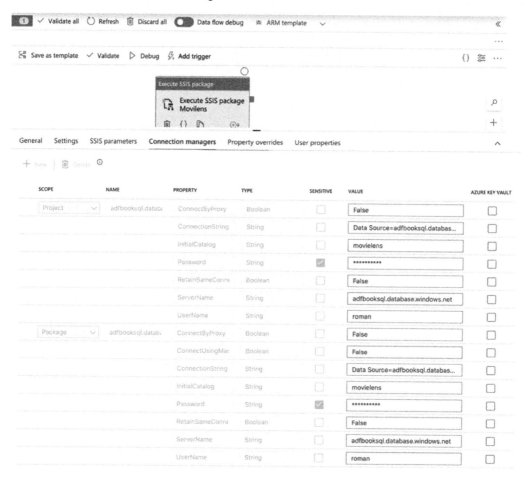

Figure 6.33 – SSIS activity connection managers

22. Publish your pipeline. Trigger the pipeline run by clicking **Trigger now**.

23. Check **Pipeline runs** for the status of the pipeline execution, as shown in the following screenshot:

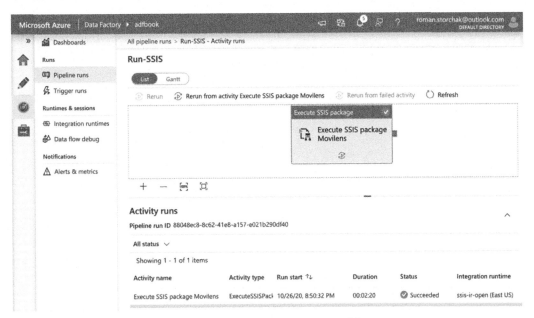

Figure 6.34 – Pipeline run successful

24. Running SSIS integration runtimes incurs extra costs. Also, it does not stop automatically. So, you have to go to **Manage**, **Integration runtimes** and pause your SSIS-IR. For production purposes, you can schedule starts and stops for Azure SSIS-IR by following this guideline: `https://docs.microsoft.com/ru-ru/azure/data-factory/how-to-schedule-azure-ssis-integration-runtime`.

How it works...

ADF is able to run SSIS packages in its own Azure-SSIS integration runtime. It runs on a number of dedicated nodes that execute packages. To start a package, you need to run SSIS-IR, and then trigger a package execution from ADF.

7
Data Migration – Azure Data Factory and Other Cloud Services

When your business needs to move data between cloud providers, Azure Data Factory presents a convenient and robust interface for this task. Microsoft provides connectors to integrate the data factory with multiple third-party services, including **Amazon Web Services (AWS)** and Google Cloud. In this chapter, we will walk though several illustrative examples on migrating data from these two cloud providers. In addition, you will learn how to use Azure Data Factory's Custom Activity to work with providers who are not supported by Microsoft's built-in connectors.

In this chapter, we will cover the following recipes:

- Copying data from Amazon S3 to Azure Blob storage
- Copying large datasets from S3 to ADLS
- Copying data from Google Cloud Storage to Azure Data Lake

- Copying data from Google BigQuery to Azure Data Lake Store
- Migrating data from Google BigQuery to Azure Synapse
- Moving data to Dropbox

Technical requirements

All recipes in this chapter assume that you have a Microsoft Azure account and an instance of a data factory. Refer to *Chapter 1, Getting Started with ADF*, for instructions on how to set up your Azure account and create a data factory.

For the recipes in this chapter, you will need accounts with sufficient permissions on third-party services. For recipes 1 and 2, you will need to set up an account with AWS. For recipes 3, 4, and 5, you will need a Google Cloud account. For recipe 6, you will require a Dropbox account.

If you do not have accounts already set up with the aforementioned services, you can do this for free:

- Go to `https://aws.amazon.com/console/` to sign up for a free AWS account.

- You will need to know this account's access key ID and secret access key. How you get this information will depend on how your account is set up (in other words, is this a root account or an IAM user?). Refer to `https://aws.amazon.com/blogs/security/wheres-my-secret-access-key/` for instructions on how to obtain this information.

- Go to `https://cloud.google.com/` to sign up for a free Google Cloud account and create your first project.

- The steps to create and configure a Dropbox account are described in the corresponding recipe.

Copying data from Amazon S3 to Azure Blob storage

In this recipe, you will learn how to copy data from an AWS S3 bucket to the Azure Blob storage container using a data factory.

Getting ready

This recipe requires you to have an AWS account and an S3 bucket. Refer to the *Technical requirements* section to find out how to set up a new AWS account if you do not have one. Once you have your AWS account set up, go to `https://s3.console.aws. amazon.com/s3/` to create a bucket. Upload the sample CSV files from `https:// github.com/PacktPublishing/Azure-Data-Factory-Cookbook/tree/ master/data` to your bucket.

How to do it...

Rather than designing the pipeline in the **Author** tab, we will use the Copy Data Wizard. The Copy Data Wizard will walk you through pipeline creation step by step, and will create and run the pipeline for you:

1. Go to the **Author and Monitor** portal in your instance of Azure Data Factory. In the **Data Factory Overview** tab, select **Copy data** from the list of tools.

2. In the first step, you will need to provide a name for your pipeline and, optionally, a description. For the purposes of this example, we will name the pipeline `pl_ copy_data_from_s3`. Leave all the other values default as they are and hit **Next**.

3. The Copy Data Wizard will help us define properties of the source (connection and the dataset). We will start by configuring the connection properties. In the interface, select **Create New Connection** and then, in the **New linked service** blade, select Amazon S3 as the connector. Then, fill in the name for your connector as well as the access key ID and secret access key. Refer to the *Getting ready* section on how to obtain the credentials if you do not have them to hand.

Your **New linked service** blade should look like this:

New linked service (Amazon S3)

ⓘ If the identity you use to access the data store only has permission to subdirectory instead of the entire account, specify the path to test connection.

Name *

AmazonS3Bucket

Description

Connect via integration runtime *   ⓘ

AutoResolveIntegrationRuntime   ⌄

Access Key ID *

Secret Access Key   Azure Key Vault

Secret Access Key *

••••••••••••••••••••••••••••••••

Service URL   ⓘ

Test connection
⦿ To linked service   ◯ To file path

Annotations
+ New

Name

▷ Advanced ⓘ

✓ Connection successful

Create   Back   🖉 Test connection   Cancel

Figure 7.1 – Creating a linked service for AWS S3

4. Test the connection and create the linked service. Hit **Next** to move to the next step.

5. Now we need to configure the dataset for our source. In the interface presented, enter the name of your S3 bucket (*adf-migration-to-azure* in our example). Use the **Browse** button to visualize the folder structure. Leave the recursive checked (we do want to copy the contents of the directory recursively), and set **Max concurrent connections** to 1. Then, hit **Next**.

6. The Copy Data Wizard will test the connection and will present you with the **File format settings** interface. Click on **Detect text format** and then check the **First row as header** checkbox to allow the Copy Data Wizard to configure the dataset for you:

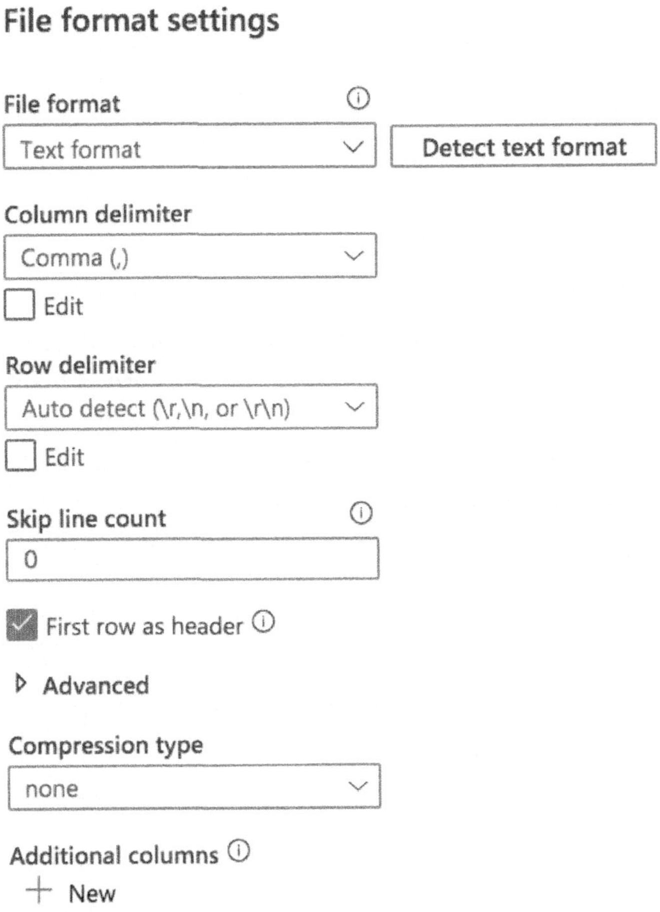

File format settings

File format   ⓘ

| Text format   ⌄ | | Detect text format |

Column delimiter

| Comma (,)   ⌄ |

☐ Edit

Row delimiter

| Auto detect (\r,\n, or \r\n) ⌄ |

☐ Edit

Skip line count   ⓘ

| 0 |

☑ First row as header ⓘ

▷ Advanced

Compression type

| none   ⌄ |

Additional columns ⓘ
+ New

Figure 7.2 – Configuring the file format in the Copy Data Wizard

With the source dataset formatted, we are ready to go to the next step.

7. Now we need to configure the **Destination** properties (as with source, both for the connection and the dataset). Let's configure the connection. Select a linked service for the Azure blob where you intend to store the data from your S3 bucket. You may have one already available if you followed one of the recipes in previous chapters. If you do not have one configured, follow the instructions in the *Using parameters and built-in functions* recipe in *Chapter 2, Orchestration and Control Flow*, for detailed instructions on how to create a linked service for an Azure blob.

8. After you have selected your connection, you will see an interface to choose the output location, as shown in the following screenshot. Type in the full path to the folder within your Azure Storage account where you want to import the files. Again, use the **Browse** button for ease of navigation:

Choose the output file or folder

Specify a folder that will contain output files or a specific output file in the destination data store.

Folder path *	datafroms3 🗁 Browse
	ⓘ If the identity you use to access the data store only has permission to subdirectory instead of the entire account, specify the path to browse.
File name	
Copy behavior	None ∨ ⓘ
Max concurrent connections	ⓘ
Block size (MB)	ⓘ

Figure 7.3 – Specifying the location for your files

9. You have set up the connection. The Copy Data Wizard will verify the connection and present you with two consecutive screens – **File Format Settings** and **Settings**. Click through both. No additional configuration is needed.

10. We have filled in the connection and dataset information for both the source (Amazon S3 bucket) and destination (Azure Blob storage) of our pipeline. Review the summary that the Copy Data Wizard presents, and verify that all the settings are correct:

Figure 7.4 – Copy Data Wizard – Summary

11. When you go to the next step, the Copy Data Wizard will run the validation to ensure that all the configurations are correct, and then run the pipeline. Click on the **Monitor** button to see your pipeline status. Once the pipeline completes execution, you should see the files in your Azure Blob storage.

How it works...

The Copy Data Wizard is simply an application that assists you in designing a simple data movement pipeline. It presents you with a series of steps, and once you have filled them all in, it creates and publishes the pipeline for you. After you have gone through the steps in this recipe, go to the **Author** tab and find the pipeline. It consists of a single copy activity that we configured with the Copy Data Wizard.

Copying large datasets from S3 to ADLS

Azure Data Factory can help you move very large datasets into the Azure ecosystem with speed and efficiency. The key to moving large datasets is data partitioning. The way you partition depends heavily on the nature of your data.

In the following recipe, we will illustrate a methodology to utilize a data partitioning table for moving a large dataset. We will use a public Common Crawl dataset, which contains petabytes of web crawl data from 2008 to the present day. It is a public dataset hosted on the AWS S3 platform. We will only use a small subset of this data for our example, enough to illustrate the power of data factory parallel processing.

Getting ready

In order to access Amazon Web Services, such as an S3 bucket, you need to have proper credentials. These credentials consist of an access key ID (for example, *AKFAGOKFOLNN7EXAMPL8*) and the secret access key itself (for example, *pUgkrUXtPFEer/PO9rbNG/bPxRgiMYEXAMPLEKEY*). In this book, we will refer to these credentials as your **AWS Account key** and **Secret**.

Even though Common Crawl data is hosted in a public repository, you will still need an AWS account and your own **Account key** and **Secret**. Refer to the instructions in the *Technical requirements* section at the beginning of the chapter on how to obtain these credentials.

We will need to create a partition table in our SQL database. Download the script to create the partitions from `https://github.com/PacktPublishing/Azure-Data-Factory-Cookbook/blob/master/Chapter07/sql-scripts/CreateCommon CrawlPartitionsTable.sql`.

You will also need access to an Azure Gen2 storage account where you plan to copy the data. Refer to this document at `https://docs.microsoft.com/azure/storage/common/storage-account-create?tabs=azure-portal` if you need to create one.

Finally, we will need an instance of the Azure SQL database, and the linked service for this instance. Refer to the *Using parameters and built-in functions* recipe in *Chapter 2, Orchestration and Control Flow*, for detailed instructions on how to create this resource and configure the connection.

Note that moving large datasets can be very expensive. We suggest that you opt for local redundancy when you create your Azure Data Lake account, and delete data that is not required as a cost-saving measure. Once you construct your pipeline and verify that it works as expected, do not run it repeatedly: you might incur considerable charges.

How to do it...

In order to copy the large dataset, we will first create a database table that will define how we partition our data. Then, we will create an outer pipeline, which will read information from the partition table and pass it to a **ForEach** activity. The **ForEach** activity will invoke an inner pipeline that will perform the data movement:

1. In **The Azure portal**, go to your Azure SQL database and open **Query Editor**, logging in with the credentials you specified when you were creating the resource. In the **Query** window, enter the following query. The text of this query is available in the `CreateCommon CrawlPartitionsTable.sql` file that you downloaded in the *Getting ready* section. We strongly advise you to copy text from the file downloaded from GitHub:

```
CREATE TABLE [dbo].[Common CrawlPartitions](
    [YearAndMonth] [varchar](255) NULL,
    [Path] [varchar](255) NULL,
    [UpdatedAt] [Datetime]
)
INSERT INTO Common CrawlPartitions (YearAndMonth,
 Path, UpdatedAt)
VALUES
('01-2019', 'cc-index/collections/CC-MAIN-2019-04/
indexes', GetDate()),
('02-2019', 'cc-index/collections/CC-MAIN-2019-09/
indexes', GetDate()),
```

```
('03-2019', 'cc-index/collections/CC-MAIN-2019-13/
indexes', GetDate()),
('04-2019', 'cc-index/collections/CC-MAIN-2019-18/
indexes', GetDate()),
('05-2019', 'cc-index/collections/CC-MAIN-2019-22/
indexes', GetDate()),
('06-2019', 'cc-index/collections/CC-MAIN-2019-26/
indexes', GetDate()),
('07-2019', 'cc-index/collections/CC-MAIN-2019-30/
indexes', GetDate()),
('08-2019', 'cc-index/collections/CC-MAIN-2019-35/
indexes', GetDate()),
('09-2019', 'cc-index/collections/CC-MAIN-2019-39/
indexes', GetDate()),
('10-2019', 'cc-index/collections/CC-MAIN-2019-43/
indexes', GetDate()),
('11-2019', 'cc-index/collections/CC-MAIN-2019-47/
indexes', GetDate()),
('12-2019', 'cc-index/collections/CC-MAIN-2019-51/
indexes', GetDate());
```

Run the query to create and populate the `dbo.Common CrawlPartitions` table.

Creating the linked services and dataset for the pipeline

Once we have created the `dbo.Common CrawlPartitions` table, we are ready to create the linked services and dataset for our pipeline. Perform the following steps to do so:

1. You can reuse the Azure SQL linked service and dataset that you created in one of the previous recipes. If you have not created any, or do not wish to reuse them, create a new one.

   Go to your **Data Factory** instance and open the **Author and Monitor** interface. Create a dataset to store the data from the partition table. From **Factory Resources** (on the left), select **New Dataset**. In the **New Dataset** blade, select **Azure SQL**. Select the appropriate subscription and test connection, and then click on **Create**.

2. Create a linked service to connect to **S3**: from the **Manage** tab, select **Linked Services**, and then click on **New**. This step is similar to *step 3* in the previous recipe (*Copying data from Amazon S3 to Azure Blob storage*), and you may reuse that connection here as well.

3. Create a dataset to refer to the **S3 Common Crawl** repository. Specify **S3** as a data store and **Binary** as a file format. Select the **S3** linked service we created in the previous step as a linked service. For the file path, enter `Common Crawl` as a bucket. Do not enter anything in the folder or file text fields:

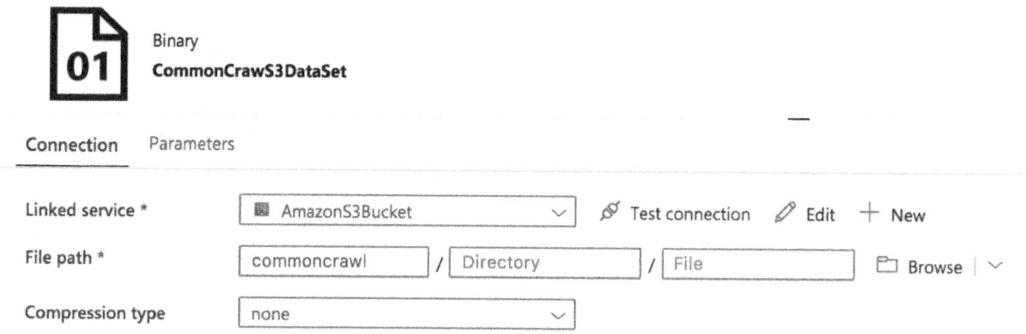

Figure 7.5 – S3 Common Crawl dataset configuration

4. Create a linked service and a dataset for the ADLS account to which you will be moving data. The steps are similar to those that you perform when creating a linked service and dataset for a common Azure Blob storage account, but instead of **DelimitedText**, select **Binary** for **Format Type**. Make the dataset parameterized (refer to the *Using parameters and built-in functions* recipe in *Chapter 2, Orchestration and Control Flow,* for instructions on how to create a parameterized dataset). Specify a single parameter, `DirName`, of the **String** type. In the **Connection** tab, enter the following text in the **Directory** part of the file path:

```
@dataset().DirName
```

The **Connection** tab for your dataset configuration window should look similar to the following screenshot:

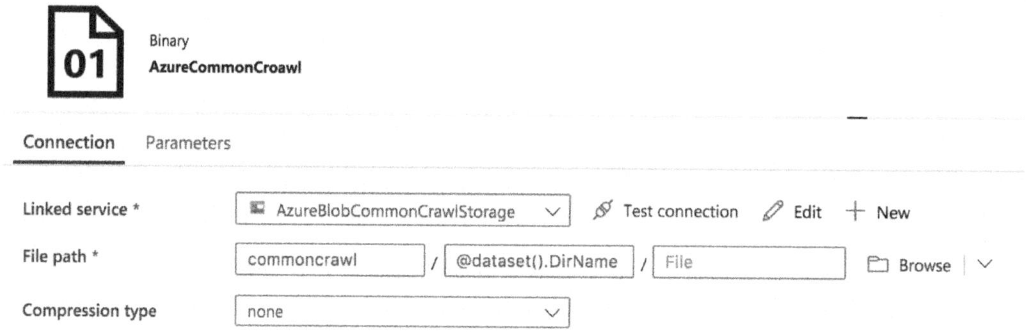

Figure 7.6 – Azure ADLS dataset configuration

Creating the inner pipeline

We now have all the components to design the inner pipeline, the pipeline that will actually copy chunks of data (defined in our partition table) from the **S3 Common Crawl** dataset into our Azure Storage account:

1. Create a new pipeline. For this example, we will call this pipeline `pl_Common Crawl_data_inner`.

2. Add the **Path** parameter to the inner pipeline. Click anywhere on the white canvas, and in the **Parameters** tab at the bottom, add a new parameter with the name **Path** of the **String** type.

    Your inner pipeline **Parameters** tab should look similar to the following screenshot:

Figure 7.7 – Adding a path parameter to the inner pipeline

3. Add a copy activity to this pipeline and name it `Copy Common Crawl from S3 to ADLS`. Next, configure the source for this copy activity. Specify the **S3 Common Crawl** dataset we created in *step 3* as the data source. In the **File Path Type** section, select the **Wildcard file path** radio button.

    In the **Wildcard Paths** section, fill in the value using the dynamic content interface. Click inside the **Wildcard folder path** text field and then select the **Add dynamic content** link to bring up the interface. In that interface, scroll down to find the **Parameters** section and select the **Path** parameter. Click the **Finish** button to finalize your choice.

    Finally, in the **Wildcard file name** text field, enter `*.gz`.

4. Configure the sink for the copy activity. Select **ADLS dataset** from *step 4 of the previous recipe*. Then, follow the instructions from *step 3* to use dynamic content to fill in the **Path** parameter text field.

Creating the outer pipeline

Next, we will build the outer pipeline. The outer pipeline reads the data partitions from the table and invokes the inner pipeline:

1. Create one more pipeline. In this example, we will refer to it by the name `pl_ Common Crawl_data_outer`.

2. Add a **Lookup activity** from the **Activities** pane on the main canvas, and name it `Get Partitions`. In **Settings**, specify the **Source** dataset that we created in *step 1* of the *Creating the linked services and dataset for the pipeline* section (which represents the Azure SQL table). In the **Query** section, check the **Query** radio button and enter the following query:

    ```
    select top 2 Path from [dbo].[Common CrawlPartitions]
    ```

    Make sure the **First Row only** checkbox is not checked.

3. Add a **ForEach** activity from the **Activities** pane and name it `For Each Partition`. In the **Settings** tab, set the batch count as `12` (the number of months), and enter the following text in the **Items** text field:

    ```
    @activity('Get Partitions').output.value
    ```

    Make sure that the **Sequential** checkbox is not checked

4. Click inside the **ForEach** activity to open the **ForEach** activity canvas. Place an **Execute Pipeline** activity on this canvas and configure it to call the `pl_Common Crawl_data_inner` pipeline. Use the dynamic content interface to fill in the **Path** parameter value. Click inside the **Value** text field for the **Path** parameter, and select the **Add dynamic content** link. In the interface, scroll down to see the **ForEach Iterator** section. Select **Current item**. This will place the word `@item()` in the textbox on top of the dynamic content interface. Append the word `Path` to it. As a result, the text in the dynamic content textbox should read `@item().Path`. Click **Finish** to finalize your choice.

    Your **Execute Pipeline** activity configuration settings should look similar to the following screenshot:

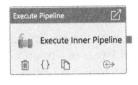

General   **Settings**   User properties

Invoked pipeline *   pl_commoncrawl_data_inner   ✎ Open   + New

Wait on completion

Parameters

Name	Type	Value
		@{item().Path}
Path	string	Add dynamic content [Alt+P]

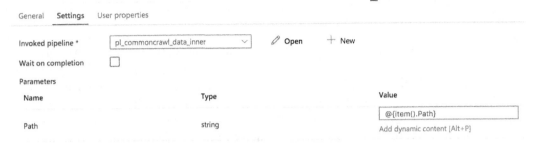

Figure 7.8 – Executing the pipeline activity configuration

5. Connect the **Lookup** activity and the **ForEach** activity.

6. Publish your pipelines and run the outer pipeline. Click on **Add trigger** and select
    the **Trigger Now** option. If you run it in debug mode, you will not see parallelism.

7. Go to the **Monitor** tab and verify that you have one instance of the outer pipeline
    and two instances of the inner pipeline running, similar to in the following
    screenshot:

Pipeline name	Run start ↓	Run end	Duration	Triggered by	Status	Parameters	Annotations	Error
pl_commoncrawl_data_inner	8/29/20, 3:08:15 PM	--	00:02:23	6c0918e1-5250-4150-83 ◉ In progress				
pl_commoncrawl_data_inner	8/29/20, 3:08:15 PM	--	00:02:23	86d64fda-aeba-49bb-ab ◉ In progress				
pl_commoncrawl_data_outer	8/29/20, 3:08:10 PM	8/29/20, 3:08:18 PM	00:00:08	Manual trigger	✅ Succeeded			

Figure 7.9 – Monitor tab

How it works...

In this recipe, we have constructed a pipeline that is capable of moving very large datasets from S3 to an Azure Storage account. For our example, we used 1 year of Common Crawl data, although we only copied over 2 months of this data (enough to validate our approach while saving the considerable cost of moving even more data). We then created the **Common CrawlPartitions** table in which we listed our partitions. This table also contained paths to the data locations.

Next, we created the inner and outer pipelines to ingest this data from locations provided in the **Common CrawlPartitions** table and copy it over to the Azure Data Lake storage. The key to parallel execution is the design of the outer pipeline: it is the **ForEach** activity that allows us to execute activities in parallel by allowing us to specify the batch count. Note that there is a limitation in terms of the degree of parallelism. If your batch count is more than 40, it is better to enhance the design by further partitioning the data and having multiple **ForEach** activities, each executing a subset of parallel sub-pipelines.

One thing to notice is that we have limited our dataset further by specifying the query in **LookupActivity** as a **select top 2** path from `[dbo] [Common CrawlPartitioning]`. We can regulate the size of our data pull by tweaking this query and, of course, by adding data to our data partitioning table.

See also

If you are interested in the Common Crawl dataset, which contains web crawl data from 2008, you can obtain more information at `https://Common Crawl.org/the-data/`.

Microsoft offers guidance on pricing for Azure Data Factory. We strongly suggest that you familiarize yourself with this information before copying large datasets: `https://docs.microsoft.com//azure/data-factory/pricing-concepts`.

Copying data from Google Cloud Storage to Azure Data Lake

In this recipe, we will use the in-built Microsoft connectors to copy the data from Google Cloud Storage to an Azure Storage account. You will learn how to configure the Google Storage account and grant permissions to allow your data factory to connect and import the files.

Getting ready

For this recipe, you will need to have a Google Cloud account and at least one Google Storage bucket:

1. To set up a free Google Cloud account and create your first project, refer to the *Technical requirements* section. Once your project is set up, go to your dashboard and copy your project ID.

2. Then, go to the Google Storage browser. It can be accessed at this URL: `https://console.cloud.google.com/storage/browser?<your-project-id>`. Be sure to replace the `your-project-id` field in the URL with the correct value.

3. In the Google Storage browser, create a new bucket. Once the bucket is created, upload the CSV files from the GitHub account (`https://github.com/PacktPublishing/Azure-Data-Factory-Cookbook/tree/master/data`) to your bucket.

4. If you do not have an Azure Storage account already available, follow the instructions at `https://docs.microsoft.com/azure/storage/common/storage-account-create?tabs=azure-portal` to set one up.

How to do it...

In order to import the data, we will first set up the Google Storage account with the correct permissions and then use the built-in data factory connectors to configure the linked services and datasets to connect to both the Google Cloud Storage bucket and the Azure Storage account:

1. Start by generating credentials to access your Google Storage bucket. The credentials are called **Access Key** and **Secret**.

    Log in to your Google Cloud Storage account and select the bucket that you want to export to Azure Storage. Select **Settings** from the menu on the left, and then go to the **Interoperability** tab in the main blade. In the **Interoperability** tab, click on the **CREATE A KEY FOR A SERVICE ACCOUNT** button:

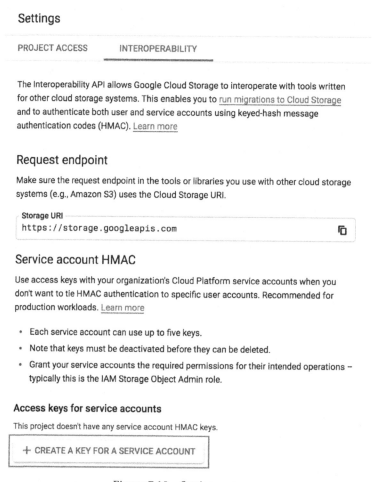

Figure 7.10 – Settings menu

2. If you do not have a service account available, you have an option to create one at this point. Make sure to assign the **Storage Admin** role to this service account to grant permissions to transfer data.

   If you have an existing service account, you can view and change its access permissions here: `https://console.cloud.google.com/iam-admin/serviceaccounts?project=<your-project-id>` (replace `<your-project-id>` with the correct value for your project).

   Select your desired service account and then click on **CREATE KEY**:

Figure 7.11 – Creating an access key and secret

   Make a note of your account key and secret; you will need these values later to create a linked service.

   We have set up the access policies on the Google Cloud service account to allow the data factory to perform a data pull. Now we can design the pipeline.

3. In The Azure portal, open the **Author and Monitor** interface of your data factory. Start by creating a linked service and the dataset for the Google Cloud Storage Bucket.

4. In the **Manage** tab, add a new linked service. Specify its type as **Google Cloud Storage (S3 API)**. Fill in the next blade, using the access key ID and secret access key values you obtained in *step 3*. In the service URL, enter `https://storage.googleapis.com`.

5. The following is an example of a filled-out Google Cloud Storage linked service creation blade:

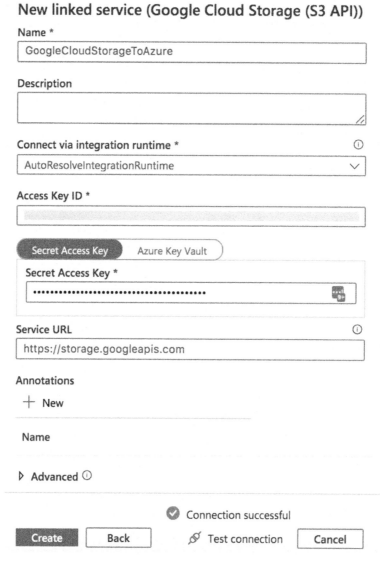

Figure 7.12 – Google Cloud linked service

6. In the **Author** tab, create a new dataset. Select **Google Storage (S3 API)** as the type, **DelimitedText** as the format, and specify the Google Storage linked service we just created as the linked service. In the **File path** text field, specify the Google Storage bucket name.

7. Create a linked service and a dataset for the Azure Blob storage account where you want to store the data from Google Cloud bucket. In the **File path** section of the dataset, specify a container where you want to transfer the files. We'll call it `datafromgoogle`. If the container does not exist, it will be created during the transfer. Your resulting dataset should look similar to *Figure 7.13*:

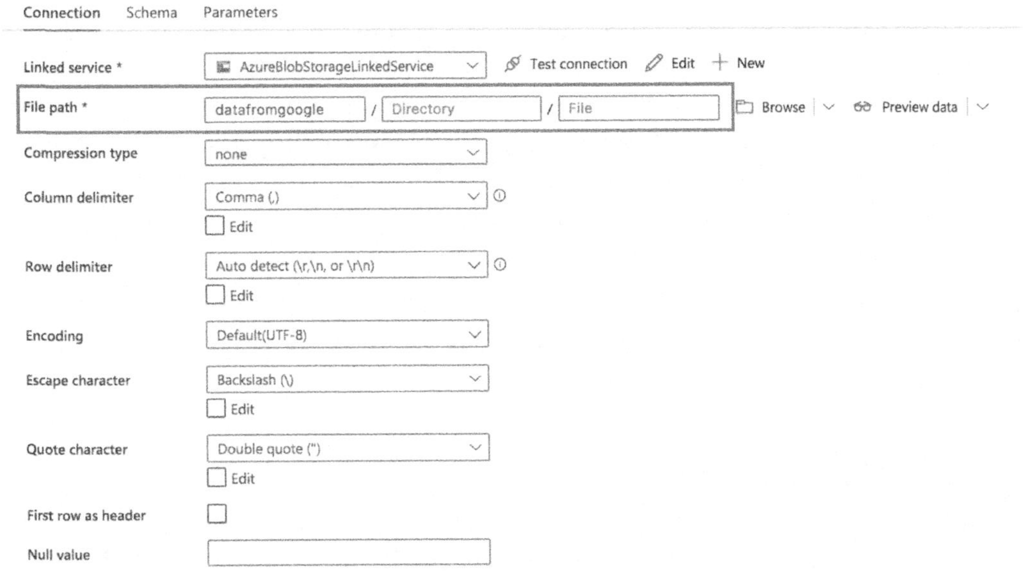

Figure 7.13 – Dataset for the Azure Storage account

8. Refer to the *Using parameters and built-in functions* recipe in *Chapter 2, Orchestration and Control Flow*, for detailed instructions.

> **Note**
> You can also use an **Azure Data Lake Storage V2 (ADLS)** account for this recipe. If you choose to do that (for example, if you want to reuse the ADLS account from the previous *Copying large datasets from S3 to ADLS* recipe), you will have to create a linked service and dataset with corresponding connectors. Refer to the previous recipe for detailed instructions on how to do that.

9. In the **Author** tab, create a new pipeline. We will call it `pl_transfer_from_gcs`. Add a copy activity to it and name this activity `Copy From GC To Azure Storage`. Configure **Source** and **Sink**. In **Source**, select the Google Storage dataset we created in *step 6*. For **File path type**, select **Wildcard file path** to copy all the files in the dataset. In **Sink**, select the Azure Blob dataset we created in *step 7*. In the **Sink** tab, make sure that the **File Extension** text field is empty. Leave all the other options as their default settings.

10. Run your pipeline in debug mode. Once it is done, you should see that the CSV files were copied from your Google bucket to the Azure Storage account.

11. Publish your changes to save them.

How it works...

In this recipe, the main challenge is to configure the Google Storage access permissions correctly. The pipeline is simple and follows all the pipeline design principles we have covered in previous recipes.

See also

Google Cloud is a vast and nimble ecosystem. To learn more about Google Cloud Storage and access management on this platform, refer to the current Google documentation at `https://cloud.google.com/iam/docs/granting-changing-revoking-access?`.

Copying data from Google BigQuery to Azure Data Lake Store

In this recipe, we will use Azure Data Factory to import a subset of a public `fdic_banks.locations` dataset from the Google BigQuery service (a cloud data warehouse) into an Azure Data Lake store. We will write the data into destination storage in Parquet format for convenience.

Getting ready

For this recipe, we assume that you have a Google Cloud account and a project, as well as an Azure account and a Data Lake storage account (ADLS Gen2). The following is a list of additional preparatory work:

1. You need to enable the BigQuery API for your Google Cloud project. You can enable this API here: `https://console.developers.google.com/apis/api/bigquery.googleapis.com/overview`.

2. You will require information for the **Project ID**, **Client ID**, **Client Secret**, and **Refresh Token** fields for the BigQuery API app. If you are not familiar on how to set up a Google Cloud app and obtain these tokens, you can find detailed instructions at the following community blog: `https://jpda.dev/getting-your-bigquery-refresh-token-for-azure-datafactory-f884ff815a59`.

   Note that these instructions include consent given by the Azure Data Factory user. Make sure that this user (the Data Factory user, the account that is signed into the The Azure portal) has correct permissions to run BigQuery user jobs. Azure Data Factory will not be able to access data in Google Cloud otherwise. To assign the correct permissions, perform the following steps:

3. Go to `https://console.cloud.google.com/iam-admin/iam?project=<your-project-name>`.

4. In the **Permissions** tab, click on **Add** and fill in the necessary information (email and role):

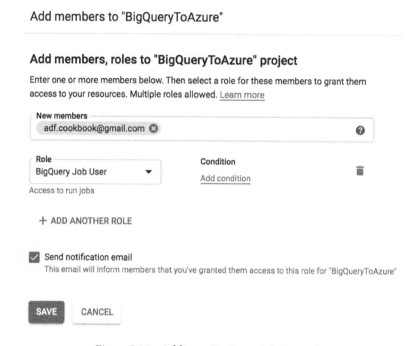

Figure 7.14 – Adding a BigQuery Job User role

5. Save the assignment.

How to do it...

Microsoft provides connectors to both Google BigQuery and Azure Data Lake storage. We will create a simple pipeline with a copy activity utilizing these built-in connectors:

1. Create a linked service for BigQuery Connection.

    From the **Manage** tab, select **Linked Services** and then click on **New**. In the new **Linked Service** blade, search for `BigQuery` and then enter the **Project ID**, **Client ID**, **Client Secret**, and **Refresh Token** information that you obtained previously (refer to the *Getting ready* section) in the blade presented. The blade should look similar to the following screenshot:

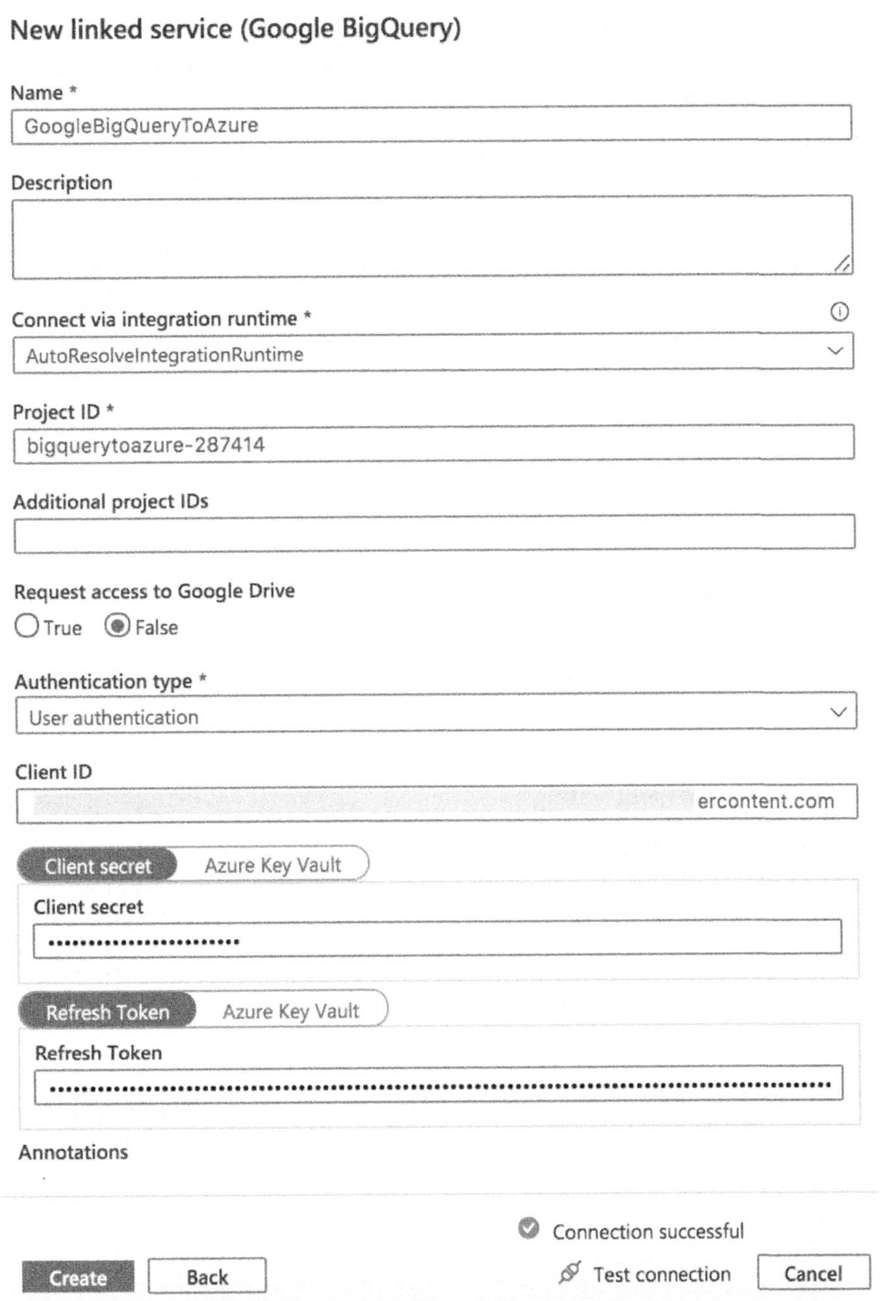

New linked service (Google BigQuery)

Name *

GoogleBigQueryToAzure

Description

Connect via integration runtime *

AutoResolveIntegrationRuntime

Project ID *

bigquerytoazure-287414

Additional project IDs

Request access to Google Drive

○ True ● False

Authentication type *

User authentication

Client ID

ercontent.com

Client secret | Azure Key Vault

Client secret

....

Refresh Token | Azure Key Vault

Refresh Token

....

Annotations

● Connection successful

Create   Back   ⌀ Test connection   Cancel

Figure 7.15 – Creating a BigQuery linked service

Test your connection and click on **Create** to save the linked service

2. Create the BigQuery dataset. From the **Author** tab, select **Datasets** and then click on **New**. In the **New Dataset** blade, search for **BigQuery**. Finally, enter a name for your dataset (for this example, we named it `GoogleBigQueryDS`) and select the **BigQuery** linked service we created in the previous step in the dropdown.

3. Create a linked service and the dataset for the **ADLS Gen 2** account where you intend to store the data. In **Select format blade**, choose **Parquet**. You can find detailed instructions on creating linked services and datasets in the *Using parameters and built-in functions* recipe in *Chapter 2, Orchestration and Control Flow*.

4. We have all the components necessary to design the pipeline. Now, create a new pipeline, `pl_bigquery_to_storage`. Add a single **Copy** activity to this pipeline and rename it to `Copy from BigQuery To Storage`.

    Configure **Source** and **Sink** for the copy activity. In **Source**, select the **GoogleBigQueryDS** dataset we created in *step 2*. Check the **Query** radio button in the **Use Query** section, and enter the following query:

    ```
    select * from bigquery-public-data.fdic_banks.locations
    LIMIT 3000
    ```

    In **Sink**, select the **ADLS2** Parquet dataset we created in *step 3*. Leave all the other options as their default settings.

    Run your pipeline in debug mode. Once the run is complete, you will see new Parquet files in your ADLS account. You can use a tool such as `http://Parquet-viewer-online.com/` to verify that this is the data from the BigQuery dataset.

5. Publish your pipeline to save the changes.

Migrating data from Google BigQuery to Azure Synapse

In this recipe, we will import a public dataset, `github_repo.files`, from Google BigQuery into Azure Synapse – formerly Azure Data Warehouse. We will create a SQL data pool, create the table to store our imported data, and configure the pipeline to migrate data from a public dataset hosted at Google BigQuery.

Getting ready

To complete this recipe, you will need a Google Cloud project with the BigQuery API enabled. Refer to the *Getting ready* section in the previous recipe for instructions on how to set those up and obtain your **Project ID**, **Client ID**, **Client Secret**, and **Refresh Token** fields.

You will also need an instance of an Azure Synapse SQL pool to import the data. Refer to the chapter on Azure Synapse on how to create and configure a SQL pool. Have the login credentials for this SQL pool to hand.

You will also need to create a table in your database to store the data we import. Download the script to create the table from `https://github.com/PacktPublishing/Azure-Data-Factory-Cookbook/blob/master/Chapter07/sql-scripts/CreateGithubRepoTable.sql`.

How to do it...

We will create a simple pipeline consisting of just one copy activity, which will use the **BigQuery** connector and **Azure Synapse** connector (both provided by Microsoft) to migrate the data from one cloud provider to the other:

1. First, let's create a table to hold the data. From The Azure portal, go to your **Azure Synapse** account and find the SQL pool where you intend to store the data. From the menu on the left, select **Query Editor** (preview), and, when prompted, log in with your credentials.

2. In **Query Editor**, execute the following script (you downloaded it from the GitHub repo in the *Getting ready* section):

```
CREATE SCHEMA github_repo
GO
CREATE TABLE github_repo.files(
    repo_name         VARCHAR(200) NOT NULL
    ,ref              VARCHAR(17) NULL
    ,path             VARCHAR(200) NULL
    ,mode             INTEGER  NULL
    ,id               VARCHAR(64) NOT NULL
    ,symlink_target VARCHAR(200) NULL
);
```

This will create a table with an appropriate schema to load data from BigQuery data.

3. Create a linked service for the **BigQuery** connection. Refer to the previous recipe (*step 1*) tor detailed instructions on how to configure a linked service for BigQuery. We named our linked service `GoogleBigQueryToAzure2`.

4. Create a dataset that uses this linked service and name it `GoogleBigQueryDataSet`. When specifying the table, check the **Edit** checkbox and then enter `bigquery-public-data.github_repos.sample_files` as the table name.

    Your dataset connection configuration should look similar to the following screenshot:

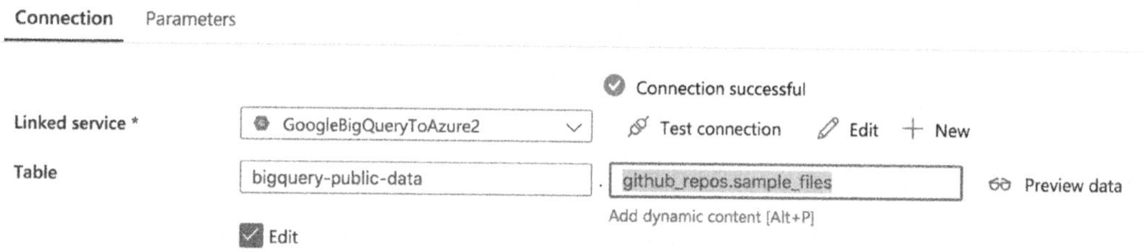

Connection   Parameters

Connection successful

Linked service *   GoogleBigQueryToAzure2   ⌄   Test connection   ✏ Edit   + New

Table   bigquery-public-data   .   github_repos.sample_files   ⚲ Preview data

Add dynamic content [Alt+P]

✔ Edit

Figure 7.16 – Configuration for the BigQuery dataset

Create a linked service to connect to Azure Synapse SQL pool. Refer to *Chapter 3, Setting Up a Cloud Data Warehouse*, on how to obtain credentials and create the linked service. Name your linked service `AzureSynapseLinkedService`.

5. Create a dataset using **AzureSynapseLinkedService** and name it `AzureSynapseDataset`. Specify `github_repo.files` for **Table**.

6. We are ready to create the pipeline. Create a new pipeline, name it `p1_bigquery_to_synapse`, and then add a copy activity to it. Specify the **GoogleBigQueryDataSet** dataset as the source and check the **Query** radio button. Enter the following query in the textbox:

```
select * from bigquery-public-data.github_repos.sample_files
limit 30
```

Important note

In order to configure and test our pipeline, we will limit the import to 30 records. Once we are sure that the pipeline works correctly, we can expand our selection.

7. Configure **Sink**. Select **AzureSynapseDataset** for the dataset. Select **Bulk Insert** as the copy method, leaving all the other fields blank.

> **Important note**
>
> **Copy Activity** supports three methods for copying data to Azure Synapse Analytics: **PolyBase**, **Copy Command (preview)**, and **Bulk Insert**. **PolyBase** and **Copy Command** are much more efficient options, although only a limited number of services support them at the time of writing. For our use case (loading data from Google BigQuery), **Bulk Insert** is the most straightforward option. It will work out of the box; no additional setup is necessary.
>
> In a production environment, where efficiency is of paramount importance, you will want to explore the **PolyBase** and **Copy** options. References to resources are included in the *See also* section of this recipe.

8. In the **Mapping** tab, click on **Import Schema** and verify that the mappings are correct.

9. Run the pipeline in debug mode. Once it completes, you should see 30 records in your Azure Synapse table.

10. We have built the pipeline and verified that it works, loading 30 records. If desired, we can now load the full dataset. To do this, just replace the query in the **Source** tab with the following:

   select * from `bigquery-public-data.github_repos.sample_files`

   However, this is optional and can be done at your discretion.

11. Publish your pipeline to save it.

See also

To learn more about the copy methods supported by the data factory's Azure Synapse connector, refer to the following resources:

- `https://docs.microsoft.com/en-us/azure/data-factory/connector-azure-sql-data-warehouse#use-polybase-to-load-data-into-azure-synapse-analytics`

- `https://docs.microsoft.com/en-us/azure/data-factory/connector-azure-sql-data-warehouse#use-copy-statement`

- `https://docs.microsoft.com/en-us/azure/data-factory/load-azure-sql-data-warehouse`

Moving data to Dropbox

As we described in previous chapters, Azure Data Factory provides many out-of-the-box connectors that integrate with various data sources both within the Azure ecosystem and outside of it (such as Amazon Web Services and Google Cloud). Sometimes, however, you need to have a destination for the reports or other data files that are not supported by Microsoft-provided connectors. How can we do that?

In this chapter, we will build a pipeline that exports the data from a table in an Azure Blob storage account into a folder in Dropbox. Currently, Microsoft does not have a preconfigured Dropbox connector. We will use Azure Data Factory Custom Activity, Azure Batch service, and a simple Python client to achieve our goals.

Getting ready

This recipe assumes that you have a Dropbox account. If this is not the case, go to www.dropbox.com and sign up for a free account.

Create an Azure Storage account, which will serve as a source storage account. In the recipe, we will refer to this account as `batchservicedata`.

How to do it...

In this recipe, we will work with Azure Data Factory Custom Activity and a simple Python client application running on Azure Batch service to copy files from an Azure Storage account to Dropbox. We'll begin by setting up a Dropbox app to enable API access, and then we'll create an Azure Batch account and a batch pool to host the Python client. Only after these steps are complete will we design a pipeline to export our data from an Azure Storage account to Dropbox.

Creating a Dropbox app and enabling API access

In order to access Dropbox folders from the Python client (and ultimately, from the ADF pipeline), we need to create a Dropbox app and generate the authentication token:

1. Log in to your Dropbox account and go to the following URL: `https://www.dropbox.com/developers/apps/create`.

    Fill in the **Create a new app** form, as shown in the following screenshot (make sure the name of your app is unique):

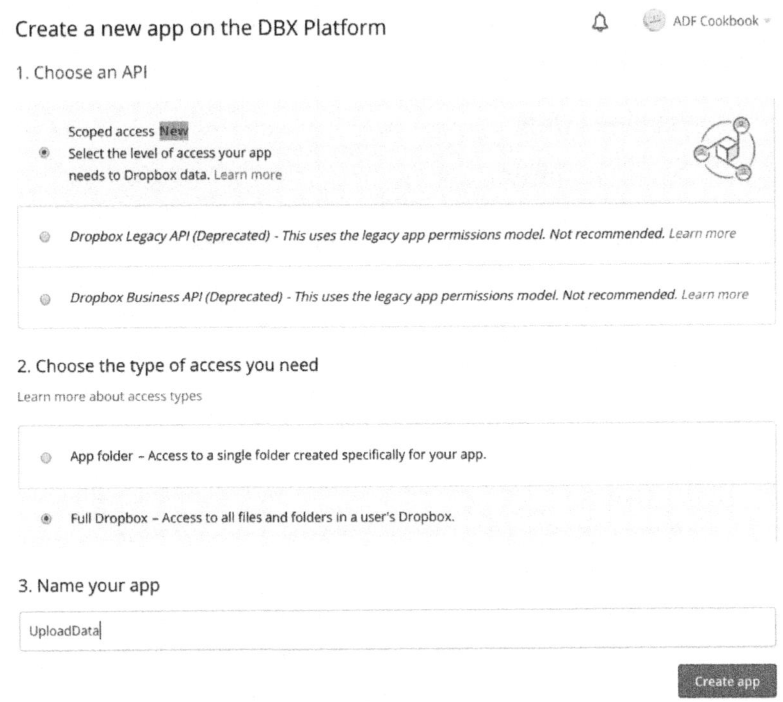

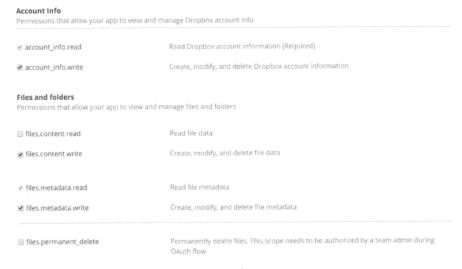

Figure 7.17 – Creating a Dropbox app

2. Once the app is created, click on it to see the settings and configurations. In the **Permissions** tab, check the file permissions, as shown in the following screenshot, and then save your changes:

Account Info
Permissions that allow your app to view and manage Dropbox account info

☑ account_info.read   Read Dropbox account information (Required)

☑ account_info.write   Create, modify, and delete Dropbox account information

Files and folders
Permissions that allow your app to view and manage files and folders

☐ files.content.read   Read file data

☑ files.content.write   Create, modify, and delete file data

☑ files.metadata.read   Read file metadata

☑ files.metadata.write   Create, modify, and delete file metadata

☐ files.permanent_delete   Permanently delete files. This scope needs to be authorized by a team admin during OAuth flow

Figure 7.18 – Edit permissions

3. In the **Settings** tab, find the **Oauth2** section, **Generated access token**. Then, click on the **Generate** button:

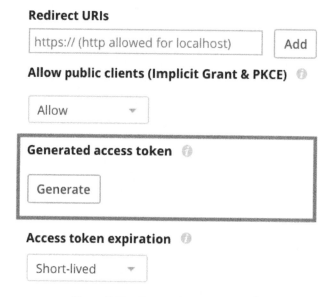

Figure 7.19 – Generating an access token

Copy and keep the value of the generated token: we will use it later in the Python client.

Customizing the Python client and setting up a storage account

The next step is to upload our Python client script and the data we intend to copy into the storage account:

1. Download the Python client from GitHub:

    ```
    https://github.com/PacktPublishing/Azure-Data-Factory-
    Cookbook/blob/master/Chapter07/python/upload_2_dropbox.py
    ```

    Open the script and edit it by replacing the words **<enter your generated access token>** with the token you generated in *step 3*.

2. In The Azure portal, find the storage account you created for this recipe (refer to the *Getting ready* section). In this example, we named this service account `batchservicedata`. In this storage account, create a new container (we named it `data`). Upload the script to this container using the The Azure portal interface.

3. In the same container, upload the CSV data that we will be copying (we used the `airlines.csv` and `airports.csv files`; you can download these from Packt's GitHub account at `https://github.com/PacktPublishing/Azure-Data-Factory-Cookbook/tree/master/data`):

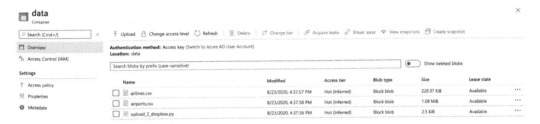

Figure 7.20 – Contents of the batchservicedata data container

4. Create a linked service for this storage account. We named our linked service `BatchServiceStorageLinkedService`. Refer to the *Using parameters and built-in functions* recipe in *Chapter 2, Orchestration and Control Flow*, for detailed instructions.

Setting up the batch account and a batch pool

> **Important note**
>
> Azure Batch service is a service that allows you to utilize the compute power of virtual machines to perform custom operations. In this recipe, we will use the **DSVM configuration** (which stands for *Data Science Virtual Machine*) for the batch pool. Although it is a more expensive option, this will simplify installation and deployment for our client. These virtual machines are already configured with Python.

Now we will create a batch account with a pool of DSVMs from an ARM template.

1. Download the `BatchServiceSqlPoolDSVM.json` file from GitHub at `https://github.com/PacktPublishing/Azure-Data-Factory-Cookbook/blob/master/Chapter07/templates/BatchServiceSqlPoolDSVM/BatchServiceSqlPoolDSVM.json`.

    Open the `https://portal.azure.com/#create/Microsoft.Template` URL.

2. From the selection, choose **Build your own template in the editor**, as shown in the following screenshot:

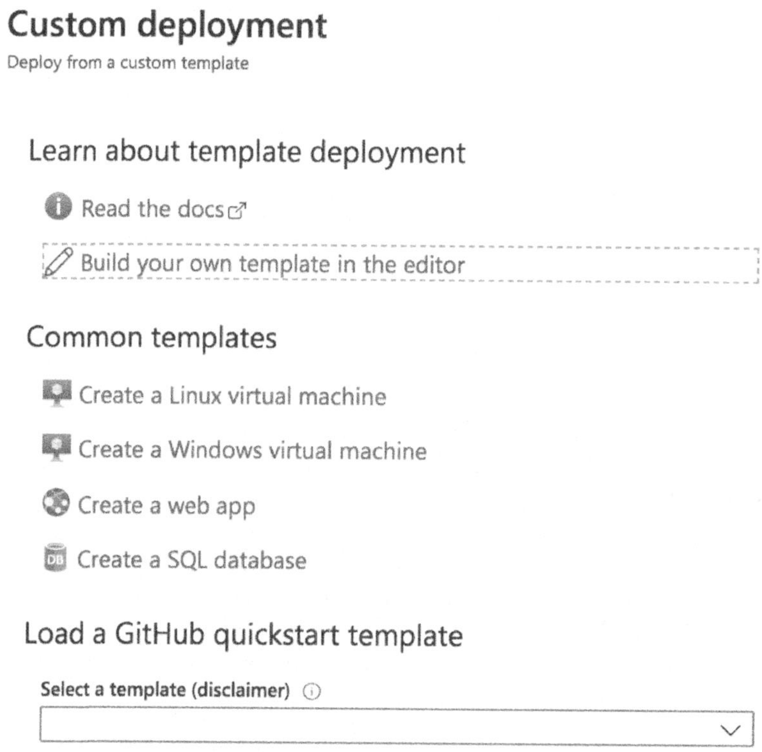

Custom deployment

Deploy from a custom template

Learn about template deployment

🛈 Read the docs ↗

✎ Build your own template in the editor

Common templates

🖥 Create a Linux virtual machine

🖥 Create a Windows virtual machine

◎ Create a web app

▦ Create a SQL database

Load a GitHub quickstart template

Select a template (disclaimer) ⓘ

[⌄]

Figure 7.21 – Deploying from the ARM template

3. You will see a JSON editor that allows you to enter or upload an ARM template. In this editor, choose the **Load File** button, upload the `BatchServiceSqlPoolDSVM.json` file, and then click the **Save** button. This will bring up the **Custom deployment** interface, shown as follows:

Home ›

Custom deployment
Deploy from a custom template

TEMPLATE

▦ Customized template			
2 resources	✎ Edit tem...	✎ Edit para...	ⓘ Learn m...

BASICS

Subscription *	Azure subscription 1 ⌄
Resource group *	⌄
	Create new
Location *	(US) West US ⌄

SETTINGS

Batch
Accounts_adfdatamigration | adfdatamigration

Pools_upload_2_dropbox_p| ^4Tm0LnZ&U188T

TERMS AND CONDITIONS

> Azure Marketplace Terms │ Azure Marketplace
>
> By clicking "Purchase," I (a) agree to the applicable legal terms associated with the offering; (b) authorize Microsoft to charge or bill my current payment method for the fees associated the offering(s), including applicable taxes, with the same billing

☐ **I agree to the terms and conditions stated above**

Figure 7.22 – Finalizing the batch service account

4. In the **Custom deployment** interface, fill in the required values – make sure to replace the hardcoded password with one of your own, which must be a strong and unique password, and then click **Purchase**. This will initiate the process of account creation and deployment of the pool nodes. This will take several minutes.

5.   Verify that the batch account has been created successfully. In The Azure portal,
     search for **Batch Accounts**. You should be able to locate your newly created account,
     adfdatamigration. When you go to it, select **Pools** from the menu on the left to
     see the compute resources allocated. You should see one pool allocated:

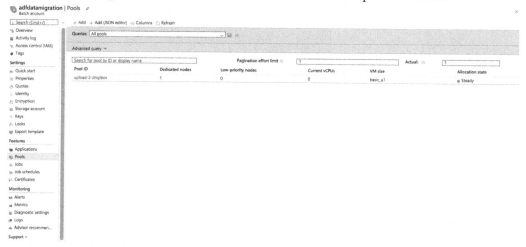

Figure 7.23 – adfdatamigration batch account and an upload-2-dropbox pool

Go into the pool. You should see that one node is allocated. It usually takes several
minutes to start. Wait until it starts and verify that it is in the **running** or **idle** state:

Figure 7.24 – Batch pool with a node in an idle state

6. Once you have verified that the account has been created, go to the main batch account interface and choose **Keys** from menu on the left. Note down both the **account key** and **account URL** fields. We will need both of those when we create a linked service in the data factory:

Figure 7.25 – Batch account keys and URL

Designing the data factory pipeline

We have configured the batch service, created a pool of virtual machines to serve our computing needs, and set up our Python client. All that is left now is to design the ADF pipeline and run it:

1. In Azure Data Factory's **Author and Monitor** interface, create a new linked service to connect to the batch account and the pool we created in *steps 8–11 of the Copying data from Amazon S3 to Azure Blob storage recipe*. Go to the **Manage** tab and add a new linked service. In the **New linked service** blade, select **Compute** and **Azure Batch**:

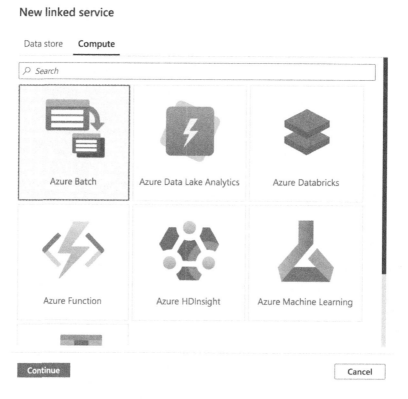

Figure 7.26 – New linked service blade

2. In the next blade, enter the required information, including the access key and the batch URL. The pool name in our example is **upload-2-dropbox**.

3. Add the `BatchServiceStorageLinkedService` linked service, which we created in the Setting up the batch account and a batch pool recipe in the **Storage linked service name** dropdown. Your Azure Batch configurations screen should look similar to the following screenshot:

New linked service (Azure Batch)

Name *

Upload2DropboxBatchLinkedService

Description

Connect via integration runtime *   ⓘ

AutoResolveIntegrationRuntime   ⌄

Account name *

adfdatamigration

(**Access key**   Azure Key Vault)

Access key *

●●●

Batch URL *

https://adfdatamigration.eastus.batch.azure.com

Pool name *

upload-2-dropbox

Storage linked service name *

BatchServiceStorageLinkedService   ⌄   🖊

Annotations

+ New

Name

▷ Advanced ⓘ

⊘ Connection successful

[Create]   [Back]   🖉 Test connection   [Cancel]

Figure 7.27 – Creating a linked service for the batch service

Test the connections (with the button on the lower right), and create the linked service.

4. Go to the **Author** tab and create a new pipeline. I will call this pipeline `pl_ upload_to_dropbox_recipe_6`.

5. From the **Activities** pane on the left, select **Custom Activity** (you can find it in the
    Batch section in the **Activities** panel on the left). Place it on the main canvas and
    configure it in the following way: in the **Azure Batch** tab, select the Azure Batch
    linked service. Then, in the **Settings** tab, in the **Command text** window, enter the
    following text:

```
python upload_2_dropbox.py
```

Then, expand the **Advanced** section and select **BatchServiceStorageLinkedService**
as **Resource linked service,** and the container with the script and files that we will
upload to Dropbox as **Folder path**.

The **Settings** tab of your custom activity should look similar to the following
screenshot:

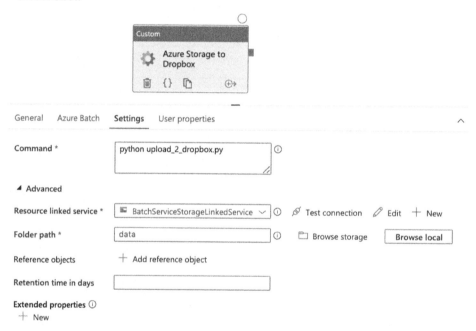

Figure 7.28 – Azure Storage to Dropbox custom activity setup

6. Our pipeline is fully set up. Run the pipeline in debug mode. Once the pipeline has
    run, go to your Dropbox account and verify that the data transfer was successful.
    In your Dropbox account, you should see a folder named the same as the Dropbox
    app that you created in *step 1* (`UploadData` in our example; your app will have
    a different name). Inside that folder, you will see a **DataFromAzure directory**,
    containing the uploaded CSV files.

7. Publish your pipeline to save it.

> **Important note**
> Do not forget to clean up your resources in Azure. Batch pools can be
> expensive, so make sure to delete the pool you created in the previous steps if
> you do not need it.

How it works...

This pipeline involved creating and configuring several components: a batch service
with a pool of nodes hosting a Python script acting as a Dropbox client, a Dropbox app,
and finally, the data factory pipeline with its usual linked services and datasets, which
are integral parts of any pipeline. The pipeline itself was simple – just one activity. The
complexity lies in the interaction between the components.

Dropbox – a popular file hosting and synching service – provides a public API, which
allows third-party users to manipulate the contents of the Dropbox account. As a common
security practice, it is necessary to configure access and grant appropriate permissions
to the application, which takes advantage of the API. An authentication token, which
we generated in *step 3 of the Creating a Dropbox app and enabling API access section*, is
a common authentication mechanism.

We used this token in the `upload-2-dropbox.py` Python script. The script acts as
a Python client and is based on the example provided by Dropbox (`https://github.`
`com/dropbox/dropbox-sdk-python/blob/master/example/back-up-`
`and-restore/backup-and-restore-example.py`). Using the Dropbox SDK, the
script uploads all the files with the extension `csv` from the local directory to the Dropbox
account specified by the access token. This is just an example client provided to illustrate
the process. For your needs, you may use custom scripts and executables, or fully fledged
third-party clients.

We used Azure Batch service as a compute layer to host our Python client. You may
learn more about Batch Service from the following resources (refer to the following *See
also* section). It is a very versatile and flexible resource. There are a multitude of options
(virtual machine configurations, the number of nodes per batch, regions where they are
hosted, and so on) that you can tweak based on your business and computing needs.
In this recipe, we have deployed the batch service and batch pool virtual machines using
Azure's Resource Template deployment functionality, with a pre-defined template. This
powerful technique allowed us to bypass lengthy setup steps and roll out an instance very
quickly. The ARM template provided in this recipe contained a specific configuration
(a pool with one DSVM node). You will need to consider your business requirements
when constructing your own batch pools.

There's more...

Sometimes, it is useful to examine the logs on your server in order to understand how the application works, or to debug an error. In this recipe, we are using a batch pool for our compute layer, and we can easily access the logs, which will give us an insight into our processing. There is an option to log in remotely to the nodes of your batch pool via SSH or a remote desktop, but you can also access the logs from the The Azure portal directly:

1. In The Azure portal, go to your batch service account, select your batch pool, and then click on **Nodes** in the left-hand menu:

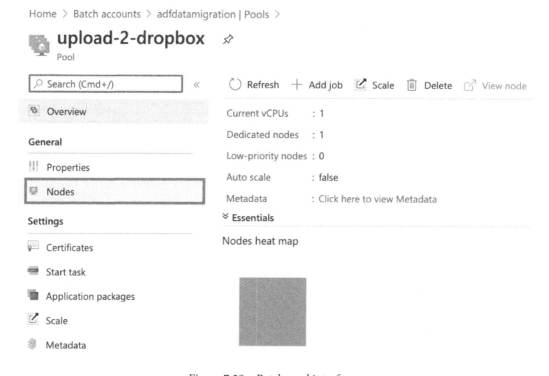

Figure 7.29 – Batch pool interface

2. Next, click on one of the nodes. You will see a list of directories accessible to you through the portal interface. The data factory pipelines will create entries in the **workitems** directory:

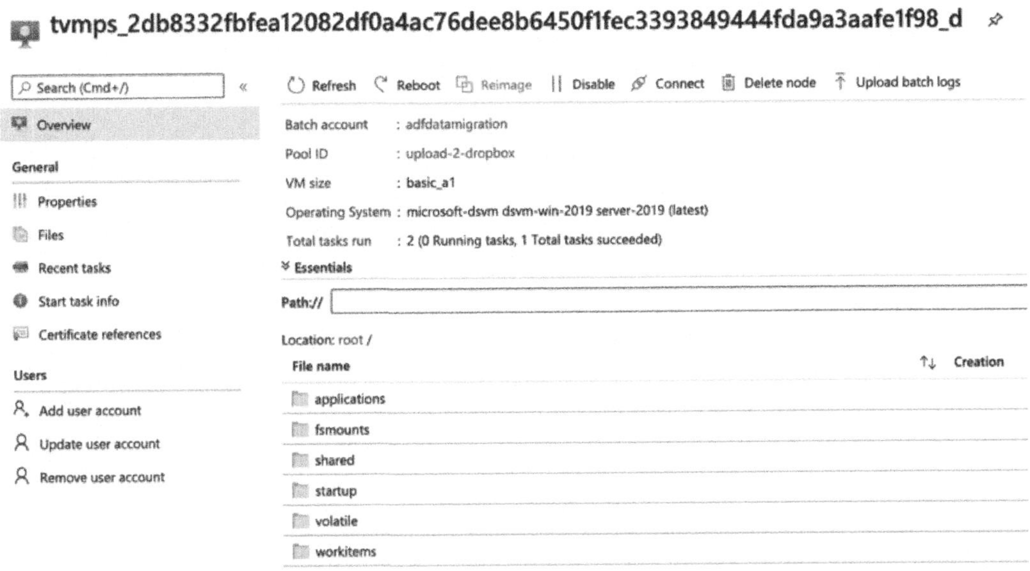

Figure 7.30 – Directories on a batch pool node

3. Click on **workitems** and explore the contents of that directory. You will find folders representing the batch service jobs and tasks. They contain valuable data: job outputs, files that were copied from the storage account onto the node, and so on. This data, including the **stdout** and **stderr** logs, can help you in debugging if your client does not work as expected:

File name	Creation time	Last modified	Size	Content type	File mode	
[..]						...
wd						...
stderr.txt	Aug 23, 16:45:14	Aug 23, 16:45:24	972 Bytes	text/plain		...
stdout.txt	Aug 23, 16:45:14	Aug 23, 16:45:24	163 Bytes	text/plain		...

Location: root / workitems / adfv2-upload-2-dropbox / job-1 / fffc6250-cc65-4d98-8b7c-7164b3a2adfc

Figure 7.31 – Contents of the workitems directory

See also

Microsoft maintains extensive documentation on using Batch Service. To learn more, start at https://docs.microsoft.com/azure/batch/ for a general overview.

8
Working with Azure Services Integration

The Azure ecosystem has a variety of different services. Most of them can be integrated and connected into **Azure Data Factory (ADF)**. In this chapter, we will cover how to do integrations of the most commonly used **Azure services** into ADF. Also, you will understand how Azure services can be useful in designing **Extract, Transform, Load (ETL)** pipelines.

You will learn how to build a pipeline that executes a logic app upon completion and how to integrate ADF with the following Azure services: Azure **Machine Learning (ML)**, Azure Web Apps, and Azure Functions.

We will cover the following recipes in this chapter:

- Triggering your data processing with Logic Apps
- Using the web activity to call an Azure logic app
- Adding flexibility to your pipelines with Azure Functions
- Automatically building ML models with speed and scale
- Transforming and preparing your data via Azure Databricks

Technical requirements

For this chapter, you will need the following:

- **An active Azure account**: It could be either your business account or a personal account. If you don't have an Azure account yet, you can activate an Azure free-trial license through Microsoft's main website: `https://azure.microsoft.com/en-us/free/`.

- **Microsoft SQL Server Management Studio**: The latest version can be found at `https://docs.microsoft.com/en-us/sql/ssms/download-sql-server-management-studio-ssms`.

- **GitHub repository**: You can download the dataset from this book's GitHub repo or you can use your own: `https://github.com/PacktPublishing/Azure-Data-Factory-Cookbook/tree/master/data`.

Triggering your data processing with Logic Apps

In this recipe, you will learn how to create an **Azure logic app** and trigger your ADF pipeline with it. One of the biggest use cases when you might want to do this is when you want to use an event-based trigger. Event-based triggers exist inside ADF; however, currently they have some limitations. For example, the only events you can do are *When a blob is created* or *When a blob is deleted*. But what if you want an event such as *When a new record is created in your SQL database* or you are dealing with SharePoint lists? The easiest way to build such an event-based trigger is via Azure Logic Apps. Azure Logic Apps opens up a world of possibilities for executing your ADF pipelines using built-in integration.

Getting ready

Before we start, please ensure that you have an Azure license and are familiar with the basics of Azure resources, such as the Azure portal, creating and deleting Azure resources, and creating pipelines in ADF. You can find more information about Azure resources in *Chapter 1, Getting Started with ADF*, and *Chapter 2, Orchestration and Control Flow*, of this book.

How to do it...

We are going to create a new Azure logic app with a create a new data factory pipeline action running inside of it. To trigger the logic app, we will use a **Hypertext Transfer Protocol (HTTP)** request with a **Uniform Resource Locator (URL)**:

1. Navigate to the Azure portal, create a new resource, and choose **Logic App**.

2. Select an active subscription and resource group, write the name of your logic app, choose the same region as the region of your data factory, and click **Review + create**, then **Create**:

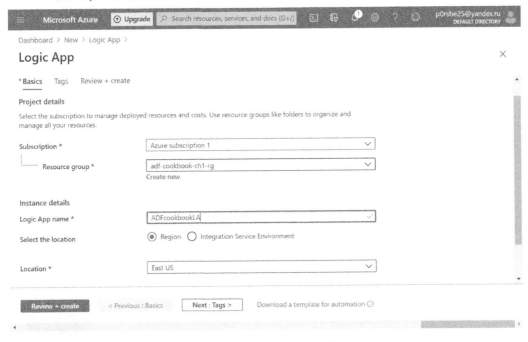

Figure 8.1 – Creating a new Azure logic app

3. When the deployment completes, click on **Go to resource** to open the logic app. Once the Logic Apps Designer opens, you need to specify a trigger for your logic app. Search for **When a HTTP request is received**. This is one of the most popular triggers for testing purposes as you don't need any additional systems set up and integrated.

4. Add a new parameter called `Method` and select **GET** from the drop-down list for **Method**:

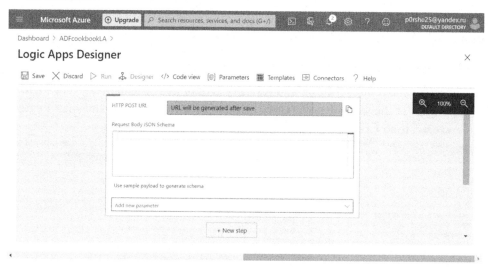

Figure 8.2 – Selecting a trigger for a logic app

5. Click on **New step** to add a new action. Search for `Azure Data Factory` and select **Create a pipeline run**. This action is used to trigger your Data Factory pipeline:

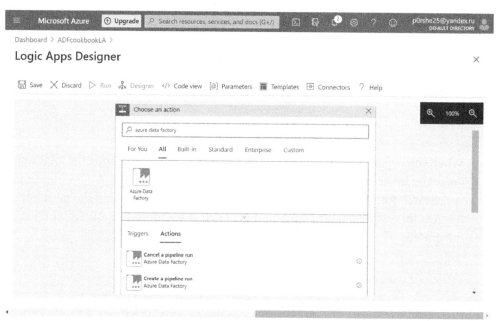

Figure 8.3 – Selecting an action for a logic app

6. In the settings of your chosen action, you need to sign in to ADF with your account. Then, you need to fill in all the required fields with your information from the following drop-down lists: **Subscription**, **Resource Group**, **Data Factory Name**, and **Data Factory Pipeline Name**. Choose a simple Data Factory pipeline (that is, consisting of one activity) that was previously created:

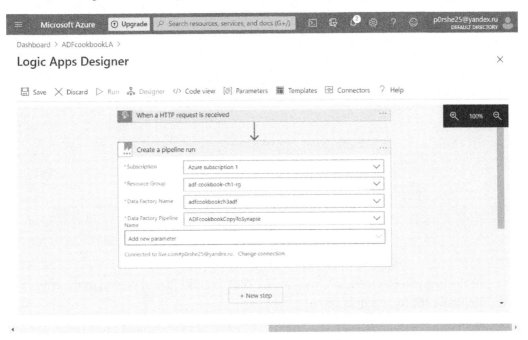

Figure 8.4 – Setting up an action for a logic app

7. After you save your logic app, an HTTP POST URL will be generated. You can copy it in the trigger section. This can be done by clicking on the copy URL button to the right of **HTTP GET URL**:

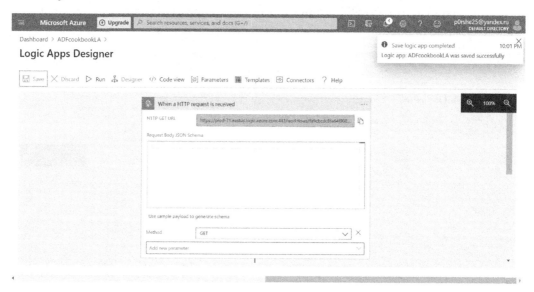

Figure 8.5 – Copying the HTTP GET URL for a logic app

In the preceding screenshot, you can see that the URL has appeared in the trigger step after the logic app is saved.

8. Paste the copied URL path into the web browser search line and press *Enter*. Though you will see a blank window, your logic app will be triggered. You can check this if you click on **See trigger history** of your logic app:

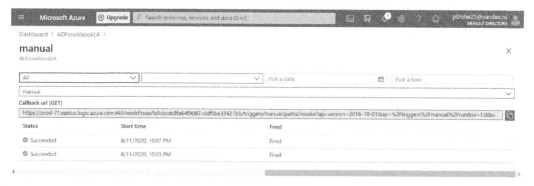

Figure 8.6 – Monitoring logic app runs

From the preceding screenshot, you can see that the logic app was fired at a specific start time. If the status is **Succeeded**, it means that all the logic app steps worked correctly, and your Data Factory pipeline was triggered. You can also check this in the **Monitor** section of ADF.

Now that we have created an Azure logic app, let's have a look at how these steps work.

How it works...

When you create and save a logic app with the **When a HTTP request is received** trigger, a callback URL is created. It is stored in the logic app settings. Every time you fire a callback URL, the logic app instance is created, and it starts executing actions of the workflow one by one.

In our logic app, we have only one action, which is **Create a pipeline run** in ADF. When the logic app instance runs this action, it uses the pre-built **Application Programming Interface (API)** connector, which uses the specified **Active Directory (AD)** account to log in to your ADF instance and run the mentioned pipeline. You can also use this action to pass parameters to your ADF pipeline via JSON code in the `parameters` field.

There's more...

You can choose different triggers for your logic apps. Here are a few such triggers you can choose from:

- When an item is modified on SQL Server
- When a code is pushed to Azure DevOps
- When there are messages in Azure Queue Storage
- When a rule is fired in Azure IoT
- When a file is created in a SharePoint folder
- When an email is received
- When a resource event occurs in Azure Event Grid

You can also use other actions for ADF in Logic Apps, such as **Cancel a pipeline run** or **Get a pipeline run**.

As there are no activities in ADF that can cancel an ADF pipeline run, the **Cancel a pipeline run** action from Logic Apps comes in handy. It can help you both reduce costs from unnecessary runs and avoid different logical errors in your pipelines. To execute this activity, you would need **Data Factory Pipeline Run Id** from the **Create a pipeline run** action.

Get a pipeline run becomes a really useful action in building a solution where the next logic app step will wait until the ADF pipeline executes completely before proceeding. For example, it could be helpful when you want to update your Power BI dataset after data preparation is completed. To do this, you need to follow these steps:

1. Initialize a variable named `Status` after the **Create a pipeline run** action and set its value as `InProgress`.

2. Create a new `Until` action and add the `Status is equal to Succeeded` break condition.

3. Inside the **Until** action, create a new **Get a pipeline run** action. Set `Data Factory Pipeline Run Id` as `runID` from the **Create a pipeline run** action.

4. Inside the **Until** action, add a **Set variable** action, choose your `Status` variable, and put the ADF status from the previous step into `Value`.

This means that the next steps of the logic app will continue only after the status of the pipeline changes to **Succeeded**.

Using the web activity to call an Azure logic app

Azure Logic Apps allows you to greatly increase the capabilities of ADF. You can use it to send emails to build a notification framework. Countless things that can't be done at this point in time in ADF you can leverage Azure Logic Apps to do.

In this recipe, you will learn how to call an Azure logic app from ADF and how to pass parameters between them to archive files from a folder in **Blob storage** and delete those files from the original location.

Getting ready

You need to have created an ADF and Azure Data Lake Storage Gen2 account. The Flights dataset (or any other dataset) should be uploaded to Storage. There should be a container called `archive` created in the **Azure Blob storage** space. You also need to be familiar with creating ADF pipelines containing the **Get Metadata**, **Filter**, and **For Each** activities. Please refer to *Chapter 2, Orchestration and Control Flow,* for guidelines on how to do that.

How to do it...

We are going to create a new Azure logic app and ADF pipeline. The logic app will have Azure Blob storage actions (**Copy Blob** and **Delete Blob**) and will be triggered via an HTTP request. The ADF pipeline will get information about blobs in storage and pass it to the logic app via a web activity:

1. Create a new logic app. You can find instructions on how to do this in the previous recipe, *Triggering your data processing with Logic Apps.*

2. After the resource is created, click **Go to Resource** and select **When a HTTP request is received** from the trigger list.

3. Inside the **When a HTTP request is received** trigger, find the **Request Body JSON Schema** field and paste the following script:

```
{
    "properties": {
        "Container": {
            "type": "string"
        },
        "FileName": {
            "type": "string"
        }
    },
    "type": "object"
}
```

4. Add a new **Copy blob** step from the **Azure Blob Storage** actions. To do this, click on **New step**, then select **All** and search for `copy blob` in the logic app actions and click on it:

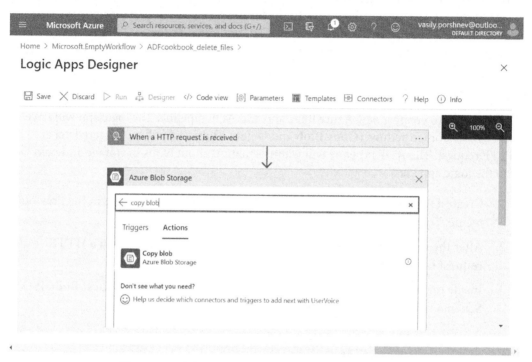

Figure 8.7 – Selecting the Copy blob action for a logic app

5. In the **Copy blob** action, click on **Manually enter connection information** below the **Create** button.

6. Create the name for your connection and paste the Azure Storage account name as well as the Azure Storage account access key:

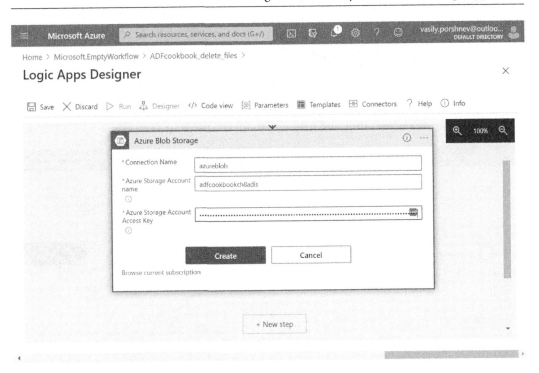

Figure 8.8 – Setting up the Copy blob action for a logic app

You can easily find this information in the access key settings of your Storage account. They are **Storage account name** and **Key** under **key1** in the following screenshot:

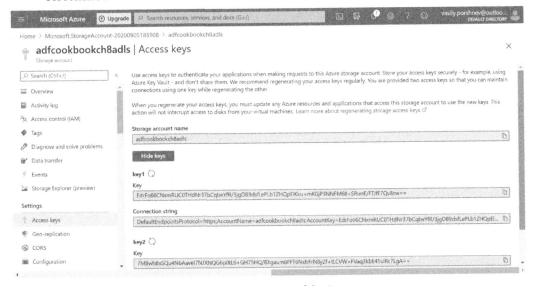

Figure 8.9 – Access key settings of the Storage account

7. After creating the Azure Blob storage connection, fill in the fields as follows:

    a. **Source url**: Choose the **Container** and **FileName** variables.

    b. **Destination blob path**: Enter `archive/` and choose **FileName** from the dynamic content.

The following screenshot will help you to fill the fields in correctly:

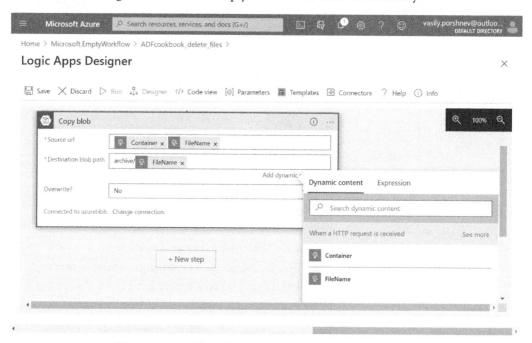

Figure 8.10 – Adding dynamic content to a logic app activity

8. Create a new **Delete blob** step and select **Container** and **FileName** in the **Blob** section.

The following screenshot will help you to fill the field in correctly:

Figure 8.11 – Setting up the Delete blob activity of the logic app

9. Save your logic app and copy the HTTP POST URL.

10. Create a new pipeline in ADF and add a **Get Metadata** activity.

11. Inside the activity, choose a dataset from your Blob storage that you would like
    to archive. The dataset should point to the file in your Blob storage (for instance,
    flights.csv in the following screenshot). Under **Field list**, add an **Item name**
    argument:

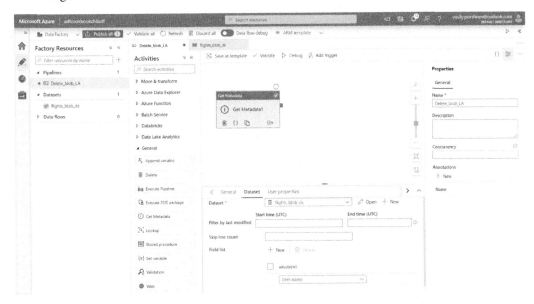

Figure 8.12 – Creating the Get Metadata activity in an ADF pipeline

12. Add an activity on success as a web activity and fill in the fields in the settings as follows:

a. **URL**: Paste the HTTP POST URL from your logic app.

b. **Method**: Select **POST**.

c. **Body**: Add the following script:

```
{
    "Container": "@{pipeline().parameters.Container}",
    "FileName": "@activity('Get Metadata1').output.itemName"
}
```

After you complete this step, you will see the following:

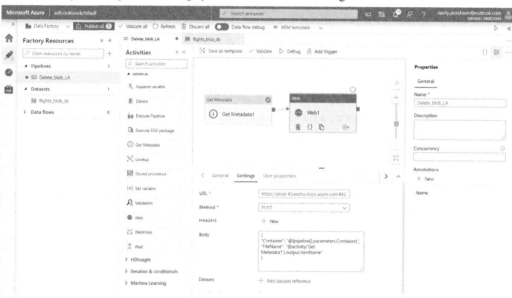

Figure 8.13 – Setting up a web activity in an ADF pipeline

13. Create a new parameter for the pipeline. To do this, you need to left-click on the blank pipeline canvas. Name it `Container` and set the default value as your container name with a backslash:

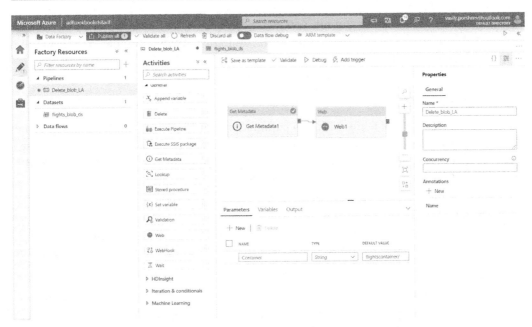

Figure 8.14 – Adding a new parameter to an ADF pipeline

14. Publish the pipeline and click **Debug**. If you refresh your Logic App overview page, you'll see that a successful run appeared in the run history:

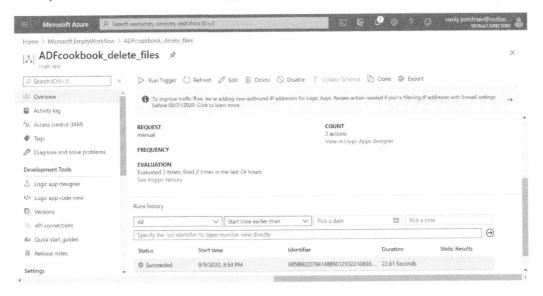

Figure 8.15 – Monitoring logic app runs

If you go to your Azure Blob storage, you will see that the specified blob has moved from the `flightscontainer` folder to the `archive` folder. You will be able to understand why this happened in the following section.

How it works...

We've created an ADF pipeline with two parameters: `Container` and `FileName`. Values for these parameters are received from the dataset specified in the **Get Metadata** activity. ADF pushes these parameters to a web activity. The web activity makes a POST method API call to the logic app using the HTTP URL (which was generated after saving the logic app). While making a POST method, ADF uses JSON code from the `Body` section (key-value pairs) of the web activity to pass the parameters to the logic app. On the left side of the JSON code, there are the keys – the names of parameters that should exist in a logic app. On the right side of the code, there are the values – parameter values from the ADF pipeline.

We've also created a logic app with an HTTP request trigger with JSON code included. This code helps us to get ADF pipeline parameters pushed into the logic app in order to use them as dynamic content for Azure Blob storage activities.

At first, the parameters inside the logic app are blank. When we execute the ADF pipeline, it sets the container parameter to `flightscontainer` and the `FileName` parameter to `flights.csv`. These parameters are pushed to the logic app using the POST method in the HTTP URL. The logic app instance fires the activity to copy the `flightscontainer/flights.csv` blob to `archive/flights.csv`, and the next activity deletes the older version of the blob from `flightscontainer/flights.csv`.

There's more...

Instead of moving just a specific blob, you can add an Azure Blob storage folder dataset to the **Get Metadata** activity and add a **For Each** activity to your ADF pipeline. Furthermore, it is useful to add a **Filter** activity before the **For Each** activity to select the desired blobs. This will help you to copy and delete more than one blob in your Blob container.

Please note that if you use a **Get Metadata** activity with an Azure Blob storage folder dataset, you need to add a **Child items** argument. You will also need to slightly change the script in the web activity:

```
{
"Container": "@{pipeline().parameters.Container}",
"FileName": "@activity('Get Metadata1').output.childItems[0].
```

```
name"
}
```

If the folder is selected in a **Get Metadata** activity, then the `itemName` argument is the name of the blob folder and the `name` argument is the name of the child item.

Adding flexibility to your pipelines with Azure Functions

In this recipe, you will learn how to create an Azure Functions app and an Azure function and call it from ADF. Azure Functions gives you the freedom to create and execute a small or moderate amount of code in C#, Java, JavaScript, Python, or PowerShell. This freedom releases you from a need to create a special infrastructure to host this development environment; however, you still need to provision an Azure Storage account and App Insights to store your Azure Functions code and collect metrics of its execution.

Getting ready...

Before we start, ensure that you have an Azure license and are familiar with the basics of Azure resources, such as the Azure portal, creating and deleting Azure resources, and creating pipelines in ADF. You can find more information about Azure resources in *Chapter 1, Getting Started with ADF*, and *Chapter 2, Orchestration and Control Flow*, of this book.

How to do it...

We are going to create a Functions app, create a new Azure function, and then create a new ADF pipeline that calls an Azure function:

1. First, you need to create a Functions app. Go to the **Resources** page, search for **Function App**, and choose **Create new**.

2. Fill in the fields as follows:

   a. **Subscription**: Select yours.

   b. **Resource Group**: Select yours.

   c. **Function App name**: Set the name you prefer.

   d. **Publish**: Choose **Code**.

   e. **Runtime stack**: Choose **.NET Core**.

Then, you should see the following:

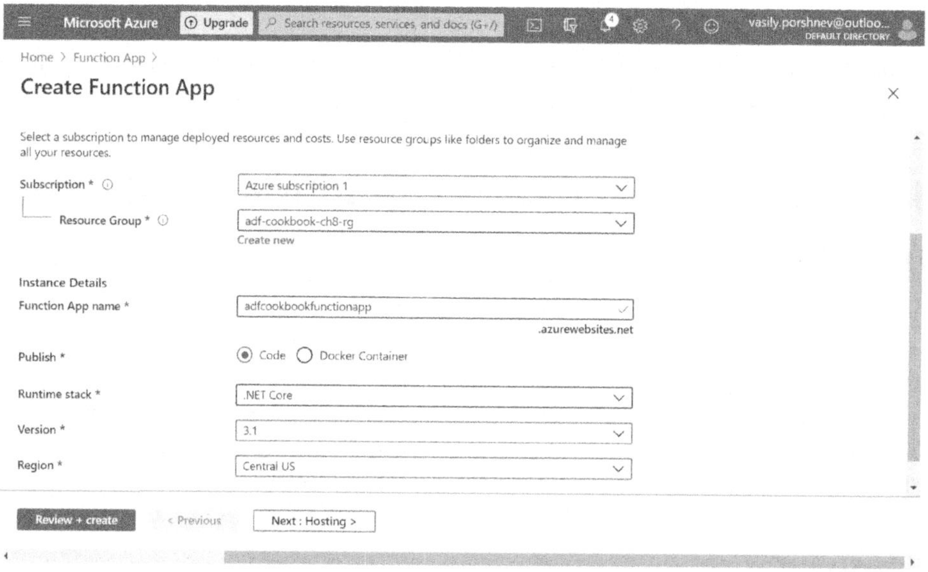

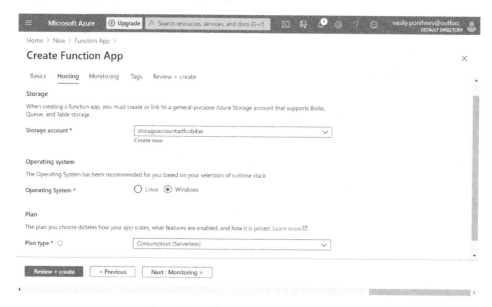

Figure 8.16 – Creating a Functions app

3. In the **Hosting** tab, choose a storage account or create a new one, then choose **Operating System** and **Plan type** options:

Figure 8.17 – Setting up a Functions app

4. In the **Monitoring** tab, you need to create application insights for your Functions app. Then, click **Review + create**:

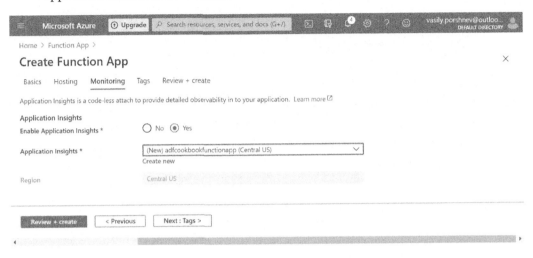

Figure 8.18 – Setting up a Functions app

5. When a new resource is deployed, go to **Resource**, click on **Functions**, and click **Add**. In the **Add function** window, choose the following:

a. **Development environment**: **Develop in portal**

b. **Template**: **HTTP trigger**:

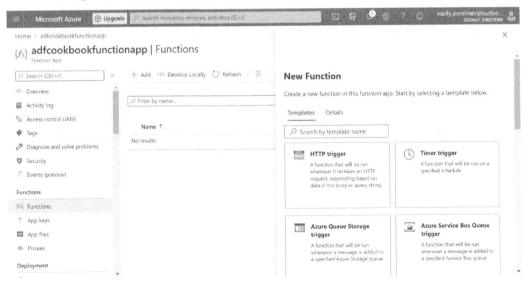

Figure 8.19 – Creating a new Azure function

6. Set the name of the new function and set **Authorization level** as **Function**, then press **Create**.

7. Use the following code inside your Azure function:

```
#r "Newtonsoft.Json"

using System.Net;
using Microsoft.AspNetCore.Mvc;
using Microsoft.Extensions.Primitives;
using Newtonsoft.Json;
using System.Text;

public static async Task<HttpResponseMessage>
Run(HttpRequest req, ILogger log)
{
    log.LogInformation("C# HTTP trigger function
processed a request.");

    string name = req.Query["name"];

    string requestBody = await new StreamReader(req.
Body).ReadToEndAsync();
    dynamic data = JsonConvert.
DeserializeObject(requestBody);
    name = name ?? data?.name;

    string responseMessage = string.IsNullOrEmpty(name)
        ? "This HTTP triggered function executed
successfully. Pass a name in the query string or in the
request body for a personalized response."
            : $"Hello, {name}. This HTTP triggered
function executed successfully.";

    var responseObj = new {result = responseMessage};
    var responseJson = JsonConvert.
SerializeObject(responseObj);
    return new HttpResponseMessage(HttpStatusCode.OK) {
        Content = new StringContent(responseJson,
```

```
Encoding.UTF8, "application/json")};
}
```

8. Go to ADF and create a new pipeline.

9. Choose **Azure Function** from **Activities**.

10. In the activity settings, you need to create an Azure Function linked service:

a. **Azure subscription**: Select yours.

b. **Azure Function App url**: Select yours.

c. **Function Key**: Copy and paste from the **Developer** tab of your Azure function:

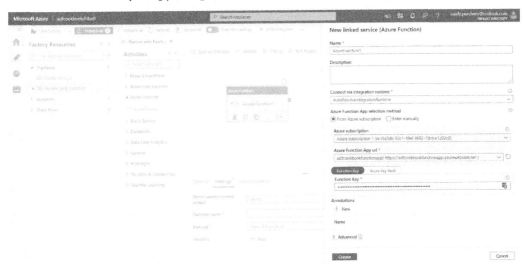

Figure 8.20 – Creating a new Azure Function linked service

11. Fill in the settings fields as follows:

a. **Function name**: Enter the name of your Azure function.

b. **Method**: POST.

c. **Body**: Add this script: { "name": "ADFcookbook" }.

Then, publish your changes to the factory:

Figure 8.21 – Setting up an Azure function activity

12. After debugging the pipeline, you can check the status of your function when you go to the **Monitor** tab of your function:

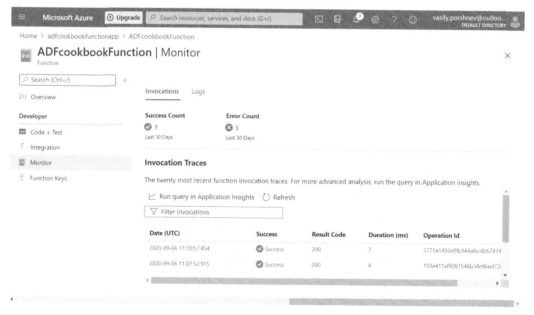

Figure 8.22 – Monitoring Azure function runs

In the next section, we will see how these steps work in the background.

How it works...

When you create a function app, a new function app URL and a function key are generated. They are used to establish a connection between your ADF pipeline and the function app via a linked service. An Azure Function linked service is used to connect from ADF to Azure Functions via a pre-built Azure Functions activity. We've created a new Azure function that is serverless and allows you to execute code on event-based triggers with no need to manage infrastructure. We've created an ADF pipeline with an Azure Functions activity and put simple JSON code into its Body section, which returns a string value.

When the ADF pipeline executes, theAzure Functions activity fires the specified Azure function and uses the API to pass the JSON code using the selected method.

There's more...

You can use an Azure function to dynamically update ADF settings. For example, it could change the schedule of pipelines or activities. To trigger an Azure function, it is helpful to use its own scheduler, which has the much more powerful and really flexible **CRON** syntax (scripts for a time-based job scheduler). With the addition of Azure Functions, ADF's potential greatly increases. Even connecting to non-Microsoft databases is possible.

Automatically building ML models with speed and scale

In ADF, it is possible to call ML algorithms to make predictive analytics as a step of the pipeline. In this recipe, you will learn how to create an Azure ML workspace and call an Azure ML experiment from ADF.

Getting ready

Before we start, please ensure that you have an Azure license and are familiar with the basics of Azure resources, such as the Azure portal, creating and deleting Azure resources, and creating pipelines in ADF. You can find more information about Azure resources in *Chapter 1, Getting Started with ADF*, and *Chapter 2, Orchestration and Control Flow*, of this book.

How to do it...

We are going to use Machine Learning Studio (classic), use an API to connect it with our ADF pipeline, run an ML experiment on a file from Blob storage, and save the results of the ML experiment to the output file:

1. First, you need to create an **Azure Machine Learning Studio** environment. Go to the Azure **Resources** page, search for **Machine Learning Studio (classic) web service**, and choose **Create new**.

2. Select **Machine Learning Studio (classic)** under **Create**. It is highlighted in the following screenshot:

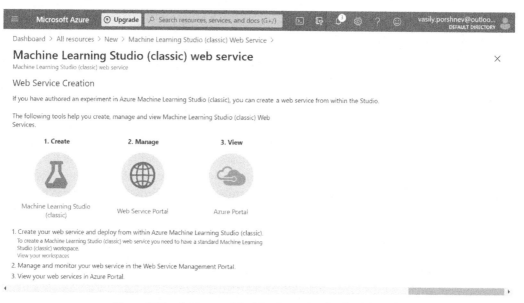

Figure 8.23 – Setting up Machine Learning Studio (classic)

3. The preceding link should transfer you to the Azure Machine Learning Studio (classic) website. In the newly opened window (`https://studio.azureml.net/`), click **Sign In** and sign in with your Azure account:

Figure 8.24 – Signing in to Machine Learning Studio (classic)

4. When Machine Learning Studio is loaded, go to **Datasets** and fill in the fields as follows:

    a. **SELECT THE DATA TO UPLOAD**: Upload a new dataset: `routes.csv`.

    b. **ENTER A NAME FOR THE NEW DATASET**: `Routes`.

c. **SELECT A TYPE FOR THE NEW DATASET**: Generic CSV File with a header
(`.csv`):

Figure 8.25 – Uploading a dataset in Machine Learning Studio (classic)

5. Click **NEW | EXPERIMENT | Blank Experiment**:

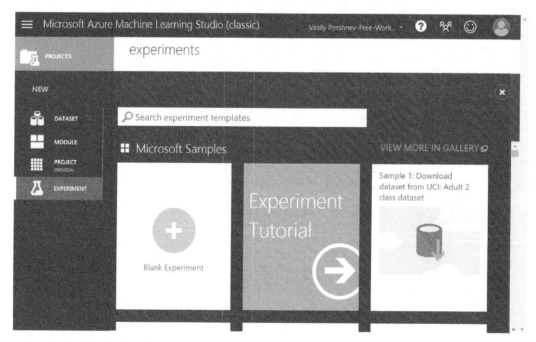

Figure 8.26 – Creating an experiment in Machine Learning Studio (classic)

6. Add your saved dataset, then drag the **Detect languages** experiment from the left menu and drop it to the canvas. Link your dataset to the **Detect languages** experiment with an arrow. Open the **Detect languages** properties and select columns of your dataset. These columns should be in text format to make it possible for the ML experiment to detect the languages of the columns. This ML experiment will automatically detect whether the language of the column values is English, French, Italian, and so on. If you're using the `routes.csv` dataset, you can select the **Airline** column. The menu for the settings is shown in the following screenshot:

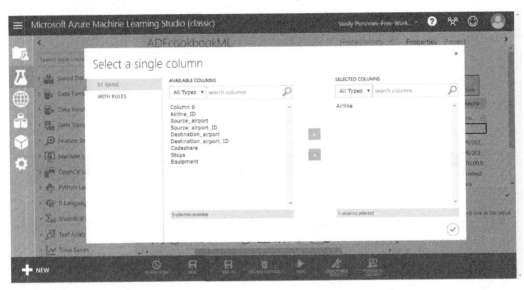

Figure 8.27– Selecting columns in the Detect languages item

7. Click **Set up Web Service**, then click **RUN**. After the run is finished, click **DEPLOY WEB SERVICE**. It is the button to the right of **RUN** in the following screenshot. Your experiment should look as in the following screenshot:

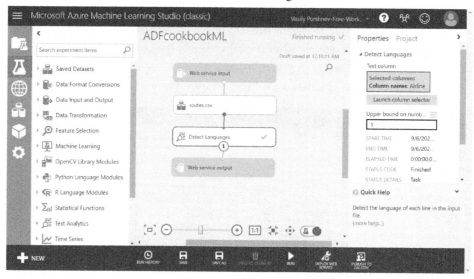

Figure 8.28 – Deploying the web service

8. You will see the web services tab opened, where you can find the API key. This tab is shown in the following screenshot:

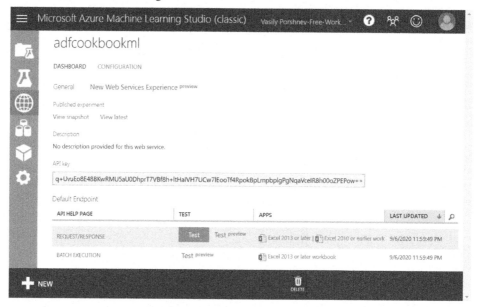

Figure 8.29 – ML experiment API key

9. Navigate to the API help page. If you click on **Batch execution**, you will find the POST method request URI. It is in the **Request URI** column in the following screenshot:

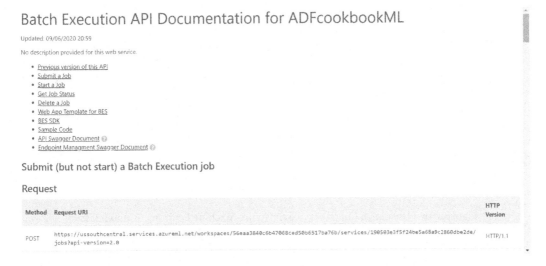

Figure 8.30 – ML experiment API documentation

10. Go to ADF and create a new pipeline. Choose **Machine Learning Batch Execution** from **Activities**.

11. Create a new linked service for Azure Machine Learning Studio (classic). Set the name of the linked service and fill in the fields as follows:

a. **Endpoint**: The POST method request URI.

b. **API key**: Paste the API key (from the web services tab).

Click on **Test connection** and then on **Create**:

Figure 8.31 – Creating a linked service for Azure Machine Learning Studio (classic)

12. Go to **Settings**:

    a. **INPUT KEY**: Add `input1` and choose the location of the `routes.csv` blob
    in your storage.

    b. **OUTPUT KEY**: Add `output1` and choose the location and name of the blob
    as an output file in your storage.

You can find the settings of these fields in the following screenshot:

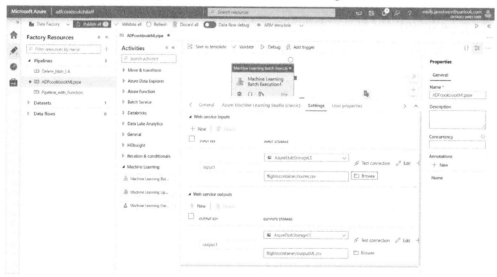

Figure 8.32 – Setting up an ML batch execution activity

13. Publish your pipeline and click **Debug**. When the debug is finished, you can check that the output file is created in Blob storage. The file is highlighted in the following screenshot. In the file, the following columns have been added: **Airline**, **Language**, and **Score**:

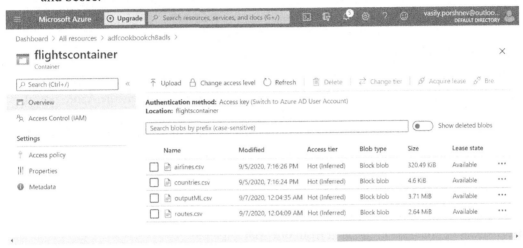

Figure 8.33 – Checking the results of the ML pipeline execution

We will look at how this is done in the following section in more detail.

How it works...

We've created an ADF pipeline with a pre-built ML batch execution activity. This activity uses a POST method request URI and API key to establish a connection between ADF and Machine Learning Studio via a linked service. When an ADF pipeline executes, it passes the file from the **INPUT KEY** settings of the ADF activity to the specified Azure ML experiment and runs the experiment. After the experiment is finished, the result of the experiment is saved as the output key in the selected storage location.

There's more...

We've used a pretty simple ML experiment that consists of only one step of Text Analytics. You can choose different items for your experiment, such as the following: different types of Text Analytics, time series anomaly detection, cleansing data using Statistical Functions, Pretrained Cascade Image Classification, clustering models, execute your own R and Python scripts, and many others.

You can even combine items and choose the output of one item as an input for another item in your ML experiment.

Transforming and preparing your data via Azure Databricks

In this recipe, you will learn how to call **Azure Databricks** notebooks from ADF pipelines.

Getting ready

Before we start, please ensure that you have an Azure license, have a basic knowledge of coding, and are familiar with the basics of Azure resources, such as the Azure portal, creating and deleting Azure resources, and creating pipelines in ADF. You can find more information about Azure resources in *Chapter 1, Getting Started with ADF*, and *Chapter 2, Orchestration and Control Flow*, of this book.

How to do it...

We are going to set up an Azure Databricks service, create a new cluster, create a Databricks notebook, and call it from our ADF pipeline:

1. First, you need to create an Azure Databricks service. Go to the **Resources** page, search for `Azure Databricks`, and choose **Create new**.

2. Select your Azure subscription, resource group, workspace name, location, and pricing tier, as in the following screenshot. Click **Review + Create**:

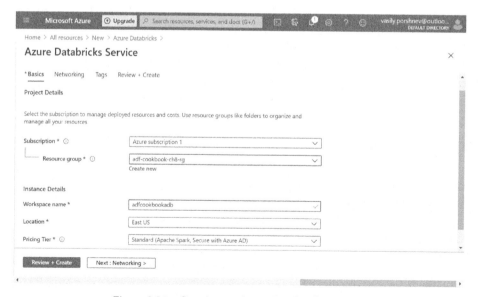

Figure 8.34 – Creating an Azure Databricks service

3. To operate in an Azure Databricks service, you need to go to the Azure resource that you created, select the **Overview** tab, and click **Launch Workspace**.

4. Go to **Clusters** and click **Create cluster**. Set the name of the cluster, **Cluster Mode**, **Databricks Runtime Version**, and the minutes of inactivity for termination. Click **Create Cluster**:

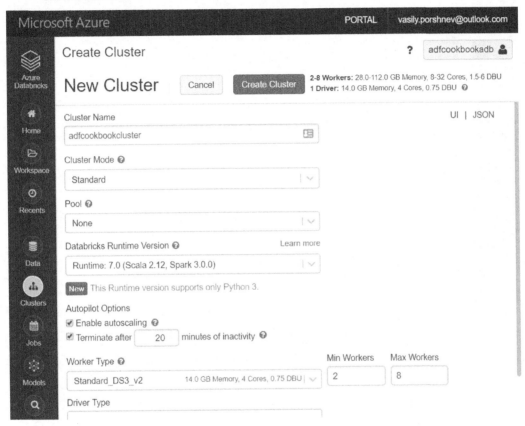

Figure 8.35 – Creating a new cluster

You need to wait for some time until the cluster starts. Usually, it takes several minutes.

5.   Click **Workspace | Create | Notebook**:

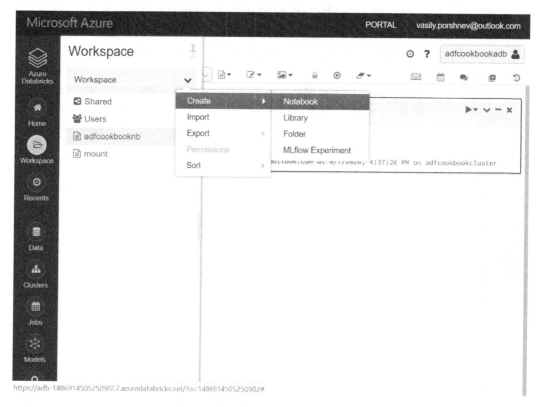

Figure 8.36 – Creating a new notebook

6.   Type the name of the notebook, attach a cluster to it, and write some simple code in Python:

```
print('ADFcookbook')
```

Here is how the screen should look:

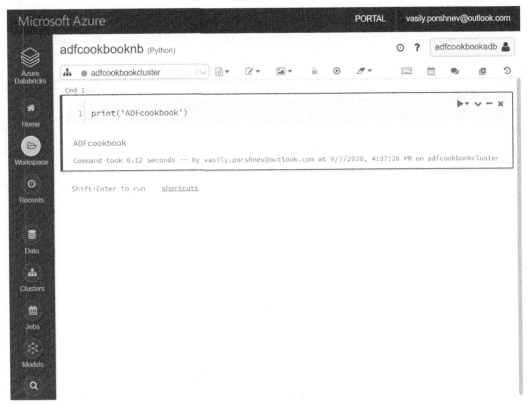

Figure 8.37 – Attaching a cluster and writing code within a notebook

7.   Go to ADF, create a new pipeline, and choose the **Databricks | Notebook** activity.

8. Create a new linked service to Azure Databricks. Type the name of the linked service, and choose an Azure subscription, Databricks workspace, and existing interactive cluster:

Figure 8.38 – Setting up an Azure Databricks linked service

To get an access token, you need to click on **User settings** in the top-right corner of the Databricks workspace. In the opened window, click **Generate New Token**, enter a comment, and click **Generate**. The comment should have some information about the purpose of this token (as in the following screenshot). You can then use this token ID as an access token in the linked service:

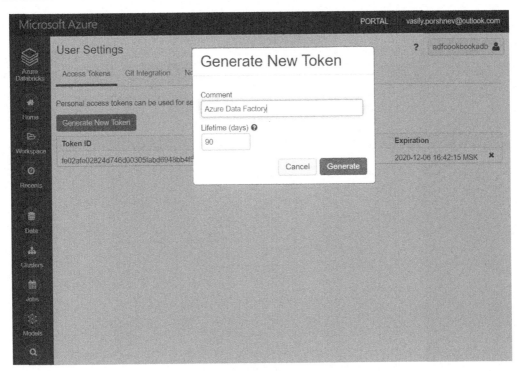

Figure 8.39 – Generating a new token

9. Go to the settings of the Databricks **Notebook** activity and browse for your notebook:

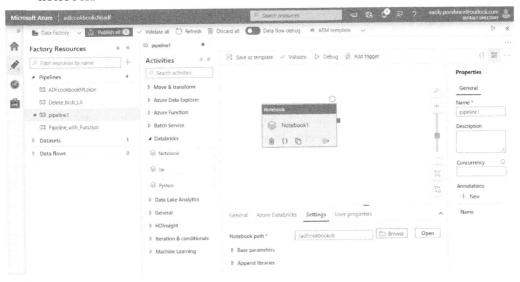

Figure 8.40 – Creating a new ADF pipeline with the Databricks Notebook activity

10. Publish your pipeline and click **Debug**. If the code is correct and the pipeline is well configured, you will see the **Succeeded** status of the pipeline:

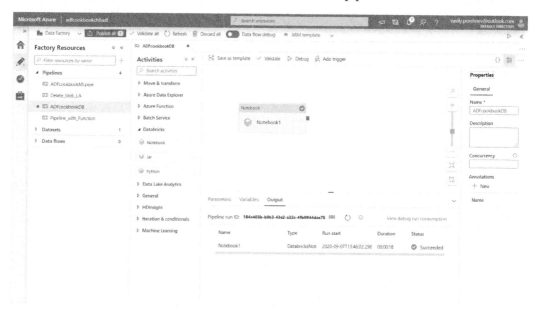

Figure 8.41 – Monitoring the status of a pipeline activity

In the next section, we will see how these steps work in the background.

How it works...

We've created an Azure Databricks service that allows you to execute notebooks with Python, PySpark, and Scala code while handling big data. As all the data engineering and analytics in Databricks is run on a special set of computation resources, we've created a cluster. We used the Databricks workspace URL, access token, and cluster name to establish a connection between ADF and Databricks via a pre-built linked service. When the ADF pipeline executes the Databricks **Notebook** activity, it calls Azure Databricks via a configured linked service, attaches the cluster used in the linked service to the specified notebook, and runs the code of the notebook.

There's more...

We've covered how to call a simple Databricks notebook from an ADF pipeline, but there could be much more complex notebooks with a bunch of code rows, preparing massive amounts of big unstructured data, resulting in a tiny **Parquet** format datamart. All of these preparations, including data extractions, transformations, copy data, and email alerts, may be used within one ADF pipeline.

Furthermore, using the **Notebook** activity in ADF, you can append new libraries to your Databricks notebooks in an ADF pipeline. You can see how to set this up in the following screenshot. On the left side of the **Notebook** activity's **Settings** tab, you can choose **LIBRARY TYPE**. On the right side of the **Settings** tab, you can add **LIBRARY CONFIGURATION** settings, such as specifying the package, repository, coordinates, and exclusions:

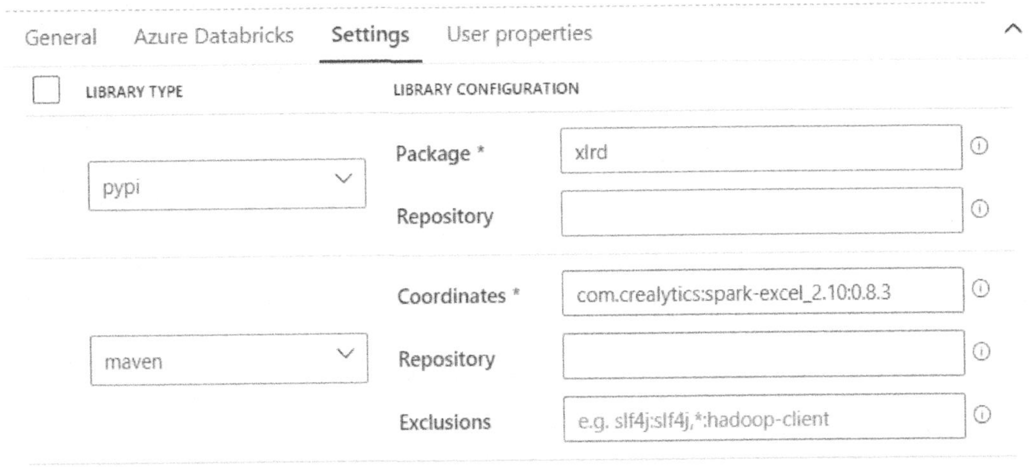

General	Azure Databricks	**Settings**	User properties		∧

☐ LIBRARY TYPE		LIBRARY CONFIGURATION	
pypi ∨		Package *	xlrd ⓘ
		Repository	ⓘ
maven ∨		Coordinates *	com.crealytics:spark-excel_2.10:0.8.3 ⓘ
		Repository	ⓘ
		Exclusions	e.g. slf4j:slf4j,*:hadoop-client ⓘ

Figure 8.42 – Appending a new library to the Databricks notebook via an ADF activity

Azure Databricks is a very important service of the Azure data platform, which allows you to do data engineering, data science, streaming analytics, ad hoc analytics, and ML.

9

Managing Deployment Processes with Azure DevOps

Azure DevOps provides a wide range of development collaboration, **continuous integration (CI)**, and **continuous delivery (CD)** tools. **Azure Repos** helps you to collaborate on code development using free public and private Git repositories, pull requests, and code reviews. **Azure Pipelines** helps you implement a build, test, and development pipeline for any app.

In this chapter, you will learn how to set up the CI and CD of your data analytics solutions in **Azure Data Factory (ADF)** using Azure DevOps. We will start by setting up an Azure DevOps account, creating an organization and projects within that, and then linking it to your **ADF**. Then, we'll go deeper into how to publish changes from Git to ADF and deploy new features using Azure Repos. Finally, you will learn how to get ready and set up the CI/CD processes of Data Factory pipelines using Azure Pipelines.

We will cover the following list of recipes in this chapter:

- Setting up Azure DevOps
- Publishing changes to ADF
- Deploying your features into the **master branch**
- Getting ready for the CI/CD of ADF
- Creating an Azure pipeline for CD

Technical requirements

For this chapter, you will need the following:

- **An active Azure account**: It could be either your business account or a personal account. If you don't have an Azure account yet, you can activate an Azure free trial license through the main Microsoft website: `https://azure.microsoft.com/en-us/free/`.

- **GitHub repository**: You may download the dataset from the book's Git repo or you may have your own one: `https://github.com/PacktPublishing/Azure-Data-Factory-Cookbook/tree/master/data`.

Setting up Azure DevOps

To get the most out of Azure DevOps integration with ADF, you first need to create an account within Azure DevOps, link it with your Data Factory, and make sure everything is set up and ready to work. This recipe will take you through the steps on how to accomplish that.

Getting ready

Before we start, please ensure that you have an Azure license and are familiar with the basics of Azure resources such as the Azure portal, creating and deleting Azure resources, and creating pipelines in ADF.

How to do it...

In this recipe, you will learn how to create an Azure DevOps account, create a new project, connect a DevOps organization with Azure Active Directory, link it with your ADF, and set up a code repository:

1. Navigate to `https://dev.azure.com`.

2. You will see the following screen. Click on **Start free** to begin creating your Azure DevOps account:

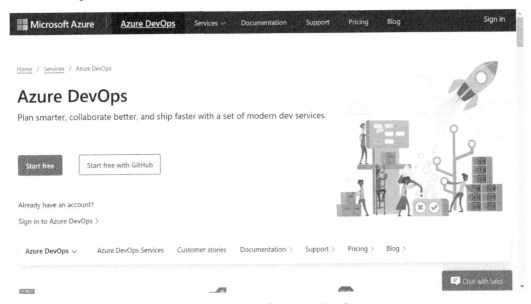

Figure 9.1 – Starting your free Azure DevOps account

3. Log in with your Azure account as we are going to connect Azure DevOps to Azure Active Directory. Choose your **Country/region** and click **Continue**:

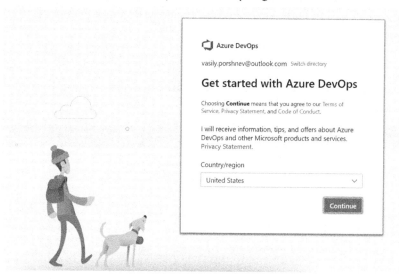

Figure 9.2 – Setting up an Azure DevOps account

4. Enter your organization name in the **Name your Azure DevOps organization** field. It is something like your account name. You need to select the location for hosting your project. It's recommended to choose the location where your ADF is hosted, otherwise, there could be syncing issues. Click on **Continue**:

Figure 9.3 – Creating an Azure DevOps organization

5. Enter a name in the **Project name** field of the project and click **Create project**:

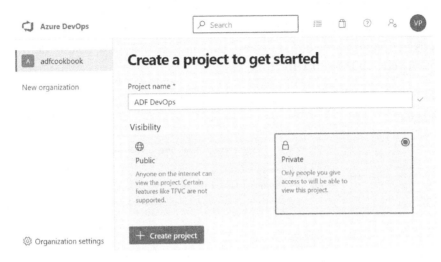

Figure 9.4 – Creating an Azure DevOps project

6. Go to **Organization settings** in the bottom-left corner (in the preceding screenshot), and you'll see the dialog box shown in the following screenshot. Then choose the **Default Directory** option in the **Azure Active Directory** field and click **Connect**:

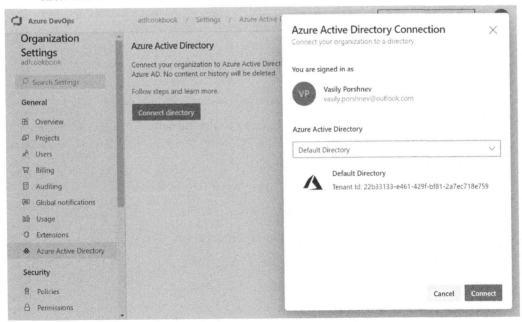

Figure 9.5 – Connecting an organization to Azure Active Directory

In this step, we have connected our organization to Azure Active Directory. It is a necessary step to link your ADF to an Azure DevOps account.

7. Then it's recommended to sign out and sign in again. If you go to the **Azure Active Directory** page of Azure DevOps, you'll see that, now, your organization is connected to **Default Directory**:

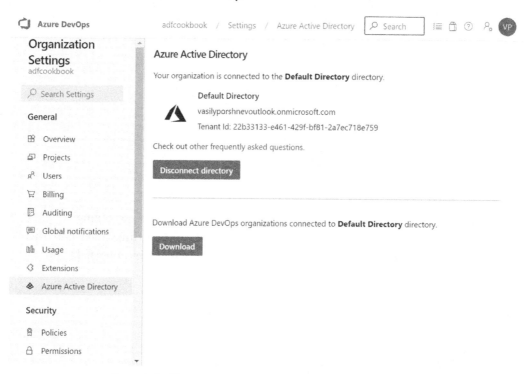

Figure 9.6 – The organization is connected to Default Directory

8. Go to your ADF and click on **Data Factory** in the top-left corner. Click **Set up code repository** as is highlighted in the following screenshot. A dialog box with the repository settings will appear.

9. In the open dialog box, you need to have the settings as follows:

    Repository type: `Azure DevOps Git.`

    Azure Active Directory: `Choose your default.`

    Azure DevOps Account: `Choose your account.`

    Project name: `Your project name.`

Repository name: You can create a new repository or choose **Use existing**, which was created by default with the creation of your project.

Collaboration branch: Choose your branch that will be used for collaboration in Git. Usually, it is called the **master branch**.

Publish branch: Choose your branch that will be used for publishing into the production environment. Usually, it is called **adf_publish**.

Root folder: / .

Import existing resource: Check.

Import resource into this branch: Use Collaboration:

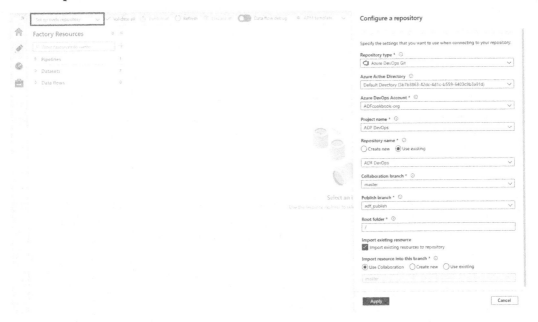

Figure 9.7 – Setting up a Git repository

10. After you click **Apply**, you will see the window to **Select working branch**. Choose **Use existing** to continue your work within the **master branch** and click **Save**. You will see that, now, your ADF is connected to **Azure DevOps Git** and **master branch** is chosen. You can find it highlighted in the following screenshot:

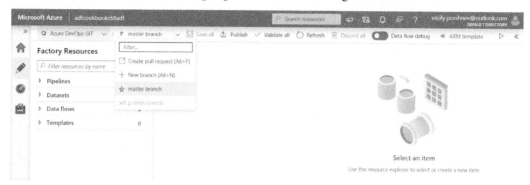

Figure 9.8 – Choosing a branch in Azure DevOps Git

In this section, we've created an Azure DevOps account with a new project, connected a DevOps organization with Azure Active Directory, linked it with ADF, and set up a code repository. In the next section, we will see how these steps work in the background.

How it works...

As we had an Azure account and an Azure DevOps account, we could connect them using an Azure Active Directory default directory. In order to make it possible to link Azure DevOps with ADF, we've connected a DevOps organization to the default Azure Active Directory. It stores the tenant ID for linking these services. After setting up the repository in Data Factory, a new repository, ADF DevOps, was created automatically in the Azure DevOps project. As we set the collaboration branch as the master, a **master branch** was automatically created in the Azure DevOps ADF DevOps repository.

Publishing changes to ADF

Collaboration on code development involves using Git. In this recipe, you will learn how to create an ADF pipeline in **Azure DevOps Git** and publish changes from your **master branch** to ADF.

Getting ready

Before we start, please ensure that you have an Azure license and are familiar with the basics of Azure resources such as the Azure portal, creating and deleting Azure resources, and creating pipelines in ADF. Also, you will need an Azure DevOps project created and linked to your ADF.

How to do it...

We are going to create a new ADF pipeline in the **master branch** of **Azure DevOps Git** and publish the changes to Data Factory:

1. Create a new ADF pipeline with the **Wait** activity in **master branch**. Please refer to *Chapter 2, Orchestration and Control Flow*, for guidelines on how to do that. Click **Save all**. Your changes will be saved in the **master branch** of **Azure DevOps Git**:

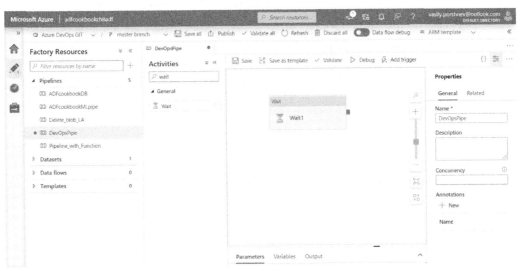

Figure 9.9 – Creating a new pipeline inside the master branch

2. Now switch from **Azure DevOps Git** to **Data Factory** mode (in the top-left corner of the following screenshot). You'll see that there are no newly created pipelines:

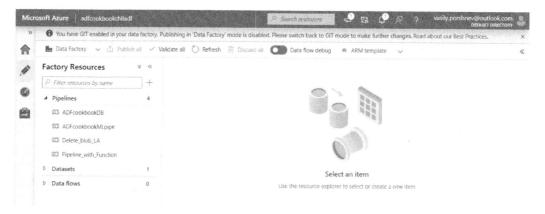

Figure 9.10 – Switching to Data Factory mode

The blank ADF canvas in the preceding screenshot means that changes are not deployed to Data Factory yet.

3. Go to Azure DevOps | **Repos** | your repository | **Files** | **pipeline**. Here, you will see your pipeline created in the **master branch**. It is saved as a JSON file in DevOps. You can also see that there is only the **master branch** created in the current repository:

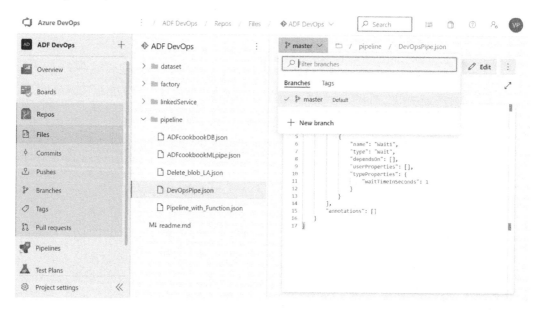

Figure 9.11 – Azure DevOps repo: pipeline created in the master branch

4. Navigate to your ADF and select **Azure DevOps Git** mode. You will see that your changes are saved in the **master branch** and you can continue working with it. Click **Publish** to publish your DevOps pipeline. **ADF** will create a new branch called **adf_publish** inside your repository and publish the changes to ADF directly. You will see the message about the `Publish` branch in the **Pending changes** dialog box as in this screenshot:

Figure 9.12 – Publishing a pipeline from the master branch

5. Click **OK**. While the publish is completed, switch to **Data Factory** mode and you will see that the pipeline is deployed to it.

How it works...

Every activity you do in ADF is saved to a JSON file (separate JSON files for datasets, pipelines, linked services, dataflows, and so on), and this file is kept in Azure DevOps.

After publishing your ADF pipeline from the **master branch** to Data Factory, the **adf_publish** branch is created automatically in the repository, and the ARM template is created and placed into the **adf_publish** branch. The ARM template is a code representation of your **ADF** and Azure resources:

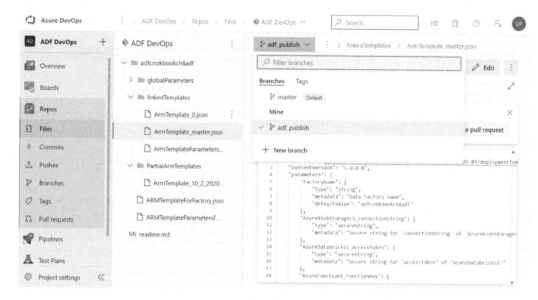

Figure 9.13 – ARM templates are created in the adf_publish branch

If you go to your project in **DevOps**, you will see that the `adf_publish` branch has been created and the ARM template of **master branch** (`ArmTemplateForFactory.json`, `ARMTemplateParametersForFactory.json`) is saved there. The templates highlighted in the preceding screenshot are stored only in the `adf_publish` branch.

Deploying your features into the master branch

Now that we have covered how to publish changes from the **master branch** to Data Factory, we are going to look at how to deploy new branches into the **master branch**. There are several reasons for creating new branches. While implementing new changes to your project, it is a common practice to create a **feature branch**, develop your changes there, and then publish them to the **master branch**. Some teams working in an Agile environment can create branches per story development. Other teams may have branches per developer. In all these situations, the main purpose is to avoid breaking changes during the release into the production environment.

Getting ready

Before we start, please ensure that you have an Azure license and are familiar with the basics of Azure resources such as the Azure portal, creating and deleting Azure resources, and creating pipelines in ADF. Also, you will need an Azure DevOps project created and linked to your ADF.

How to do it...

In this recipe, we are going to create a new branch, make changes in this branch, create a pull request, and merge the changes with the **master branch**:

1. To create a new branch, go to your ADF, choose **Azure DevOps Git mode**, then click on **master branch** and then **New branch** (highlighted in the following screenshot):

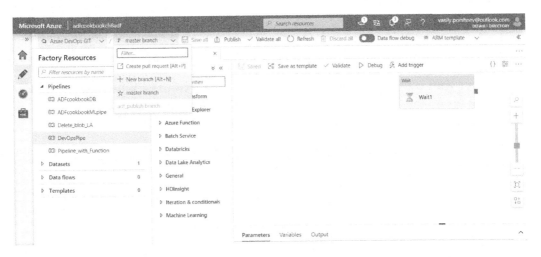

Figure 9.14 – Creating a new branch in Azure DevOps Git

2. Type the name of your feature in the field that appears in the dialog box (see the following screenshot) and click **Save**:

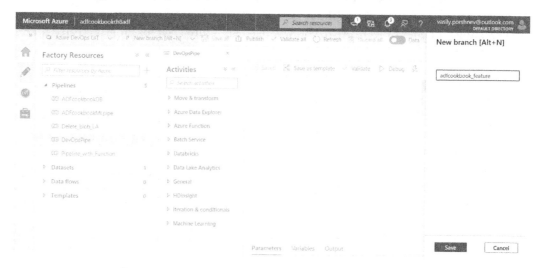

Figure 9.15 – Creating a feature branch in Azure DevOps Git

3. Open your **feature branch** and create a new dataset with a CSV file from your **Blob storage**. In the following screenshot, you can see that **adfcookbook_feature** is selected and the changes are made to this branch:

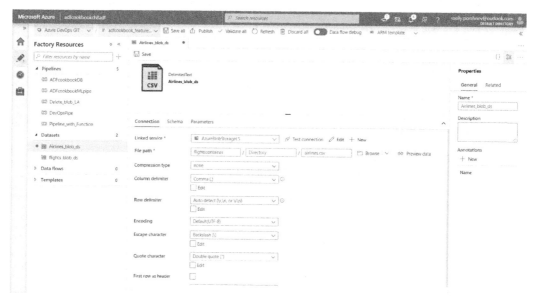

Figure 9.16 – Creating a dataset in the feature branch

Let's assume that your deployment is completed, and you want to publish it to ADF. If you try to publish your changes from the feature branch, ADF will not allow you to do so. It is only possible to do so from the collaboration branch, which is the **master branch**:

Figure 9.17 – Publishing changes from the feature branch

4. Before publishing your changes to ADF, you need to first publish them to the **master branch**. To do so, click **Save all**, then click on your **feature branch** and choose **Create pull request** (highlighted in the following screenshot):

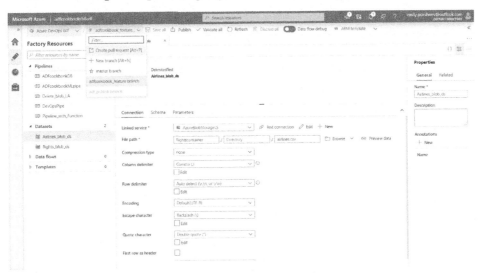

Figure 9.18 – Creating a pull request from ADF

5. This option will take you to your Azure DevOps account and we'll navigate the steps of how to do a pull request. You need to enter the title and description (they are created by default). If you're working within an organization, you can also choose **Reviewers** for your deployment (that is, Team Leader, Senior Engineer, and so on):

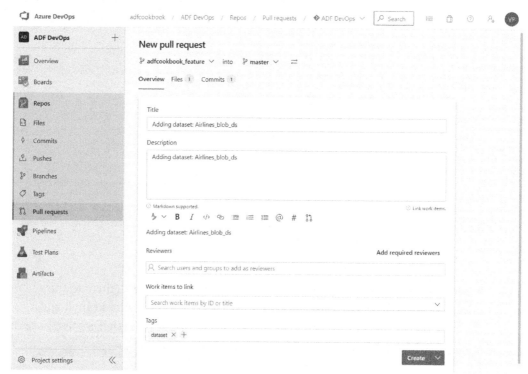

Figure 9.19 – Creating a pull request in Azure DevOps

In the **Files** tab, you will see the changes that are being deployed as a JSON file (as in the following screenshot):

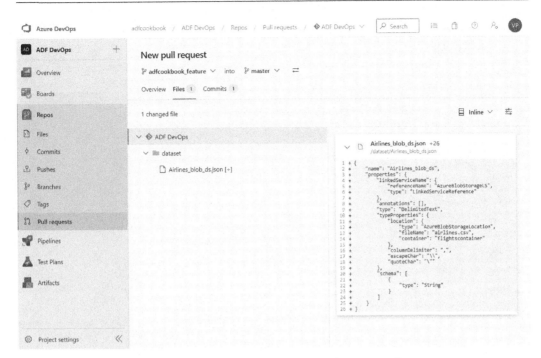

Figure 9.20 – The changes are deployed as a JSON file

To proceed with the pull request, click **Create** on the **Overview** tab.

6. You will see a new active pull request in the **Pull requests** section of your repository:

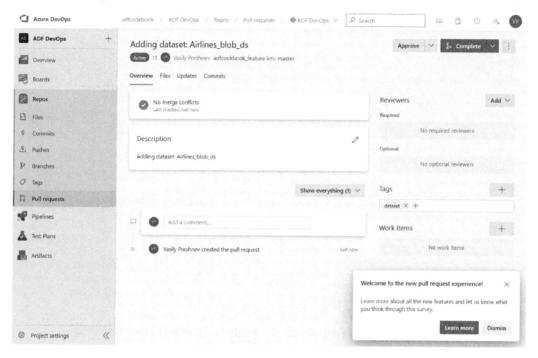

Figure 9.21 – An active pull request form

7. You can **approve** the pull request on your own if you don't have any other approvers (if you have any reviewers, you will need to wait until they approve your pull request before merging). Then, click **Complete**. The dialog box for completing the pull request will appear:

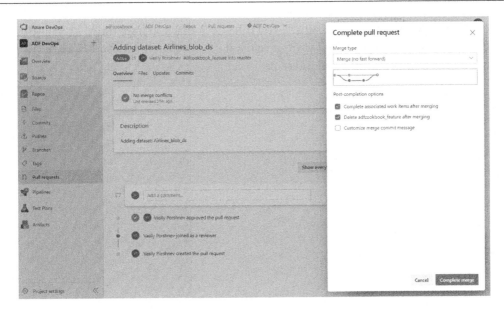

Figure 9.22 – Approving a pull request

8. You can delete the source branch on the completion of the pull request by selecting
    the appropriate checkbox if you don't need this branch anymore. Once you click
    Complete merge (as seen in the preceding screenshot), the feature code will be
    merged with the **master branch**:

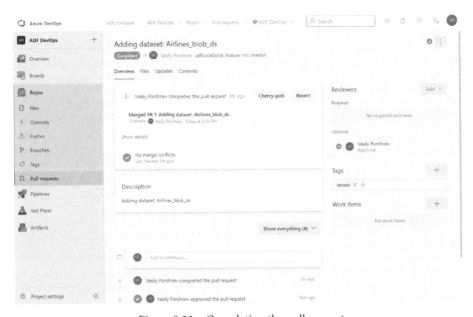

Figure 9.23 – Completing the pull request

9.   Now if you go to your repository, you can check that you have only two branches as the feature was deleted and your developed dataset is in the **master branch**. You can check the same in the ADF interface:

Figure 9.24 – Changes are merged into the master branch

10. When you go back to ADF, you will see that the current working branch was deleted. To use the existing **master branch**, click **Save**:

Figure 9.25 – Deleting the feature branch

11. In the opened **master branch**, click **Publish**, then click **OK**:

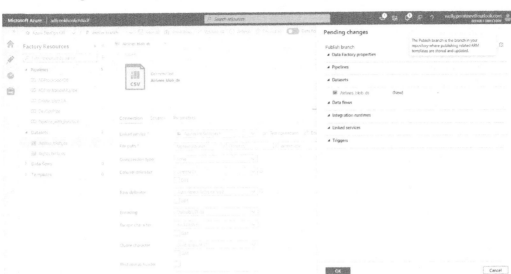

Figure 9.26 – Publishing changes from the master branch to the adf_publish branch

12. After publishing is completed, you can switch to **Data Factory** mode and check that the dataset has been added to the **adf_publish** branch.

In this section, we have created a feature branch and successfully merged changes from the new branch to the **master branch** and **publish branch**. Now let's take a look at how it works.

How it works...

When you click **Create a new branch** in ADF DevOps GIT mode, a new branch is created inside the Azure DevOps repository. When you add a new feature in the feature branch, it is saved as a JSON file in this branch of the Azure DevOps repository. In order to release your feature from Git to Data Factory, you need to merge the changes with the **master branch** first (as it is selected as a collaboration branch) via a pull request. The pull request needs to be approved and completed by a reviewer. After completion of the pull request, the JSON file of the new feature will be copied into the appropriate folder of the **master branch**. If we tick the **Delete feature branch after merging** checkbox, the feature branch will be deleted. After publishing the changes from the **master branch**, the JSON file of the new feature will be copied into the appropriate folder of the publish branch.

Getting ready for the CI/CD of ADF

CD includes the deployment of ADF pipelines between different environments, that is, development, testing, and production. The best practice and most secure way of configuring your pipelines in the CI/CD process is using **Azure Key Vault (AKV)** instead of a connection string. In this chapter, you will learn what you need to set up before creating a CD process and how to establish AKV and connect it with ADF and an Azure storage account.

Getting ready

Before we start, please ensure that you have an Azure license and are familiar with the basics of Azure resources such as the Azure portal, creating and deleting Azure resources, and creating pipelines in ADF.

How to do it...

In this section, we are going to create and set up two resource groups – development (DEV) and testing (UAT). Inside of each resource group, we'll create access policies, and secrets on ADF, an Azure storage account, and AKV:

1. You need to have created two resource groups: ADFCOOKBOOK-DEV-RG and ADFCOOKBOOK-UAT-RG. Please refer to *Chapter 2, Orchestration and Control Flow*, for guidelines on how to do that.

2. Inside of each resource group, there should be these resources: ADF, an Azure storage account, and AKV. Inside of the DEV resource group, there will be the following: ADFCOOKBOOK-DEV-ADF, ADFCOOKBOOK-DEV-AKV, and adfcookbookdevadls. Inside of the UAT resource group, there will be the following: ADFCOOKBOOK-UAT-ADF, ADFCOOKBOOK-UAT-AKV, and adfcookbookuatadls.

3. To create an **AKV** resource, search for it in the Azure portal, choose a **Subscription** option, choose a resource group, fill in **Key vault name**, and choose a **Region** option and a **Pricing tier** option, as shown in the screenshot:

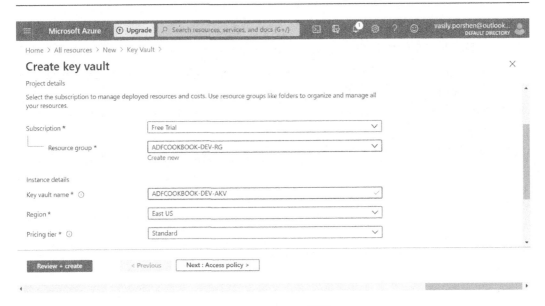

Figure 9.27 – Creating an AKV resource

4.   In **access policy**, you need to create a new access policy for ADF. Click **Add access policy**. For **Secret permissions**, select **Get** and **List**. In the **Select principal** section, select a principal for your development environment data factory. Click **Add**:

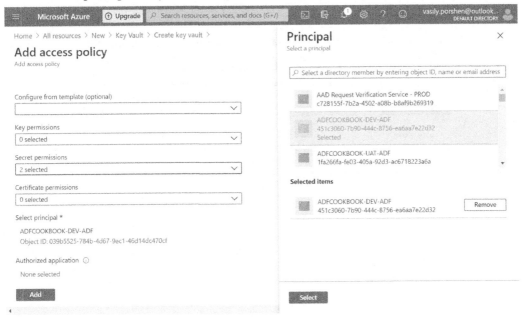

Figure 9.28 – Adding an access policy to Data Factory

5.   To create a new access policy, click **Create**. Now, when your Dev data factory refers to **Dev Key Vault**, it will have access to the stored secrets.

6.   It is common practice when using Azure DevOps pipelines to configure linked services via AKV. To set this up, you need to copy the connection string from **Access keys** in your Azure storage account settings and store it in the secret of AKV:

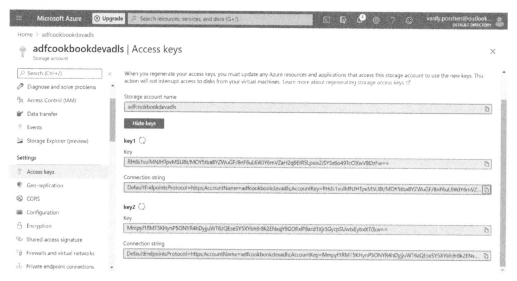

Figure 9.29 – Copying a connection string to an Azure storage account

7.   Go to **AKV | Secrets**. Click **Generate/Import**, type the name of the secret, and paste the connection string copied from **Access keys**:

Figure 9.30 – Creating a secret with a connection string in AKV

8. Link your `Dev` data factory with your DevOps project.

9. Go to **master branch** in your **Azure DevOps Git** and create a linked service for your AKV using an **Azure subscription** method:

Figure 9.31 – Configuring a linked service to AKV

10. Create a linked service to Azure Blob storage via AKV. Choose your **AKV linked service** and the secret name you created with the connection string to **Azure Blob storage**:

Figure 9.32 – Configuring a linked service to Azure Blob storage via AKV

11. Create a **Copy data** activity in your Dev data factory, which will copy a CSV file from the input folder of the Blob container into the output folder. Datasets should be configured via the linked services created in the previous steps:

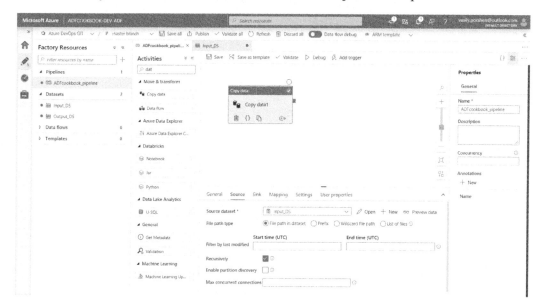

Figure 9.33 – Creating a pipeline with datasets using the linked services created

12. In the **Source** tab of the **Copy data** activity, there should be an Azure Blob storage DelimitedText dataset with the following properties:

a. **Name**: Input_DS

b. **Linked service**: ADLS_DEV_LS (the linked service created in *step 10*)

c. **File path**: adfcookbookcontainer/input/airlines.csv

d. **First row as header**: Check

e. **Import schema**: None

13. In the **Sink** tab of the **Copy data** activity, there should be an Azure Blob storage DelimitedText dataset with the following properties:

a. **Name**: Output_DS

b. **Linked service**: ADLS_DEV_LS (the linked service created in *step 10*)

c. **File path**: adfcookbookcontainer/output

d. **First row as header**: Check

e. **Import schema**: None

14. Click **Save all** and **Publish** to publish your developed linked services, datasets, and pipeline to your **ADF**.

Now that we've set up all the necessary resources, you will be able to understand how it works in the following section.

How it works...

CI/CD processes between two technical environments in Azure usually involve having separate resource groups with the same set of resources: ADF, an Azure storage account, and AKV. Using AKV is the best practice for CI/CD as you don't need to store connection strings in your code; you can manage access via parameters and pass them between resource groups automatically and connection strings will also change. We've created secrets for storing connection strings in an Azure storage account in AKV. These secrets are used to configure linked services from ADF to an Azure storage account. To make your Data Factory have access to the stored secrets in AKV, we've created a new access policy.

Creating an Azure pipeline for CD

The Pipelines service of Azure DevOps helps you automate your release cycle between different environments, that is, development, testing, and production. In this recipe, you will learn how to create an Azure pipeline and connect it with Azure data factories related to different environments.

Getting ready

Before we start, please ensure that you have an Azure license and are familiar with the basics of Azure resources such as the Azure portal, creating and deleting Azure resources, and creating pipelines in ADF. Also, you will need an Azure DevOps project created and linked to your ADF.

How to do it...

We are going to create a new pipeline in Azure DevOps and set it up to release changes from development to the testing environment:

1. Go to your Azure DevOps account, and click **Pipelines | Releases | New release pipeline | Start with an empty job.** You will see the following screen:

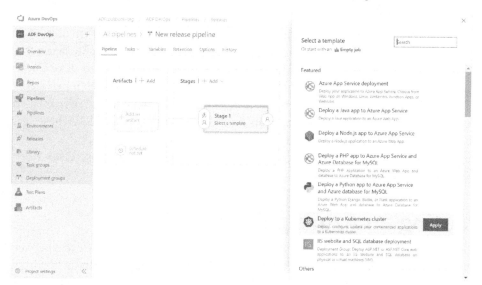

Figure 9.34 – Creating a new release pipeline

2. You can give a name to your pipeline and have **Stage name** as UAT:

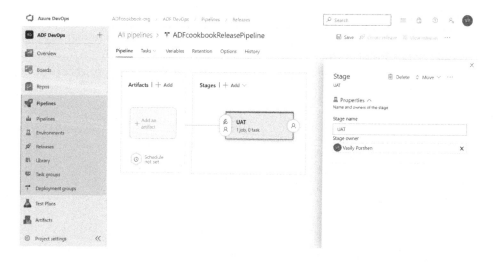

Figure 9.35 – Creating a UAT stage

3. Click **Add an artifact**. Fill in the fields as follows:

    Source type: **Azure Repos Git**

    Project: Your project

    Source (repository): Your repository (**ADF DevOps**)

    Default branch: Your default branch (`adf_publish`)

    Default version: **Latest from the default branch**

    Source alias: `_ADF DevOps`

    Click **Add**:

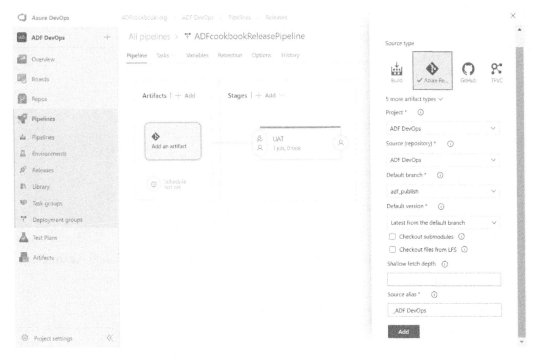

Figure 9.36 – Configuring an artifact

4. Click on **1 job, 0 task** (you can find it under the UAT stage of the pipeline in the preceding screenshot). Then click on the plus sign to the right of **Agent job**, search for ARM Template deployment, and click **Add**:

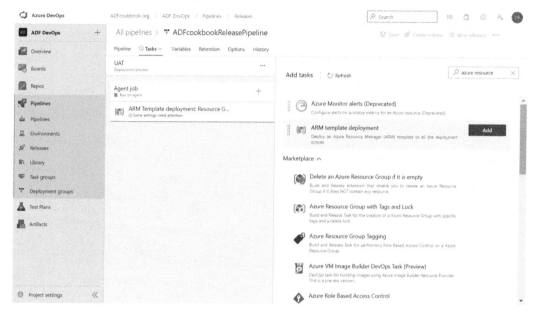

Figure 9.37 – Adding a new task for the job

5. Then you need to change some settings here:

    Deployment scope: Resource Group.

    Azure Resource Manager connection: Your Azure subscription. Click **Authorize**.

    Subscription: Your Azure subscription.

    Action: Create or update resource group.

    Resource group: ADFCOOKBOOK-UAT-RG .

    Location: The location for deploying the resource group.

    Template location: Linked artifact:

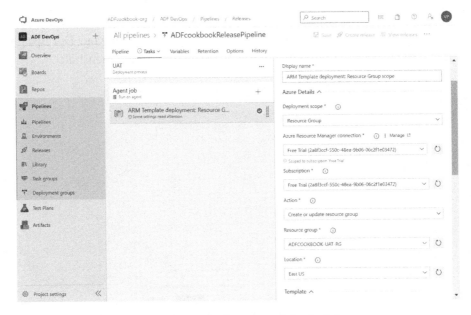

Figure 9.38 – Setting up a task for the job

6. **Template**: Select **Browse template** and the `ARMTemplateForFactory.json` file from your DevOps project. It should be stored in **Linked artifacts** as in the following screenshot:

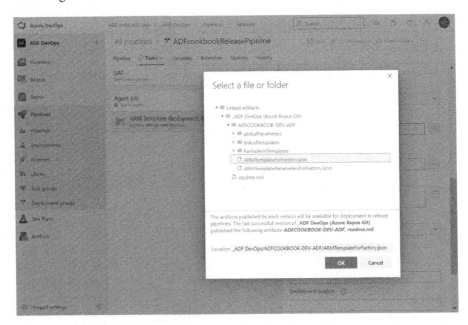

Figure 9.39 – Choosing a file for the template from the DevOps project

7. **Template parameters**: Select **Browse template** and the
   `ARMTemplateParametersForFactory.json` file from your DevOps project.
   It should be stored in **Linked artifacts** as in the following screenshot:

Figure 9.40 – Choosing a file for template parameters from the DevOps project

8. **Override template parameters**: You need to change your DEV parameters to UAT
   parameters: `ADFCOOKBOOK-UAT-ADF`, `https://ADFCOOKBOOK-UAT-AKV.
   vault.azure.net/`, and `adfcookbookuatadls-secret`. These parameters
   should be entered in the **Value** column, as in the following screenshot:

Figure 9.41 – Setting up override template parameters

9. Click the **Save** button (at the top of the page below the **Search** box) and **OK**.

10. To start executing your release pipeline, go to **Releases** and click **Create release |**
Create:

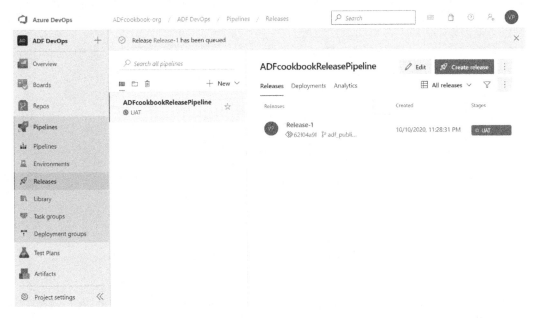

Figure 9.42 – Creating a release

11. You can monitor the status of the release if you click on **Release-1**. Here, you can
see how many tasks are deployed already:

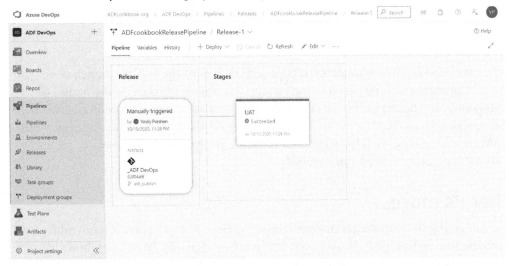

Figure 9.43 – Release is completed

12. If you go to your UAT data factory, you can check that the pipeline and datasets were deployed successfully:

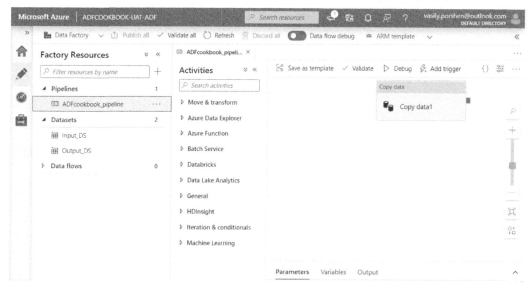

Figure 9.44 – Deployment to the UAT environment is complete

In the preceding screenshot, you can see that the pipeline is deployed to the UAT environment as stated in the top-left corner. All the configurations were automatically changed to UAT resources because of the template parameters that are used in the release pipeline.

In the next section, we will see how these steps work in the background.

How to do it...

When the release pipeline executes, it copies JSON files in the publish branch of the development resource group to the production resource group. As the names of configurations (such as linked services, Blob storage paths, and so on) differ between different resource groups, we've used parameters in ARM templates. That means when ARM templates are copied from the DEV resource group to the UAT resource group, configurations are changed automatically.

There's more...

You can configure more stages in your release pipeline. For example, you can add a production environment. In this case, artifacts from the adf_publish branch will be deployed to the UAT stage and after that to the **PROD** stage.

Instead of performing a release manually, you can automate your release pipeline. There are two options for how to do this. The first one is setting up **Continuous deployment trigger**. If you enable it, a release will be created every time a Git push happens in the selected repository. You can also filter the branch to track **Pushes to**. Moreover, there is the possibility to enable **Pull request trigger**, which will perform a release every time an artifact appears in the pull request workflow. You can find this option in the **Continuous deployment trigger** dialog box in the following screenshot. A dialog box will appear after clicking on the lightning icon on the _ADF DevOps artifact:

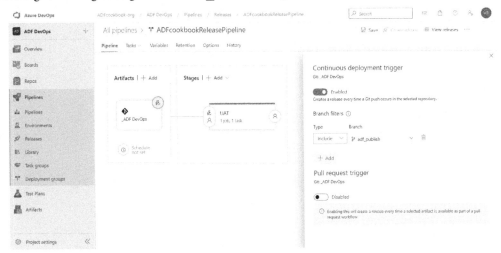

Figure 9.45 – Creating a continuous deployment trigger

The second option for release pipeline automation is enabling **Scheduled release trigger**. It means that the release will be created at the specified time:

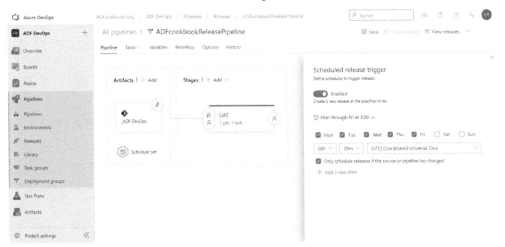

Figure 9.46 – Creating a scheduled release trigger

The preceding screenshot shows the **Scheduled release trigger** dialog box, which will appear after clicking on **Schedule set** below the `_ADF DevOps` artifact. You can also set the trigger to work only if the source or pipeline has changed.

10
Monitoring and Troubleshooting Data Pipelines

Azure Data Factory is an integration tool that helps engineers transfer data between multiple data stores, both within and outside of the Microsoft Azure ecosystem. Data integration is rarely straightforward. In this chapter, we will introduce tools to help you manage and monitor your Data Factory pipelines. You will learn where and how to find more information about what went wrong when a pipeline failed, how to debug a failed run, how to set up alerts that notify you when there is a problem, and how to identify problems with your integration runtimes.

The following is a list of the recipes in this chapter:

- Monitoring pipeline runs and integration runtimes
- Investigating failures – running pipelines in debug mode
- Rerunning activities
- Configuring alerts for your Data Factory runs

Technical requirements

We will be examining Data Factory tools and working with existing pipelines. Specific instructions on how to create or import the pipelines to work with are provided in the *Getting ready* section of each recipe.

You will need access to an Azure Data Factory instance and a GitHub account to access the files and templates we provide for the recipes. If you do not have a GitHub account, you can sign up for a free one at `https://github.com/`.

Monitoring pipeline runs and integration runtimes

Data integration can be tricky, and it is helpful to be able to visualize progress or evaluate inputs/outputs of the pipelines in your Data Factory. This recipe will introduce you to the tools that help you gain an insight into the health and progress of your pipelines.

Getting ready

In this recipe, we will give you an overview of the features of the **Monitor** tab in the Azure Data Factory **Author** interface. If you have access to a data factory with a few pipelines already configured, you will be able to follow along. Otherwise, create a new data factory instance and design and run two or three pipelines. If you followed the first two or three recipes from *Chapter 2, Orchestration and Control Flow*, you will have sufficient material to understand the capabilities of the **Monitor** interface.

How to do it...

Without further ado, let's explore the **Monitor** tab interfaces and customize them for our needs:

1. In the **Author and Monitor** interface, go to the **Monitor** tab. You will see that this tab has several sections: **Runs, Runtime and Sessions**, and **Notifications**. Let's start with the pipeline runs. In this interface, you can see the history and progress of your pipeline runs. *Figure 10.1* shows a typical **Pipeline runs** interface with three pipelines running and one pipeline that completed successfully:

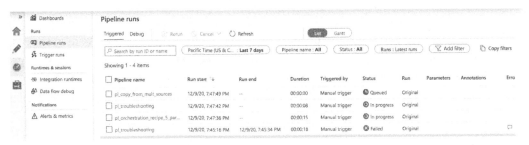

Figure 10.1 – The Monitor tab – Pipeline runs

Note that you have to manually refresh the view by clicking the **Refresh** button when you want to see updates: auto-refresh is not supported at the time of writing:

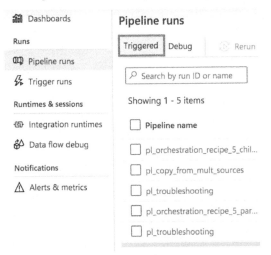

Figure 10.2 – Triggered versus debug mode pipelines

You can start a pipeline run either in debug mode or by a trigger (scheduled or manual). In the **Monitor** tab, triggered and debug pipelines are placed under their respective tabs.

2. We will customize this view to place **Duration**, **Status**, and **Error** immediately after the pipeline name, and remove the **Run ID** column from the view.

> **Note**
>
> **Run ID** is a unique identifier of a particular run and can prove very useful in analyzing it. In this recipe, we do not have a practical use for the information provided by the run ID, so we remove that column from the interface.

First, let's edit the columns that we want to display. Click on the **Edit columns** button to bring up the **Edit columns** blade. In the **Edit columns** blade, drag the **Duration** field to be immediately after the **Pipeline name** field. Similarly, rearrange the **Status** and **Error** fields to follow **Duration**. Finally, delete the **Run ID** field. Click the **OK** button to save your changes. After this, your interface will look similar to the following:

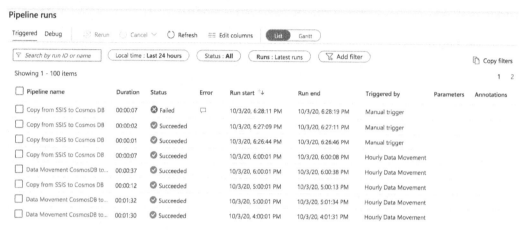

Figure 10.3 – The Pipeline runs table with edited columns

3. If you hover over any of the pipelines, you will see additional buttons:

Figure 10.4 – Additional buttons in the pipelines

The first one, which looks like a play button encircled in arrows, is the rerun button (we will explore the rerun functionality in a later chapter). The second one, which looks like a miniature table, is for the consumption report. Click on it to examine the units consumed during the run:

Pipeline run consumption ✕

	Quantity	Unit
Pipeline orchestration		
Activity Runs	4	Activity runs
Pipeline execution		
Azure integration runtime		
Data movement activities	0.0000	DIU-hour
Pipeline activities	0.0167	Execution hours
External activities	0.0333	Execution hours

Learn more ☐
Pricing calculator ☐

Figure 10.5 – Consumption report

4. Now, let's apply some filters to our pipeline list. We have several filtering options: by the pipeline name, by the time window, by status, and so on. Let's adjust the interface to show only the pipelines that have failed. Click on the **Status** button and select the **Failed** checkbox. Now, only the pipelines that have failed are shown.

We can customize the interface even more. Data Factory allows us to create custom annotations for our pipelines. In this recipe, we shall annotate the pipelines we created in *Chapter 2*, *Orchestration and Control Flow*, with annotation orchestration.

To annotate a pipeline, go to the **Author** tab and select the pipeline you want to update. Click on the **Properties** symbol, which is located at the top right of the window (it is pointed out by the red arrow in the following screenshot). This will bring up the **Properties** blade. In the **Properties** blade, click on the **New** button under **Annotations**, and type Orchestration in the text field:

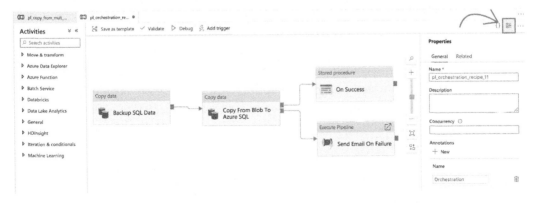

Figure 10.6 – Adding an annotation

Publish your changes. Next, run the pipeline that you annotated. You will not see the annotations in the **Monitor** tab until the pipeline has been run again.

5. Go to the **Monitor** tab and look at your pipeline runs again. You should see that the pipelines that you annotated show a little tag icon.

6. We can now filter our pipelines based on custom annotations. To do this, click on the **Add filter** button and choose **Annotations**. Select **Orchestration** from the list:

Figure 10.7 – Filtering on user-defined annotations

After applying this filter, you will only see the pipelines that have the **Orchestration** tag.

7. Finally, let's have a look at our integration runtimes. Under **Runtimes & sessions**, select **Integration runtimes**. By default, the interface shows you all of your available integration runtimes. You can switch to the **Self-Hosted**, **Azure**, or **Azure-SSIS** tab to view only the integration runtimes of a particular type:

Figure 10.8 – Integration runtimes interface

If you have a self-hosted integration runtime, you can click on its name in the interface to see the details about the computer nodes on which the integration runtime is installed, the software version, memory consumption, and networking state.

How it works...

The **Monitor** tab gives us tools to understand the functioning of our data factory, including to examine the progress of our pipeline runs, look into the status and health of the integration runtimes, and investigate which resources the data factory is consuming and how they are being used.

The interface is very useful and flexible without any modification, but customizing it gives you even more power. In *steps 2* through *5*, we changed the order of the columns and filtered displayed runs based on status. This allowed us to focus on the attributes of the pipelines that were of most interest to us. Custom annotations, which we created in *step 6*, give you even more filtering options: you can use business logic to filter your list and enhance your interface.

The consumption reports (such as the example we gave in *Figure 10.5*) is especially convenient when you need to control costs. The pipelines we used in this chapter for illustration are not moving a lot of data, and therefore should not incur many costs. However, in a real production environment, when tera- and petabytes of data are moved, cost is an important consideration, and the consumption report will help you identify the most expensive resources and activities and strategically apply your optimization efforts for maximum impact.

When we work with pipelines that access on-premises servers/SSIS, it is necessary to configure self-hosted integration runtimes (you learned about these pipelines in *Chapter 6, Integration with MS SSIS*). When such a pipeline has issues, it is not unusual to discover that a corrupted or unavailable node in the self-hosted integration runtime is the culprit:

Figure 10.9 – Self-hosted integration runtime overview

The integration runtime overview interface, which we encountered in *step 7*, is very helpful in investigating these problems. For example, the preceding screenshot shows an integration runtime where both nodes are unavailable and will therefore cause problems if a pipeline is using those integration runtimes to access on-premises data stores.

Investigating failures – running in debug mode

When your Data Factory pipeline does not work as expected, it is useful to have tools to examine what went wrong. The debug mode allows us to run a pipeline receiving immediate feedback about its execution.

In this section, we shall investigate a pipeline failure utilizing the capabilities of the debug mode. We will learn how to look for errors, understand error messages, and troubleshoot activities to fix a failed pipeline.

Getting ready

In order to prepare your environment for this recipe, follow these steps:

1. Set up an Azure SQL server and create `Airline`, `Country`, and `PipelineLog` tables and an `InsertLogRecord` stored procedure. Use the `CreateAirlineTable.sql`, `CreateCountryTable.sql`, and `CreateActivityLogsTable.sql` scripts to create these objects. These were also required for *Chapter 2, Orchestration and Control Flow*. If you followed the recipes in that chapter, you should have the database and table stored procedures already set up.

2. Create a new data factory. Download the template from `https://github.com/PacktPublishing/Azure-Data-Factory-Cookbook/blob/master/Chapter10/ADF-template.json`.

   Next, go to `https://portal.azure.com/#create/Microsoft.Template` and select **Build your own template** in the editor option. Copy the contents of the template file into the space provided and click **Save**. You should see a form similar to the one in *Figure 10.10*:

Custom deployment

Deploy from a custom template

Select a template   **Basics**   Review + create

Template

Customized template ☐
2 resources

✎ Edit template   ✎ Edit parameters

Deployment scope

Select the subscription to manage deployed resources and costs. Use resource groups like folders to organize and manage all your resources.

Subscription * ⓘ	Azure subscription 1	⌄

└── Resource group * ⓘ		⌄

Create new

Parameters

Region * ⓘ	West US	⌄

Data Factory Name ⓘ	[concat('datafactory', uniqueString(resourceGroup().id))]

Location ⓘ	[resourceGroup().location]

Storage Account Name ⓘ	[concat('storage', uniqueString(resourceGroup().id))]

Blob Container ⓘ	[concat('blob', uniqueString(resourceGroup().id))]

[Review + create]   [< Previous]   [Next : Review + create >]

Figure 10.10 – Deploying a data factory from a template

Choose a resource group where you want your data factory to be created, and click on **Review + create**. On the next screen, wait until validation is done, and hit **Create**. Wait until your factory is created.

3. Create an *AzureSQ Database linked service* in this new data factory. The steps to do so are described in detail in *Chapter 2, Orchestration and Control Flow*, in the *The power of dynamic pipelines* recipe.

4. Create a pipeline from the template. First, download the `pipeline_debugging.zip` file from `https://github.com/PacktPublishing/Azure-Data-Factory-Cookbook/blob/master/Chapter10/pipeline_debugging.zip`.

Next, go to the data factory you created in *step 2* and open the **Author and Monitor** interface. In the **Author** tab, hover over **Pipelines** in the **Factory Resources** section. As you hover, you will see three dots: this is the **Actions** menu:

Figure 10.11 – The Actions menu

Click on the three dots and select **Pipeline From Template** from the presented options. Then, click on the **Use local template** button (see *Figure 10.12*) and select the pipeline_debugging.zip file that you downloaded:

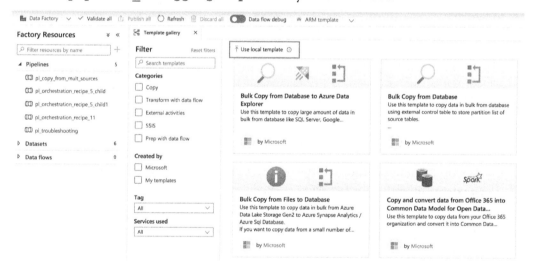

Figure 10.12 – Creating a pipeline from a template

5.   After you have selected the template, you will see the **Preview** interface, similar to the following:

pl_troubleshooting

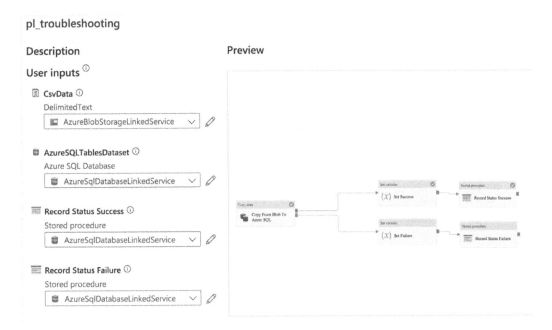

Figure 10.13 – Creating a pipeline from a template

This pipeline first backs up the files in a storage account, then copies the contents of the files into a table in the Azure SQL database. If the copy activity succeeds, we set the **Status** pipeline variable to **Success**; otherwise, the value is set to **Failure**. Finally, the last activity records the status and some other metadata about this run into the `PipelineLog` Azure SQL table.

6. Fill in the user inputs from the dropdowns by selecting the drop-down options as shown in *Figure 10.13*. Click on **Use this template** to create the pipeline.

7. Publish to save your changes.

> **Note**
> Even though we execute the pipeline in debug mode, the data is still being moved! Be sure not to run any pipelines in debug mode in your production environment. Rather, create test linked services and datasets, and only debug on a small set of data to save on costs. Once your pipeline is fine-tuned, you can use connectors that point to the real data sources and sinks.

How to do it...

In this recipe, we will run a failing pipeline, look for the root cause of the failure, fix the error, and rerun the pipeline to ensure that that our fix worked:

1. Start by running the pipeline in debug mode. Open the factory that you created in the *Getting ready* section and open the **Author and Monitor** interface. In the **Author** tab, open the **pl_troubleshooting** pipeline.

2. Click on the **Debug** button at the top of the authoring canvas to run your pipeline in debug mode:

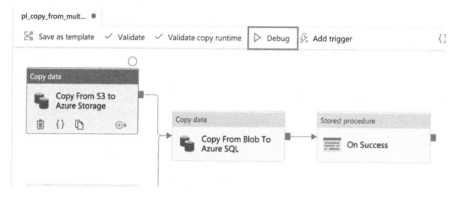

Figure 10.14 – Debug button

This will start your pipeline run. Note that after you have started the pipeline, the **Debug** button is replaced with a **Cancel options** button. You can use this if you need to stop/cancel your pipeline run:

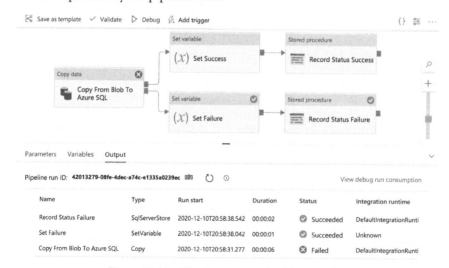

Figure 10.15 – Pipeline running in debug mode

3. Uh-oh! The pipeline failed! Click anywhere on the canvas to bring information about the activities in the **Output** pane at the bottom. In the **Output** pane, hover with your cursor over the row representing the **Copy from Blob to Azure SQL** activity. You will see additional icons appearing between the activity's **Name** and **Type** columns:

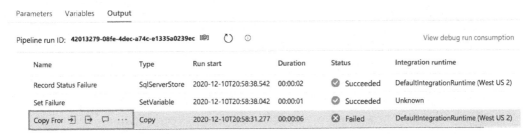

Figure 10.16 – Examining input, output, and error messages

The additional icons are buttons that will help us to gather even more information about what went wrong:

Figure 10.17 – Activity input, activity output, and error message (detail)

Click on the error message button and enlarge the window. You should see an error message similar to the following:

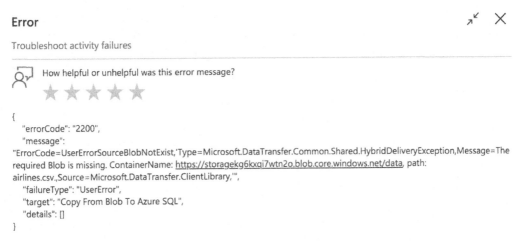

Figure 10.18 – Error message

> **Note**
>
> At the top of the error message, there is a link to the Microsoft documentation. This really comes in handy when you are investigating activity failures!

4. Read the error message. The message says **The required Blob is missing**, and gives further details about the missing file: the container is the storage account that we created in the *Getting ready* section, and the file is `airlines.csv`.

    Examine the **Copy from Blob to Azure SQL** activity. Click on it and then go to the **Source** tab at the bottom. You will see that the activity uses the `CsvData` dataset. `CsvData` requires a filename as a parameter, and the current configuration specifies `airlines.csv` as the filename. The `CsvData` dataset represents the Azure Blob storage account we created in the *Getting ready* section. We did not create any containers in that Blob storage account, nor did we upload any files!

5. To fix this error, open another tab in your browser to the Azure portal (`https://portal.azure.com`), go to the storage account you created in the *Getting ready* section, and create a container called `data`. Next, download the file called `airlines.csv` from `https://github.com/PacktPublishing/Azure-Data-Factory-Cookbook/blob/master/data/airlines.csv` and upload it to the `data` container.

6. Rerun your pipeline in debug mode. It should succeed this time: we have found and fixed the error.

How it works...

If your pipeline does not behave as expected – or fails – you need to spend some time to understand what went wrong. The **Debug** interface helps you do that. As we illustrated in this recipe, you can perform test runs before finalizing your design, and use the **Output** pane to view the execution results as your pipeline progresses from activity to activity.

In the **Output** pane, each row represents an activity and shows you the activity name, status, when it started, how long it has been running for, which integration runtime it is using, and the run ID.

In *step 3*, when we examined the **Output** pane, we saw that the first activity, **Backup SQL Data**, succeeded, but the second activity in our pipeline, **Copy from Blob to Azure SQL**, failed. Following that, subsequent activities succeeded, which means that the state of the run was captured by the stored procedure.

This gave us a clue that the problem occurred in the **Copy from Blob to Azure SQL** activity. With the help of the **Output** pane, we identified the root cause by examining the error message. Finally, we were able to correct the error by providing the required data to the data source: uploading the `airlines.csv` file, and verified that we indeed fixed the error by running in debug mode again and seeing that the run succeeded.

There's more...

After going through the preceding steps, your pipeline is configured correctly and can copy data from source to destination. Open the pipeline and click anywhere on the canvas to display the pipeline run information in the **Output** pane. Hover over the **Copy From Blob to Azure SQL** activity (similar to what we did in *step 3* in the *Monitoring pipeline runs and integration runtimes* recipe). Instead of an error icon, you will see a spectacles icon, as shown in the following screenshot:

Name	Type	Run start	Duration	Status	Integration runtime	Run ID
Set Success	SetVariable	2020-10-05T03:13:23.050	00:00:01	Succeeded	Unknown	008fd98e-a2
Copy From Blob	Copy	2020-10-05T03:13:15.152	00:00:07	Succeeded	DefaultIntegrationRuntime (West US 2)	1c6d6eb2-2c
Backup SQL Data	Copy	2020-10-05T03:13:07.607	00:00:07	Succeeded	DefaultIntegrationRuntime (East US 2)	d5aa0b73-6:

Figure 10.19 – Copy activity details

Click on it. You will see the **Copy Activity Details** report, which contains lots of useful information about the copy activity data transfer. The following screenshot shows the report:

Figure 10.20 – Copy activity performance report

Use this report when you are designing and refining data transfers containing the copy activity. You can view it while the data movement is in progress, too, and you will gain insight into the process: the number of rows read versus the number of rows written to the sink connector, the number of open connections, the degree of parallelism, and so on. This report is very helpful when you need to identify data transfer bottlenecks between connectors.

See also

Microsoft maintains an extensive collection of troubleshooting guides, which will be of great help to you if and when you encounter errors. Here are the links to some of the guides that can serve as starting points:

- Troubleshooting activities:

  `https://docs.microsoft.com/azure/data-factory/data-factory-troubleshoot-guide`

- Troubleshooting connectors:

  `https://docs.microsoft.com/azure/data-factory/connector-troubleshoot-guide`

- Troubleshooting integration runtimes:

  Troubleshooting self-hosted integration runtimes: `https://docs.microsoft.com/azure/data-factory/self-hosted-integration-runtime-troubleshoot-guide`

  Troubleshooting SSIS integration runtime management in Azure Data Factory: `https://docs.microsoft.com/azure/data-factory/ssis-integration-runtime-management-troubleshoot`

  Using the diagnose connectivity feature in the SSIS integration runtime: `https://docs.microsoft.com/azure/data-factory/ssis-integration-runtime-diagnose-connectivity-faq`

Rerunning activities

When our data transfers fail for one reason or another, we frequently need to rerun affected pipelines. This ensures the appropriate data movement is performed, albeit delayed. If our design is complex, or if we are moving large volumes of data, it is useful to be able to repeat the run from the point of failure, to minimize the time lost in the failed pipeline.

In this section, we will look at two features of Data Factory that help us to troubleshoot our pipelines and rerun them with maximum efficiency. The first feature is breakpoints, which allow us to execute a pipeline up to an activity of our choice. The second feature is rerunning from the point of failure, which helps to minimize the time lost due to a failed execution.

Getting ready

Preparing your environment for this recipe is identical to the preparation required for the previous recipe in this chapter, *Investigating failures – running in debug mode*. We will be using the same Azure Data Factory template, but a different pipeline template.

The template for this recipe is `pipeline_rerunning.zip`. It can be found at `https://github.com/PacktPublishing/Azure-Data-Factory-Cookbook/blob/master/Chapter10/pipeline_rerunning.zip`. Refer to the aforementioned recipe for detailed instructions on how to import a pipeline from an existing template.

Note that if you have completed the previous recipe already, you will not need to create the data factory from the template again; however, it is necessary to reverse the "fix" that we applied after debugging a failing pipeline. To do that, go to the storage account that was established as you created the data factory in the previous recipe, and remove the data container and its contents. (If you skipped the previous recipe, this step is not required.)

How to do it...

In the following steps, we shall again deal with a failed pipeline and learn how to set a breakpoint to pipeline execution, and then rerun the pipeline from any point of our choosing:

1. Go to the data factory you set up in the *Getting ready* section and open the **Author and Monitor** interface. Go to the **Author** tab and run the pipeline that you imported in debug mode. Wait until it completes (it will fail).

2. We see from that it is the **Copy From Blob to Azure SQL** activity that fails. Let's run the pipeline again, but stop execution after this failing activity. To do this, click on it – you will see a hollow red circle above it:

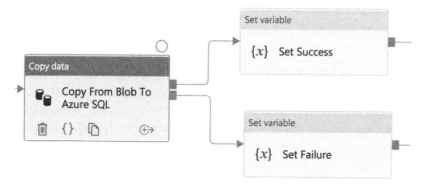

Figure 10.21 – Selected activity in the Author interface

Click inside this circle. It will fill in red, and subsequent activities become faded, as shown in the following screenshot. This indicates a breakpoint in your pipeline:

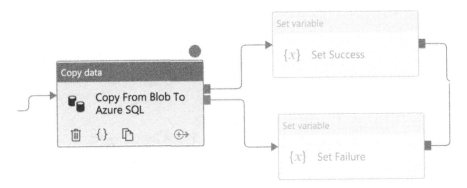

Figure 10.22 – Setting up a breakpoint

Now, run your pipeline in debug mode (refer to the *Investigating failures – running in debug mode* recipe in this chapter if you are unsure of how to do that). You will see that the execution only continues up to the breakpoint; neither the **Set Success/ Failure** activities nor the **Record Status** activities are executed.

3. Let's now rerun this pipeline from the point of failure. After all, we know that the **Backup SQL Data** activity succeeded, and we do not need to rerun it again.

    Before you can rerun your pipeline, you need to publish and trigger it. Publish your pipeline, and, once it is published, trigger it to start a run. Do not use the **Debug** mode this time.

    Once your pipeline has run, go to the **Monitor** tab. There, under the **Pipeline Runs** section, you will see a list of rows, each row representing a run of this pipeline. Make sure you are looking under the **Triggered** tab (we went over the structure of the **Pipeline runs** section in the *Monitoring pipeline runs and integration runtimes* recipe). When you hover over a row, you will see the edit, rerun, and consumption buttons:

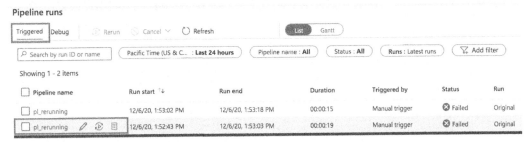

Figure 10.23 – Rerun and consumption buttons

4. If we click on the rerun button here, the data pipeline will rerun starting from the very first activity. Instead, click on the pipeline name; this will open the pipeline run details interface:

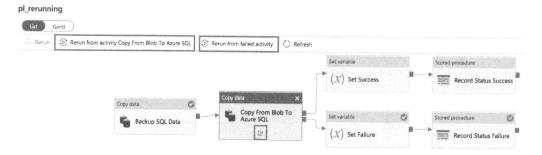

Figure 10.24 – The pipeline run details interface

Here, you can see the rerun options: we can rerun from the selected activity or we can rerun from the failed activity (in our case, this is the same activity, since we selected the activity that failed). Click on any of these buttons (in our case, they all will rerun the pipeline from the **Copy from Blob to Azure SQL** activity).

After your rerun is completed, the graphical representation of your pipeline looks like this:

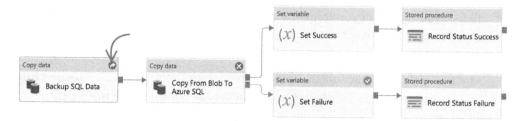

Figure 10.25 – Pipeline after rerun from failed activity

Note the grayed-out arrow in the **Backup SQL Data** activity. This indicates that this activity was not executed; we rerun from the point of failure, bypassing the first activity.

How it works...

In this recipe, we tried out two very intuitive but powerful features of Azure Data Factory. If your pipeline failed, setting a breakpoint as we did in *step 2* allows you to execute only the problematic portion of your pipeline – the activities that failed, or the ones that require your scrutiny. There is no need to waste time waiting for the whole pipeline to finish if you know that the activities beyond the breakpoint function perfectly.

After you have performed an investigation and fixed your pipeline, you can rerun it from the point of failure (or from any activity within the pipeline) to verify that you corrected the error. This feature is very useful when your pipeline takes some time to complete. For example, many pipelines move data to a staging area and then perform data transformation. If the transformation activity (or activities) failed for some reason, but export to the staging area was successful, rerunning the pipeline from the beginning will be both lengthy and costly, and, ultimately, unnecessary. You can avoid both the wait and the extra expense by rerunning from the point of failure and skipping successful steps.

Configuring alerts for your Data Factory runs

When a failure in data processing happens, we have to react as fast as possible to avoid impacting downstream processes. Data Factory gives us tools to automate monitoring by setting up alerts to inform the engineers when there is a problem. We already introduced a custom email alert in the *Branching and chaining* recipe in *Chapter 2, Orchestration and Control Flow*. It sent a notification if that particular pipeline failed. In this chapter, we shall create an alert that will notify on-call engineers via email or a phone call whenever any of the pipelines in our data factory have a problem.

Getting ready

In order to follow this recipe and configure the alerts, we first need to register with the Insights resource provider:

1. In the Azure portal, go to your subscription, and from the menu on the left, select **Resource providers**.

2. Use the **Filter by name...** text field to search for the `microsoft.insights` resource provider.

3. Select `microsoft.insights` as the provider and click on the **Register** button:

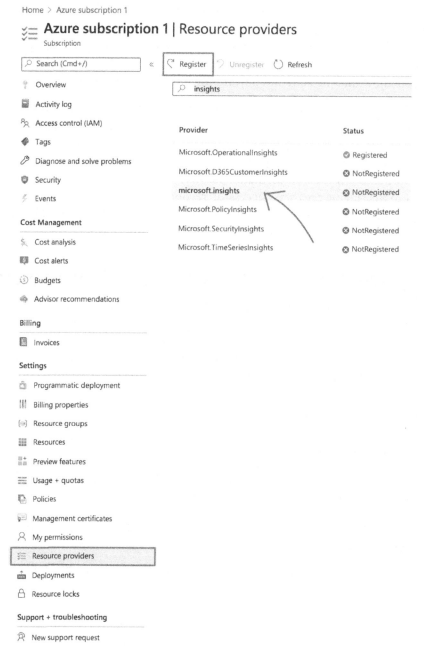

Figure 10.26 – Registering the microsoft.insights resource provider

4. Wait until the registration is complete.

After we go through the recipe and configure the alert, we will test it on a failed pipeline. We shall use the pipeline that we designed in *Chapter 2, Orchestration and Control Flow*, in the *Using parameters and variables in a pipeline* recipe. If you did not go over that recipe, do so now so that you have a simple pipeline handy. Alternatively, if you already have a simple pipeline you know well and can make fail, you can use it for this recipe.

How to do it...

In this recipe, we shall configure an alert that notifies on-call engineers when any of the pipelines in your data factory have a failure:

1. Go to your data factory instance and open the **Author and Monitor** interface. Then, open the **Monitor** tab.

2. In the **Monitor** tab, select **Alerts & metrics** in the **Notifications** section, as shown in the following screenshot. Then, click on **New alert rule** in the interface:

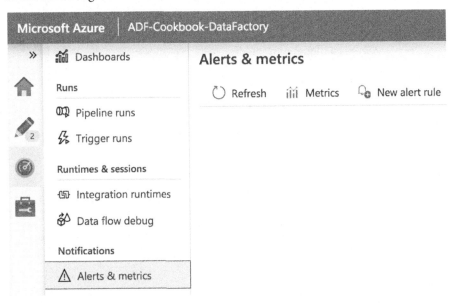

Figure 10.27 – Alerts and metrics interface

3. In the **New alert rule** blade, configure your new alert. Name your alert `Pipeline Failures Detected`. From the **Severity** drop-down option, choose **Sev2**.

4. Next, we shall configure the target criteria. Click on **Add criteria** under the **Target criteria** section. You will see a long list of metrics that you can utilize in order to configure your alerts. Select **Failed activity runs metrics**; this will give us the most general failure metrics:

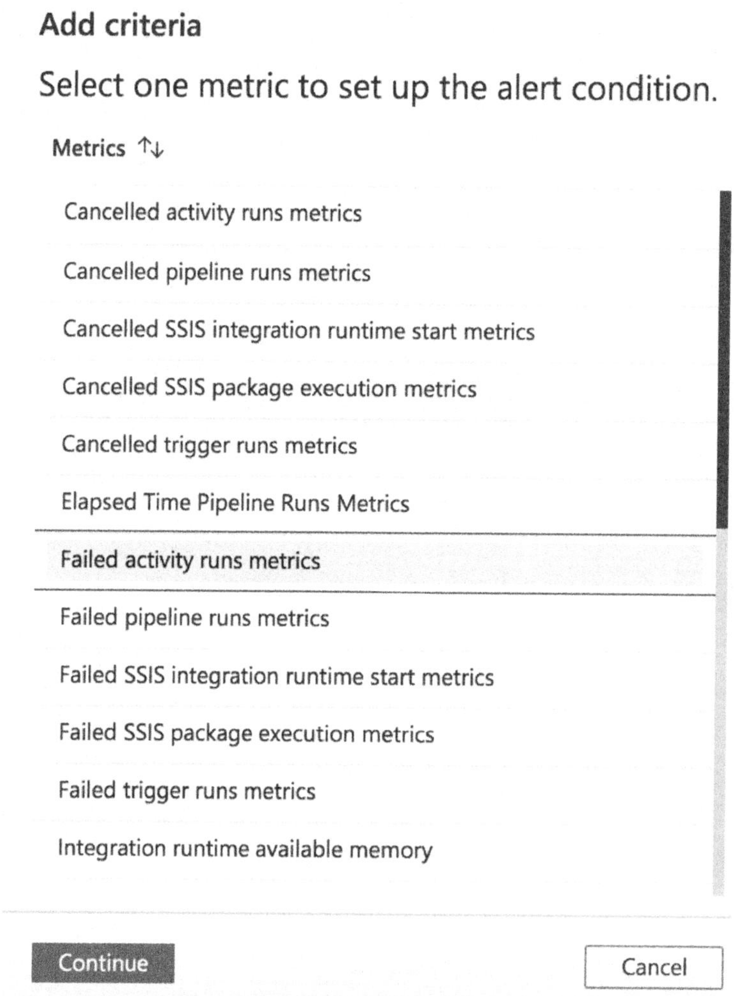

Add criteria

Select one metric to set up the alert condition.

Metrics ↑↓

Cancelled activity runs metrics

Cancelled pipeline runs metrics

Cancelled SSIS integration runtime start metrics

Cancelled SSIS package execution metrics

Cancelled trigger runs metrics

Elapsed Time Pipeline Runs Metrics

Failed activity runs metrics

Failed pipeline runs metrics

Failed SSIS integration runtime start metrics

Failed SSIS package execution metrics

Failed trigger runs metrics

Integration runtime available memory

Continue   Cancel

Figure 10.28 – Alert condition metrics

5. Hit **Continue**. This will take you to the blade where you can set up additional alert logic. At this time, we shall leave all the values at their defaults to make sure that we receive a notification whenever there is any type of failure in any of the activities. Click the **Add criteria** button to finalize the target criteria and return to the alert configuration:

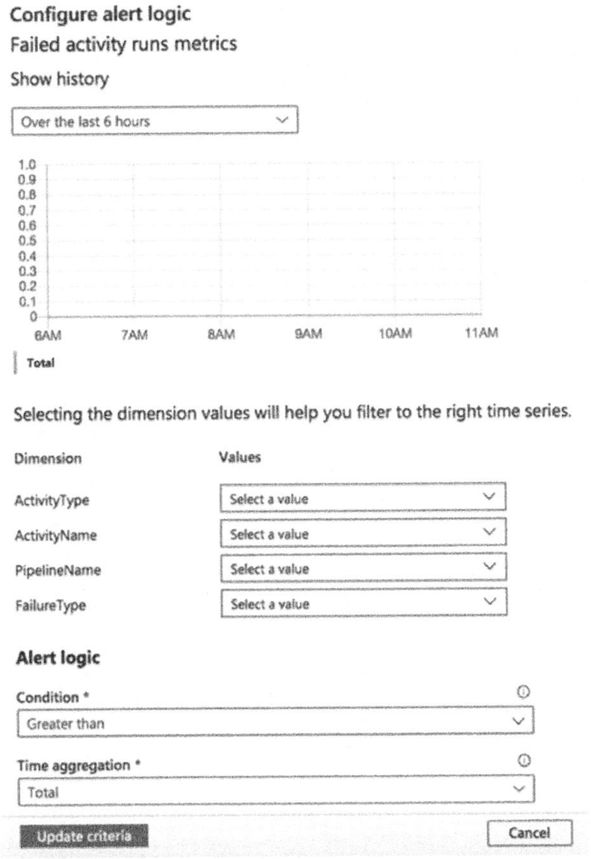

Configure alert logic
Failed activity runs metrics

Show history

| Over the last 6 hours | ⌄ |

Selecting the dimension values will help you filter to the right time series.

Dimension	Values
ActivityType	Select a value ⌄
ActivityName	Select a value ⌄
PipelineName	Select a value ⌄
FailureType	Select a value ⌄

Alert logic

Condition *   ⓘ

| Greater than | ⌄ |

Time aggregation *   ⓘ

| Total | ⌄ |

| Update criteria | | Cancel |

Figure 10.29 – The Configure alert logic blade

6. Next, specify the notification method. Click on **Configure notification**. We shall create a new action group to send our notifications to. Enter On-call Engineers as your action group name for this recipe, and On-call for **Short name**. Next, click on the **Add Notifications** button.

7. You will see the **Add notification** blade. Here, you can set up how you want to receive your alert. In this recipe, we shall send alerts to email and SMS so that the engineers know as soon as possible if there is a problem.

    Fill in the fields in the **Add notification** blade, as shown in the following screenshot (fill in the appropriate contact email and phone number):

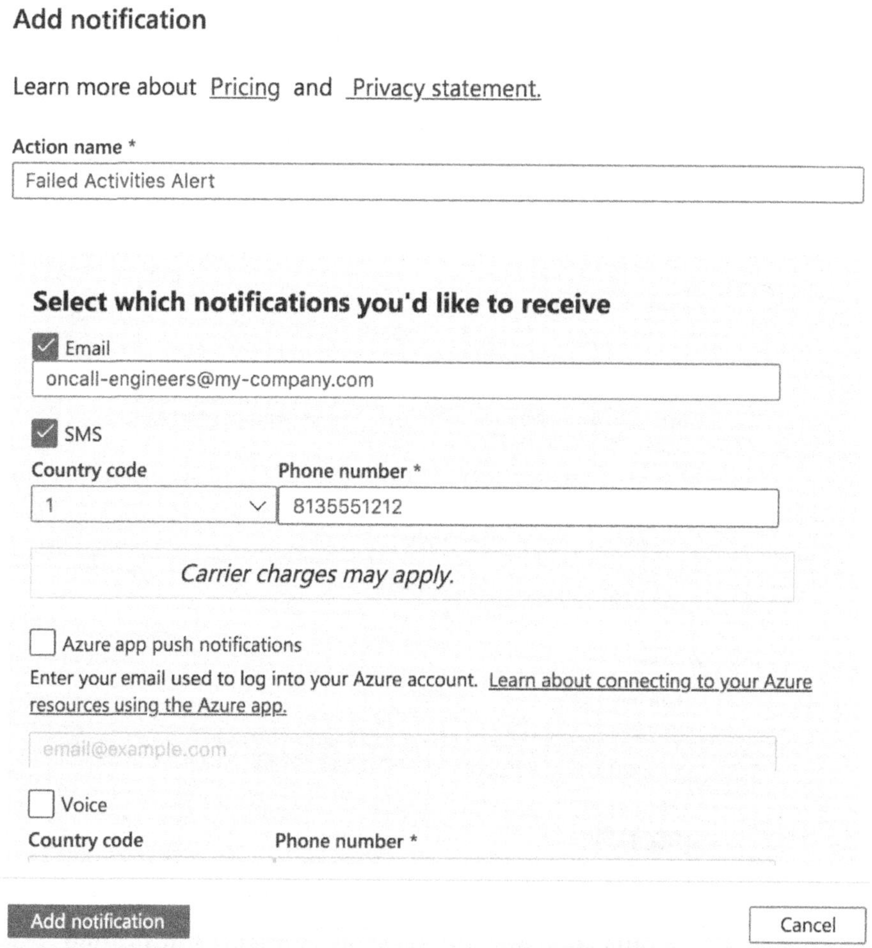

    ## Add notification

    Learn more about <u>Pricing</u> and <u>Privacy statement.</u>

    Action name *

Failed Activities Alert

    ### Select which notifications you'd like to receive

    ☑ Email

oncall-engineers@my-company.com

    ☑ SMS

Country code	Phone number *
1 ⌄	8135551212

Carrier charges may apply.

    ☐ Azure app push notifications

    Enter your email used to log into your Azure account. <u>Learn about connecting to your Azure resources using the Azure app.</u>

email@example.com

    ☐ Voice

Country code	Phone number *

    [Add notification]   [Cancel]

    Figure 10.30 – Add notification configuration

    Click on the **Add notification** button to return to the **Configure notification** blade.

8. We have specified an action group and notification method for our notifications. Click on the **Add action group** button to finalize this action group and return to the **New alert rule** blade. Review your alert rule configuration; it should look similar to the following:

New alert rule

Alert rule name *

Pipeline Failures Detected

Description

Alert on-call engineers that one or more pipelines failed

Severity *

Sev2 ⌄

Target criteria	Actions
Whenever Activity Failed Runs metric is Greater Than to 0	✏️ 🗑️

+ Add criteria

🛈 *There will be a monthly rate for the configured criteria. Learn more about* *Pricing*

Notifications	Action group type	Actions
On-Call Engineers		🗑️

+ Configure notification

Enable rule upon creation

🔘 On

| Create alert rule | Cancel |

Figure 10.31 – Configured alert rule

9. Click on **Create alert rule** to finalize your new rule and create an alert. You should see this alert in the **Alerts & metrics** interface:

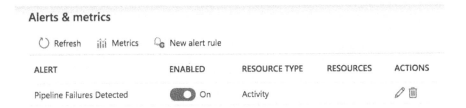

Alerts & metrics

🔄 Refresh   ılıl Metrics   🔖 New alert rule

ALERT	ENABLED	RESOURCE TYPE	RESOURCES	ACTIONS
Pipeline Failures Detected	🔘 On	Activity		✏️ 🗑️

Figure 10.32 – Alert rule in the Alerts & metrics interface

Your action group has been created, and members of that group will receive an email and an SMS informing them they have been added to the group. This is what you will see after the group is created:

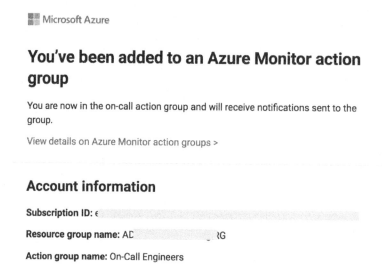

Figure 10.33 – Informational email

10. Let's test this alert. Take a simple pipeline we designed in *Chapter 2, Orchestration and Control Flow*, in the *Using parameters and variables in a pipeline* recipe, and make it fail. All we need to do is to change the `tableName` parameter in **Source dataset** for the **Backup SQL Data** activity. Do not forget to publish our changes!

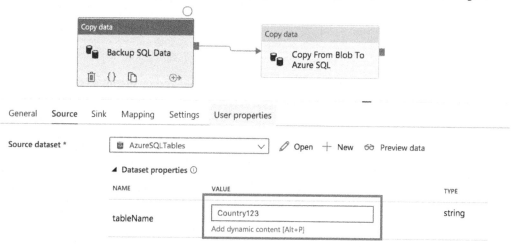

Figure 10.34 – Entering an incorrect tableName value to cause pipeline failure

After publishing, trigger the pipeline. It will fail, because it won't be able to find the `Country123` table. After it fails, the alert will send an email and an SMS to the addresses/phone numbers you specified in *step 7*.

A sample email alert looks like this:

Microsoft Azure

⚠ Your Azure Monitor alert was triggered

Azure monitor alert rule Pipeline Failure Detected was triggered for ADF-Cookbook-DataFactory at September 28, 2020 21:17 UTC.

Alert rule description	Alert on-call engineers that one or more pipeline failures detected
Rule ID	/subscriptions/a6/resourcegroups/ADF-Orchestration-RG/providers/Microsoft.Insights/metricalerts/Pipeline%20Failure%20Detected View Rule >
Resource ID	/subscriptions/ea6/resourcegroups/ADF-Orchestration-RG/providers/Microsoft.DataFactory/factories/ADF-Cookbook-DataFactory View Resource >

Alert Activated Because:

Metric name	ActivityFailedRuns
Metric namespace	factories/ADF-Cookbook-DataFactory
Dimensions	ResourceId = /SUBSCRIPTIONS//RESOURCEGROUPS/ADF-ORCHESTRATION-RG/PROVIDERS/MICROSOFT.DATAFACTORY/FACTORIES/ADF-COOKBOOK-DATAFACTORY
Time Aggregation	Total
Period	Over the last 1 mins
Value	1
Operator	GreaterThan
Threshold	0
Criterion Type	StaticThresholdCriterion

Figure 10.35 – Sample email notification

Examine the email that you received. Click on the **View Resource** link in the email; it will take you right to the data factory where the failure occurred, and you can start debugging immediately.

How it works...

Azure Data Factory gives you a sophisticated interface to allow fine-grained control over your alert logic. We configured a very general alert in *steps 4* and *5*, to illustrate how to receive a notification when any problem occurs. For your business and engineering needs, you can use the same interface to refine the target criteria of your alerts and specify many parameters, such as which pipelines or activities you want to monitor, what types of failures you are interested in, and how frequently the data factory should be polled to determine whether there is a problem.

In *steps 6* to *8*, we configured the information about our responders. We entered the email and SMS information of the people to be notified when a pipeline fails. This interface allows great flexibility in setting up the notifications; you can specify any combination of email, SMS, voice, or Azure app push notifications. Note also that you can easily configure several notifications per alert using the same interface. For example, in case of a problem, you may wish to send both an email and an SMS to on-call engineers and just an informational email to the rest of your engineering team.

There's more...

It is always useful to have the ability to notify the user (or an on-call engineer) if a failure occurs. In this book, we have shown a way to notify the user if a failure occurs in a certain activity within one pipeline (refer to *Chapter 2*, *Orchestration and Control Flow*, the *Branching and chaining activities* recipe), and how to set up an alert if one or more pipelines fail in a certain data factory. What if we want to be notified whenever a failure occurs in any of our data factories?

One way is to configure separate alerts in all the data factories we need to monitor. There is another way, which offers much more sophisticated control over the metrics you want to monitor: you can use the Azure Monitor service. Azure Monitor lets you configure the export of the logs to several platforms, including Azure Log Analytics. Once you export your logs to Log Analytics, you can use this robust platform to gain insight into your pipeline runs or configure alerts based on data gathered across resources.

See also

If you are interested in exploring the Azure Monitor or Log Analytics services for your data factory alerts, there is no better place to start than the following link:

```
https://docs.microsoft.com/azure/data-factory/monitor-using-
azure-monitor
```

Other Books You May Enjoy

If you enjoyed this book, you may be interested in these other books by Packt:

ETL with Azure Cookbook

Christian Cote, Matija Lah, Madina Saitakhmetova

ISBN: 978-1-80020-331-0

- Explore ETL and how it is different from ELT
- Move and transform various data sources with Azure ETL and ELT services
- Use SSIS 2019 with Azure HDInsight clusters
- Discover how to query SQL Server 2019 Big Data Clusters hosted in Azure
- Migrate SSIS solutions to Azure and solve key challenges associated with it
- Understand why data profiling is crucial and how to implement it in Azure Databricks
- Get to grips with BIML and learn how it applies to SSIS and Azure Data Factory solutions

Mastering Azure Machine Learning

Christoph Körner, Kaijisse Waaijer

ISBN: 978-1-78980-755-4

- Setup your Azure Machine Learning workspace for data experimentation and visualization

- Perform ETL, data preparation, and feature extraction using Azure best practices

- Implement advanced feature extraction using NLP and word embeddings

- Train gradient boosted tree-ensembles, recommendation engines and deep neural networks on Azure Machine Learning

- Use hyperparameter tuning and Azure Automated Machine Learning to optimize your ML models

- Employ distributed ML on GPU clusters using Horovod in Azure Machine Learning

- Deploy, operate and manage your ML models at scale

- Automated your end-to-end ML process as CI/CD pipelines for MLOps

Leave a review - let other readers know what you think

Please share your thoughts on this book with others by leaving a review on the site that you bought it from. If you purchased the book from Amazon, please leave us an honest review on this book's Amazon page. This is vital so that other potential readers can see and use your unbiased opinion to make purchasing decisions, we can understand what our customers think about our products, and our authors can see your feedback on the title that they have worked with Packt to create. It will only take a few minutes of your time, but is valuable to other potential customers, our authors, and Packt. Thank you!

Index

Made in the USA
Monee, IL
21 October 2022